D0631896

ART ON SITE

COUNTRY ARTWALKS
FROM MAINE TO MARYLAND

Discover Sculpture Gardens,
Environmental and Architectural Gems,
Painters' Landscapes, and
Art and Craft in Process

MARINA HARRISON and LUCY D. ROSENFELD

Drawings by Lucy D. Rosenfeld

Michael Kesend Publishing, Ltd., New York

Copyright 1994 © by Marina Harrison and Lucy D. Rosenfeld First Publication 1994

Published by Michael Kesend Publishing, Ltd.
          1025 Fifth Avenue, New York, NY 10028

Harrison, Marina 1939–
    Art on site: country artwalks from Maine to Maryland/Marina Harrison and Lucy D. Rosenfeld.
        p.   cm.
    Includes indexes.
    ISBN 0-935576-42-8: $16.95
    1. Art, American—Northeastern States. 2. Art, Modern—19th century—Northeastern States. 3. Art, Modern—20th century—Northeastern States. 4. Artists' studios—Northeastern States. 5. Gardens—Northeastern States. 6. Northeastern States—Tours. I. Rosenfeld, Lucy D., 1939-   . II. Title.
N6513.H37 1993
709'.74—dc20   93-23511
                                                                CIP

942282

CONTENTS

In the Artists' Footsteps: Painters' Views of the World Around Them

Unusual Visions of Landscapes: Environmental Art and Archaeology

Architectural Pleasures: Unique Communities and Eccentric Monuments, Old and New

Works in Process: Studios, Foundries and Workshops

Artistic Gardens: Formalizing Nature

Master Painters and Sculptors of the Past: Artists' Homes and Ateliers

Indoor and Outdoor Collections: Art in Public Settings

LIST OF ILLUSTRATIONS

LIST OF ILLUSTRATIONS

FOREWORD

Welcome to *Art on Site!* In the following pages we will take you on forty-eight voyages of exploration into the artists' varied worlds—from the intimate confines of their working studios to the grand sites of their works. These have been outings of discovery for us—as we hope they will be for you.

We call this book *Art on Site* because each of our outings has a sense of place, whether as a site for art or artist. As you walk across a sculpture park, or follow in the footsteps of a landscape painter, or wander through a garden designed after a Chinese painting, we hope you will have a true sense of the artist's space and individual vision.

Our country's artists have historically had a deep and complicated relationship with their land—ranging from romantic views picturing the nation's natural beauty to abstractions of the landscape to environmental works, in which the landscape itself has become art. These outings will take you, for example, to the panoramic sites of the Hudson River painters, or to a planned architectural community by Frank Lloyd Wright, or to a quarry sculpture of an environmental artist.

To be an artist in America has rarely been easy. Some have worked together in colonies—like the impressionists of Connecticut or the abstractionists of East Hampton; others have struggled alone, taking their inspiration from the natural scenery and resources around them. For every illustrious Augustus Saint-Gaudens sculpting at his glorious New Hampshire estate, there have been dozens of artists with creative visions and cold studios tucked away in small towns and rural valleys. Even today there is tremendous variety in how American artists live and work—as you will see when you visit both the studios of the past and the artists' workshops of the present.

We have used a broad definition of art in these outings. The lines separating art from craft have long ago blurred, and environmental and landscape art have touched the boundaries of architecture. We have similarly tried to include a wide variety of artistic styles, and to give fair representation to younger, less known artists, as well as to the great names of past and present. In our search for unique sites that have a sense of history or visual appeal or unspoiled charm, we have purposely omitted the more frequented spots in our region. We hope you will not find masses of tour buses or tourist trappings in the places we have selected.

This book is for those of you who have a taste for art and architecture, as well as curiosity for exploring unusual places of artistic interest. You need not be a connoisseur to appreciate the aesthetic pleasures of *Art on Site*.

We do not pretend that this is a comprehensive guide to the region's many artistic treats. From the numerous places we visited we have selected these outings because they captured our imaginations. In your wanderings you might well discover additional places that we would be happy to know about.

As in our previous two books together, we have had a wonderful time working on this project and are grateful to the many people who have helped and encouraged us along the way. Among these we wish to thank in particular Cristina Biaggi, Andy Boose, Midge Boyle, Judy Dales, Jim Harrison, Elaine Kobos, Wani Larsen, Don Mallow, Robin Mooring-Frye, Peter Rosenfeld, Susan Stainback, and our always supportive publisher, Michael Kesend.

HOW TO USE THIS BOOK

Art On Site is a special kind of guidebook. It will take you through a large, eleven state area, exploring many out-of-the-way places, while avoiding well-known urban art centers. It is meant to be a guidebook of artistic discovery, rather than a comprehensive listing of every studio and collection throughout the region. With this aim in mind, we invite you to join us in seeking the unusual, inspiring, eccentric, wonderful world of America's artists.

We hope that you will use this book in a variety of ways. Perhaps you will take it along as you travel, choosing a detour or outing not far from your route. Maybe, with the help of our book, you will plan day-trips or weekend jaunts to sites of interest to you. Devotees of a particular style of art or artist may choose artwalks relating to their special interest. Even if you live in this region, we doubt you are familiar with all of the fascinating sites in your own state; perhaps our book will guide you to people and places you will want to visit again and again near your own hometown. We have ourselves already used our "finds" to delight foreign guests—to whom vast sculpture parks, for example, are a new and intriguing sight. But perhaps you are simply an armchair reader, content to explore in your mind by reading about distant pleasures. This book is for you, too.

We have divided our collection of artwalks into seven sections exploring different aspects of art on site. Our first group of outings follows in the footsteps of American artists, seeking the characteristic—often magnificent—views they painted. Next we take you to the most modern of conceptions: works of environmental art. In the third part you'll find artwalks exploring whole communities of special architectural interest.

The next selection includes a series of fascinating visits to studios and workshops to watch contemporary artists and artisans at work. The fifth part introduces special gardens, in which nature's beauty has been artistically designed or formalized. In the sixth section we take you to visit the evocative homes and ateliers of artists of the past. And in the final group of outings you'll find the spectacular sculpture gardens and other public art that is increasingly taking its place in the American landscape.

We provide you with a map of the entire region, and at the end of each chapter, directions from the nearest city. We recommend that before setting out you check our occasional "in the vicinity" suggestions at the end of some chapters, and our additional listings (And Bear in Mind . . .) in the back of the book. You'll find a guide to "choosing an outing" at the end, as well as an index of artists and sites of interest. Telephone numbers are included in each entry; it is a good idea to call before you leave home, to be certain that the site is open; outdoor art sites may be closed in bad weather.

Most of the private studios require a telephone call for an appointment, but you will find the artists and artisans we have chosen welcoming and enthusiastic in describing their work. (You are not expected to buy artworks when you visit private studios!) Public places may charge an admission fee, though many are free; we have identified the (often changing) fees as inexpensive (under $5.00), moderate (under $10), or expensive (more than $10). Needless to say, they may have risen from the amount listed at the date of publication.

We have tried to invite you into the many different worlds of American art and to make our book easy to use and enjoyable to read. We hope you will savor these artwalks as we have.

In the Artists' Footsteps: Painters' Views of the World Around Them

1

Landscape and History on the Hudson Highlands

West Point, New York

The Hudson River painters, the great romantics who glorified America's natural wonders on canvas, were inevitably drawn to the Hudson Valley Highlands. In their quest for what they called the "sublime landscape," they sought vistas that embodied their aesthetic and philosophical ideals. These nineteenth century artists, who flourished between 1820 and 1880, were dazzled by the scenic grandeur of the West Point region, where dramatic mountain ranges meet the majestic Hudson. Here they captured the spectacular scenery in its many variations.

This is a walk of views and imagination. We will locate some of the sites and vistas the artists immortalized. The actual scenes may not be precisely those depicted in the paintings—artists often use artistic license in their interpretation of nature—but will still be easily identifiable. We will concentrate on four areas, all within walking distance of one another, but you may prefer to drive to and from them and enjoy a walk within each site instead. And if time and energy are no problem, you may also visit additional spots that the artists painted nearby and just across the river.

When you arrive at West Point you might begin your outing at the Visitors' Center, where you can get a map and other materials. Our first art site is the nearby Regina Hall (once Ladycliff Building), the single officers' quarters, just up the hill from the museum. Although visitors are not encouraged to walk about here (as a sign clearly indicates), a discreet person can take a peek looking south from the river side of the building to the valley below—as we were told to do at the Visitors' Center. The Hudson River master John Frederick Kensett captured this vast panorama in his *View near Cozzens Hotel, West Point, New York* (Figure 1) and no doubt stood on this very spot. Although the Cozzens Hotel is long since gone, the natural landscape remains the same and is as spectacular as ever. Kensett, trained as an engraver, was greatly admired for his muted and natural colors and for the atmospheric lights and shadows he created in his works. As you can see, this landscape lends itself to his harmonious and almost impressionistic interpretation.

Our next stop is Fort Putnam, high above the West Point campus. To reach Fort Putnam (and you might prefer to drive, rather than walk), you must go past the Visitors' Center, continuing straight through Thayer Gate. Proceed left on Mills Road all the way up the hill. Bear left at Michie Stadium and take another left at Delfield Road. You will find a small parking area just below the fort and a little asphalt path leading to the fort. Fort Putnam can be visited year-round. It is perhaps most picturesque when the trees are leafy and the river blue, but even if you come during the winter months you can still walk around it at will and enjoy the spectacular panoramas. There are also walking trails nearby that take you through the woods to the valley below.

Fort Putnam was erected during the Revolutionary War to defend the Highlands at West Point. Called the "Gibraltar of North America," its strategic location made it an important defense site of the region, and its surrender to the enemy the object of Benedict Arnold's treason.

Fort Putnam, which could now be described as a "romantic ruin," was a subject that greatly appealed to the Hudson River artists, as can be seen from the number of landscape works it inspired. (In fact, an exhibition of Hudson River paintings frequently includes several versions of the same vista.) Its intriguing history, picturesque setting, and extraordinary views made it an ideal setting for artists of the period.

1. John Frederick Kensett. *View from Cozzen's Hotel, West Point, New York.* 1863

Robert Havell, Jr. was one of the painters who climbed to Fort Putnam to record its remarkable panoramic view. A native of England who engraved Audubon drawings for a time, Havell turned to painting later on in his career, settling in a home across the Hudson and devoting himself to painting landscapes of the area.

His *West Point from Fort Putnam* (Figure 2) creates a sweeping panoramic scene with the timeless Storm King Mountain, Constitution Island, and Pollopel Island, as well as the now-gone Roe's Hotel (in the foreground) and simple military encampments (to the right). The grandeur of the site is clearly appreciated by the three figures depicted at the left of the painting, all of whom are standing on the fort's ramparts in apparent awe.

Other views from the same site include Kensett's muted, subtle *View of Storm King from Fort Putnam* (at the Metropolitan Museum of Art) and John Ferguson Weir's *View of the Highlands from West Point* (New-York Historical Society). Weir, son of Robert Weir, the drawing teacher at West Point, painted almost precisely the same scene as Havell, but included neither fort nor people. (For more about Weir see chapter 39.)

Storm King Mountain was prominent in many of these landscapes. You should be able to view what those painters saw by scrambling up as high as you can so that the fort is below you, on your right. (For another view of Storm King looming over the Hudson, see chapter 2.)

From Fort Putnam it's a bit of a drive down to Trophy Point, at water's edge. Find the large parking area nearby and walk east toward the river, to the Kosciuszko Monument off Cullum Road. The well-known monument is easily recognizable, though the top portion was added on after it was painted by the Hudson River artists.

This monument honors the Lithuanian-born and Polish-educated Thaddeus Kosciuszko (1746–1817), who was appointed by George Washington as engineer in the Revolutionary Army to supervise the building of defenses at West Point. In 1828, twelve years after his death, a pedestal and shaft were erected by the cadets of West Point on the site of Fort Clinton, the center of the fortifications at West Point. The fort had been strategically located to fire on the enemy during the war and

2. Robert Havell, Jr., West Point, c.1850

prevent their access to Constitution Island. On this very spot the famous chain was stretched all the way across the Hudson to impede the enemy ships (as is indicated in a commemorative plaque).

It was only in 1913 that the statue atop the monument was added, hence many years after Samuel Lancaster Gerry's painting, *West Point, Hudson River* (Figure 3). To replicate the view of this charming work—which records a genteel walk by the Hudson shore on a pleasant summer afternoon rather than a bloody event—you can look north from below the monument or from the area around the cannons to the right.

From the monument, continue walking north on the main road to the spectacular overlook, for another favorite river scene depicted by Hudson River artists. Looking north, you will see the exact view that Thomas Doughty painted in his *Hudson River near West Point* (at the Montclair Art Museum). This follower of Thomas Cole was a leading landscape painter in Boston who traveled widely and painted many natural scenes. He has been criticized for not having been a careful enough observer of nature and for having painted from memory all too often. If that is the case, his memory must have been prodigious indeed, for his recording of this view is absolutely accurate.

Though you may be weary from all the walking from one site to the next, we hope you appreciate the inspiration the Hudson River and its surroundings provided for these artists. The river was, in fact, their "muse."

INFORMATION: The Visitors' Center at West Point is open daily from 9:00 A.M.-4:45 P.M. Telephone: 914-938-2638.

DIRECTIONS: From New York City cross the George Washington Bridge and take the Palisades Parkway north. At Exit 15 take Route 6 to Route 9W north. In the village of Highland Falls you'll see signs for West Point; follow signs to Visitors' Center.

In the vicinity . . .
There are two additional sites you might want to visit within West Point itself: Flirtation Walk and the Kosciuszko Garden.

Flirtation Walk. While visiting the Kosciuszko monument, you can take a small detour along the so-called Flirtation Walk (a romantic spot for cadets). A gravel and rock footpath about

3. Samuel Lancaster Gerry. West Point, Hudson River. 1858

three-quarters of a mile long, it has the inevitable magnificent views at every turn. From Cullum Road walk down the cliff to the river, past the lighthouse to the site where the great ship-stopping chain was actually anchored.

Kosciuszko Garden. This pleasant terrace near the south end of Flirtation Walk was a favorite reading spot of Kosciuszko's. Here he built a little fountain after discovering a living spring. Later, ornamental shrubs and seats were added, making this an ideal place for relaxing in pretty surroundings.

Storm King Art Center. Just a few miles away is the incomparable sculpture park (see chapter 46).

Of similar interest . . .
Other Hudson River artist sites include Kaaterskill Falls (see chapter 5), Olana (see chapter 37) and Cold Spring, just across the river (see chapter 2).

Samuel Colman's Vision of Storm King Mountain

Cold Spring, New York

One of the most dramatic views of the Hudson Valley is from the village of Cold Spring on the eastern riverbank, looking toward Storm King, the notable rock-faced mountain on the opposite shore. Storm King's looming presence is always mesmerizing, and particularly so in stormy weather or at dusk, when light and shadows give it an especially poetic look.

Just as the Hudson River artists chose to paint river vistas from West Point (see chapter 1), they also crossed the river to view the scenery from the opposite side. It was from the small, charming village of Cold Spring that the best views of Storm King could be had. Here, at the foot of the village's main street, was an unobstructed panorama of the river and its mountainous shore.

Among the notable mid-nineteenth century painters to capture this view was Samuel Colman, a well-known painter of the "second generation" of Hudson River artists. A student of Asher B. Durand, Colman also traveled and studied for many years in Europe seeking more exotic subject matter. But he is best known for his atmospheric landscapes of Hudson River scenery in both oil and watercolor.

Colman had a successful career, becoming a member of the National Academy of Design, and in 1866 the first president of the American Water Color Society. Colman's luminescent oil

4. Samuel Colman. *Storm King on the Hudson.* 1866

painting reflected his skillful enjoyment of watercolor, a medium which he preferred during the last twelve years of his life.

Storm King on the Hudson (Figure 4) was painted in oil in 1866. Its poetic depiction of the imposing mountain and various boats, dredges, and fishermen on the river is a study in light and atmospheric reflection. (A nineteenth century critic said that Colman's painting has "some very strong effects of light and shade, and his coloring has a brilliance that is so harmonious as to influence one like a strain of music.") In fact, in works like this one Colman realized the major objective of so many landscapists of his era: to capture a romantic vision of nature's beauty (with just a touch of industrial progress).

You can see this view across the river to Storm King—and perhaps even a dredge or boat or two—by walking to the end of Cold Spring's Main Street and out to the bandstand at the riverfront at West Street. Choose a day when the sun is breaking through the clouds over the river and you will not be disappointed by this romantic panorama.

You may also enjoy a brief visit to other sites of interest in this historic village; a small walking-tour flyer is available at many of the little shops. Cold Spring has a long and interesting background as an iron foundry center, and the town is filled with unusually well-preserved old houses dating back to its riverfront prominence as a steamboat port.

DIRECTIONS: From New York City take the George Washington Bridge to the Palisades Interstate Parkway north to the Bear Mountain Bridge. After crossing the bridge, take Route 9D along the river for nine miles for a scenic route to Cold Spring. An alternative route is to take the Henry Hudson Parkway, which becomes the Saw Mill River Parkway, to Route 9D.

In the vicinity . . .
Just across the river via the Bear Mountain Bridge is West Point, a focal point for Hudson River painters (see chapter 1). Not far from West Point is the Storm King Art Center (see chapter 46).

Of similar interest . . .
Other art sites favored by Hudson River painters are described in a visit to Kaaterskill Falls (see chapter 5) and West Point (see chapter 1).

Modernists in
The Adirondacks

Lake George, New York

Lake George, a picturesque spot in New York State's Adirondack Mountains, was the inspiration for works by two important modernists: painter Georgia O'Keeffe and sculptor David Smith. On this outing we visit the sites where they worked.

When you think of Georgia O'Keeffe's work, vivid images of nature come to mind—from the sensual flowers and stark animal skulls for which she is well-known, to her powerful panoramas in which she expresses the physical world in its most elemental form. Although much of her inspiration came from the vast southwest desert of New Mexico, O'Keeffe also lived and painted in New York State.

For years she and her husband, the renowned photographer Alfred Stieglitz, spent each summer and fall on a rustic farm property on Lake George, where her creative output was prodigious. Some of her most abstract works of the 1920s were painted by the lake. She enjoyed the wonderful natural surroundings, turning the landscape around her into abstract shapes and vibrant colors. "Objective painting is not good painting unless it is good in the abstract sense," she wrote. "A hill or tree cannot make a good painting just because it is a hill or a tree. It is lines and colors put together so that they say something . . . the abstraction is often the most definite form for the intangible thing in myself that I can only clarify in painting."

5. Georgia O'Keeffe. *From the Lake No. 1.* 1924

Like many artists of earlier times, O'Keeffe was fascinated by changing light and movement of the lake. The tradition of landscape painting (and beautiful lake views) was well established in the Adirondacks. The unspoiled scenery of upstate New York had long fascinated many painters ranging from the Hudson River artists to Winslow Homer; it was Georgia O'Keeffe who transformed the prettiness of Lake George into a series of dramatic abstractions.

Drawing on nature as a symbolic representation of inner emotions (she and Stieglitz referred to their nature works as "equivalents"), she turned landscape views into majestic, monumental visions. O'Keeffe spent hours studying the lake under different weather conditions and then painting various abstract versions of the same theme.

One of the brilliant studies in this series is *From the Lake No. 1*, painted in 1924 (Figure 5). Its swirling forms and deep colors create the ominous mood of an impending storm over water. Others in the series are similarly dramatic, with varying colors and symbolic forms.

O'Keeffe's revolutionary contributions to the art of landscape painting are particularly noteworthy if you compare the painting shown here with another view of Lake George by the nineteenth century artist John W. Casilear, who painted a similar vista in 1857. His canvas called *Lake George* (at the Brooklyn Museum) views the lake from the southern end; it was a highly regarded painting for its "pure light, neat outline, and distinct grace and grandeur," according to a critic at the time. O'Keeffe's abstract landscapes were seen by many of her contemporaries as equally grand and graceful, but by more conservative critics as shocking.

The O'Keeffe/Stieglitz farmhouse still exists today. But unfortunately, like so many artists' sites in our country, it has fallen victim to "progress"; it has become the office of a luxury condominium complex that includes much of the original property. But you can still see the house and view the lake from the same vantage point as O'Keeffe did, by walking through the grounds of the condominium complex. (The people in the office seem to be used to O'Keeffe enthusiasts coming around.)

Since the town of Lake George is no longer the quiet little lakeside resort it once was, you may like to travel north and

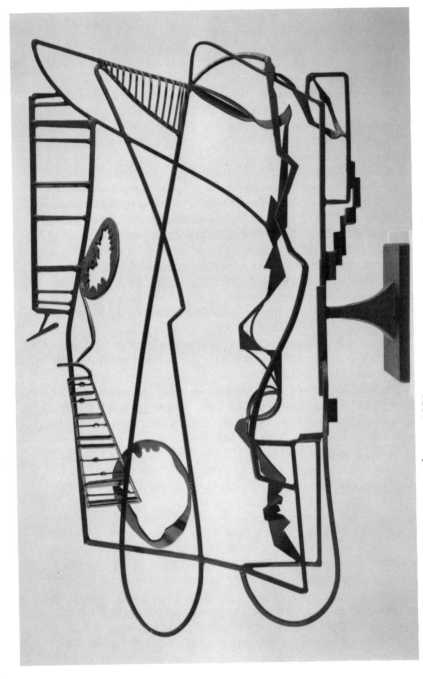

6. David Smith. *Hudson River Landscape*. 1951

view the Lake from a variety of unspoiled locations on both sides. Among them is a particularly pretty spot at Boltons Landing. This small picturesque town just north of Lake George on the west shore of the lake was for many years home to the noted American sculptor David Smith. Smith's whimsical and rhythmic iron works that he called "drawings-in-space" took American sculpture into new and significant forms. Combining found objects, shapes from the machine age, and free linear patterns, many of Smith's works like *Hudson River Landscape* (Figure 6) were loosely tied to the landscape around him.

Though the estate with its sculpture-dotted grounds is no longer open to the public, Boltons Landing has for many years been associated with Smith, and is well worth a stop. Here you will see a more appealing lakeside village, and perhaps can capture something of the aura of the artist's habitat.

If you return several times, you will see the same changing colors and light on the lake, and the same unspoiled vistas that inspired these original and independent artists.

INFORMATION: You can phone the condominium called "Quarters at Four Seasons" for information: 518-668-4901; or the Chamber of Commerce in Lake George: 518-668-5755.

DIRECTIONS: *To Lake George:* From Albany take Route 87 north (Northway) to Lake George (exit 22) to Route 9N. Quarters at Four Seasons is located on Route 9N along the lake, about ½ mile from the town of Lake George.
To Boltons Landing: From Lake George take Route 9W north.

In the vicinity . . .
Hyde Collection, 161 Warren Street, Glens Falls, N.Y. This unusually fine collection housed in a gracious mansion includes paintings and sculpture by European and American masters from Renaissance through twentieth century.

Of similar interest . . .
You'll find other David Smith sculptures noted in chapters 41, 44, and 46.

4

Fitz Hugh Lane, Luminist of the Northeast Seacoast

Gloucester, Massachusetts

Among the prettiest spots on the Eastern seaboard is Gloucester on Cape Ann, with its views of the sea, its inlets and bluffs, and its charming houses lining the harbor. Dozens of artists—ranging from the earliest American primitives to John Sloan, Stuart Davis, and Milton Avery—have painted its landscapes and seascapes in their own distinctive styles. (A collection of Gloucester views by American artists has been published by the Grace Borgenicht Gallery in New York.)

But no one is more identified with Gloucester than the nineteenth century seascape artist Fitz Hugh Lane, a native son and perhaps the nation's finest marine painter. It is fortunate for us that Lane's Gloucester paintings are in large part collected in the town itself, and that the sites and vistas that he painted are mostly still there and little changed.

Fitz Hugh Lane was a truly "American" painter of the last century, a "luminist," to whom the seascape provided an opportunity to convey the beauty of changing light over water. With its emphasis on landscape light, luminism was an outgrowth of the Hudson River School of painting and flourished in the mid-nineteenth century. But it was also a different way of seeing, an attitude—not only to light but to things in nature—a subjective mode of expression that created a mood of tremendous intensity.

Lane's seascapes are startlingly still. Trained as a lithographer, he was a deft and realistic draftsman. He skillfully combined the topographical view—then among the most popular forms of art in America—with a mastery of the nuances of light and sea in different weather and seasons. He combined these carefully observed and recorded panoramas with a delicate stillness, an aura of transcendental peace or arrested time. Lane's paintings show a distinctive and lucid admiration of nature. Some art historians consider him to have been the visual counterpart of Ralph Waldo Emerson.

Begin your visit in Gloucester at the Cape Ann Historical Association. You will be able to view some of the forty Lane works housed there. In addition, the Historical Association shows a half-hour film about Lane. Pick up a map and set out on a walk to find the sites of some of the views he painted. Though Lane was crippled (probably by childhood polio), he worked from a wide variety of locations.

Your first stop is Lane's house, on Harbor Loop atop a hill in the park at Duncan Point. Built of granite blocks in 1849, this house has had a number of lives, including a stint as a jail; it is known as the Old Stone Jug. Lane's studio was on the top floor, from which he could see the harbor. The house is not open to visitors.

Next, make your way to Stage Fort Park, where the earliest settlers in Gloucester are supposed to have landed in the 1620s. This is a site of several Lane paintings.

You will see Stage Fort Park from another vantage point when you visit the former site of Brookbank, the Sawyer Homestead (now gone). In Lane's view, which almost seems to be seen by the artist through glass, you can spot Stage Fort Park (left), Gloucester (center), Ten Pound Island and lighthouse (right), and Dolliver's Neck on the far right.

Rocky Neck, the oldest continuous art colony in the country, is another Lane site, as well as a spot frequented by many other artists attracted by its view of the busy harbor.

Farther out of town are a series of beaches, including Good Harbor Beach, that Lane used for outdoor sketching and panoramas of the sea.

There are several other Lane sites that the Historical Society can suggest to you, including a place called "Norman's Woe" and a site along the Annisquam River at the drawbridge. A particularly pleasant way to see Lane's subjects is by harbor boat; Lane was an avid sailor who toured up and down the coastline, sketching. You can arrange such a tour with the whale-viewing boats in town.

Also in Gloucester are three other sites of interest which may be visited as you walk through town. The Sargent–Murray–Gilman–Hough House at 49 Middle Street was built by Winthrop Sargent in 1768; it eventually became the home of the daughter of the noted American painter John Singer Sargent. You will find some of his paintings hanging here and much to interest historians and architectural buffs, as well.

The Hammond Museum at 80 Hesperus Avenue is one of those Renaissance–Gothic style castles that can frequently be found in unlikely places in the United States; this one contains many fine European design elements, including a fifteenth century Spanish tile ceiling, a fourteenth century Italian bed, a Great Hall and a Gothic Room, and a Renaissance era courtyard and reflecting pool. The museum is also the home of one of the great Hammond organs of the world. It has ten thousand pipes and 144 stops; well-known organists occasionally give concerts here.

Beauport, on Eastern Point Boulevard, is another large castle-style mansion that invites visitors to tour its forty rooms. Each of these interiors is a replica of a different era of American design and architectural style, with an emphasis on the eighteenth century.

INFORMATION: The Cape Ann Historical Association is located at 27 Pleasant Street, Gloucester. Telephone: 508-283-0455.

DIRECTIONS: From Boston take Route 128 thirty miles north to Cape Ann. Exit 12 will bring you into the town of Gloucester. Pleasant Street intersects Main Street in downtown Gloucester.

5

The Hudson River Painters at Kaaterskill Falls

Kaaterskill, New York

There is probably no area in the East that has been so immortalized by artists as the Hudson River valley and the Catskill mountain area nearby. Fortunately, much of its glorious scenery remains unspoiled and open to the adventurous walker. In fact, a hike to the sites so beloved by Hudson River painters is an experience in both natural and artistic beauty not to be missed. Once you leave your car you will feel that you are treading on the same paths and seeing the same views of a century or more ago. And when you come upon these marvelous vistas you will understand why the Hudson River artists were so inspired and why American landscape painting caught the attention of the world.

> Nature has spread for us a rich and delightful banquet. Shall we turn from it? We are still in Eden; the wall that shuts us out of the garden is our own ignorance and folly.

Thomas Cole, America's first important landscapist, wrote these words in his 1835 *Essay on American Scenery*. His colleagues described the natural beauty of the Hudson Valley as evidence "of the hand of God" in the glories of America. This combination of religious exaltation and nationalism characterized their enthusiasm for the unspoiled wilderness scenery and added immeasurably to the nineteenth century American perception that this was a golden land with a special destiny.

As artists packed their easels and paintboxes to set out for the countryside, a new appreciation for nature—and for works done at the scene itself—took hold. A loosely-knit band of painters became known as the Hudson River School—though there was no actual school involved. While it paralleled the French interest in landscape (the Barbizon School) and the romantic realists of England, the Hudson River School was quintessentially American—an attempt to capture the very spirit of the nation. Even the experience of nature became important, as the artists trudged up mountainsides or paddled canoes into the forests to "catch" in sketchbooks or on canvas the wilderness unspoiled. (And soon a typical—and lasting—American debate over progress versus unspoiled scenery ensued. For another view of this issue see chapter 6 on the Starrucca Viaduct.)

Though the Hudson River painters eventually spread their wings and explored New England and other regions, most began their outdoor painting in the Catskill Mountain region and along the great river's banks and bluffs. The area they chose lies along Kaaterskill Creek, a meandering stream that makes its way between rolling mountains just above the Hudson Valley.

A winding mountain road known as Rip Van Winkle Trail (you can now drive most of the way) leads to Kaaterskill Clove, the site of many well-known paintings. ("Clove" means ravine or gully, from the Dutch word "cleft.")

Here, at the scenic convergence of narrow gorge, winding river, magnificent trees and jutting rocks, Asher Durand painted his *Kindred Spirits* (in the collection of the New York Public Library)—probably the most famous Hudson River School painting of all. (Other views of this spot include Thomas Cole's *The Clove, Catskills,* in the collection of the New Britain Museum of Art, and *Kauterskill Clove* by Sanford Gifford in the Metropolitan Museum of Art.)

But even more dramatic vistas brought the artists to this region. At the top of the craggy mountains were both a miraculous waterfall and thrilling panoramic views of the Hudson Valley. The area was "discovered" (and the Hudson River "school" launched) by Thomas Cole. In 1825 Cole made a rewarding sketching trip to the region. When he returned to the city his works were shown in a Manhattan shop. Colonel John Trumbull, president of the American Academy of Fine Arts, the portraitist and writer William Dunlap and Asher B. Durand, soon to be a leading landscapist, came upon Cole's paintings.

"This youth," said the illustrious Trumbull, "has done what I have all my life attempted in vain." And William Cullen Bryant summed up the artistic community's admiration at seeing Cole's Kaaterskill pictures: "Here . . . is a young man who does not paint nature at second hand . . . here is American nature and the feeling it awakens."

Soon other artists were following Cole's lead to the Catskills and to the discovery of nature as a subject. Many of them came to stay at the Mountain House Hotel, a legendary inn atop a craggy site near the spectacular Kaaterskill Falls. Taking a train from New York, the artists could disembark quite near the falls, or take a horse and buggy to sketch them up close. (We took a footpath, which is clearly indicated, since conservationists have rightly closed public roads into this wilderness.)

They found Kaaterskill Falls a magical spot with a two-part cascade over a rosy stone mountainside. Unlike the great falls at Niagara, Kaaterskill seems a private place, hidden deep in the forest, exciting to discover. Its colors, delicate rippling fall, and the spectacular foliage around it have made it one of the most famous American landscape subjects.

On this outing you will also find a spot known as Artist Rock—another grand view that must have enthralled the painters. Here, high above the Hudson Valley (you can see the river below) is a vista that literally takes your breath away. It is, fortunately, easy to reach along a comparatively flat path that winds through exquisite woods and rocky outcroppings. You will easily imagine the artists setting out from the Mountain House, sketchbooks in hand, to record this scenic wonder.

The Mountain House—once an elegant columned inn—is no longer there. Like so many spots made famous by artists, it eventually became too expensive for them, and a few bought homes in the area instead of staying there. It has long since disappeared. Now its dramatic location remains free of building. You can walk to the site and look out over the magnificent landscape, with the Hudson a bright ribbon of light in the distance, while massive trees and rocky crags spread out below you—a panorama just as it must have looked to the painters who congregated on its grand terrace.

In the following paragraphs we will take you on this three-part walk to explore some of the most beloved scenes of the Hudson River painters. This walk can be divided into parts, for some of it is rough going, while in other places you can drive to a level terrain and walk easily along a flat path. Some of the sites painted by the Hudson River school are now unreachable, including about ¼ mile of the Escarpment Trail that the artists once took from the Mountain House across the mountain to the top of the falls. But many of the locations seen in the paintings are easily accessible to walkers. In each of these sections we will point out the setting for the artists' works; this is one of those rare outings where time and progress seem to have spared the unspoiled beauty of the scenery.

This walk, being one of our more rugged outings, is recommended for fit walkers in sturdy shoes. Bring along drinking water; you will not find refreshment stands in this wilderness! We recommend the fall foliage season as the best time, when the scenery is unsurpassed. Early summer is also very lovely, but try to go on a weekday if you want total solitude, for hikers and campers know this route. Do not try this outing in winter or early spring because of wet and muddy trails.

Park your car at the public parking area on Route 23A, about 3½ miles after leaving Palenville and Route 32. Walk downhill about ¼ mile to a small bridge overlooking Kaaterskill Creek and Bastion Falls, which are quite pretty and worth a second glance. You will see a smallish sign indicating Kaaterskill Falls to be ½ mile up from there. (We should add that it's a very long uphill ½ mile! Remember the artists came by buggy above the falls.) Before you set out, cross the road to see a wonderful view of Kaaterskill Clove, perhaps one of the same views admired and painted by the artists.

Start your walk uphill, following the rather sporadic yellow trail markers, which lead you more or less parallel to the creek all the way up to the falls. (If you lose sight of the trail markers, which is likely, just keep walking alongside the creek and you won't get lost.) The going can be quite arduous, as the "path" (which can hardly be called one in some places) has been eroded and footing is uneven. You will be clambering over large rocks, twisted tree roots, decaying branches and leaves, which may be slippery. The seat of the pants is a good way to negotiate the worst of these hazards. Even though the distance is short, the trek will be difficult for those who are not in fairly good physical condition and might prefer parts two and three of this walk. (We saw some poor souls trying to negotiate their climb on all fours, and one in high heels!)

But your efforts are well rewarded. The forest is dense with hemlocks and many deciduous trees that are brilliant in fall and romantically green in spring and summer. As you make the rugged but exhilarating climb you feel somewhat like an explorer in a primeval forest. Finally, you reach a large boulder in the middle of the creek bed from where you get a full front view of the falls in all their splendor. And what majestic falls they are! At 260 feet, they are the highest in New York State (including Niagara Falls, which, of course, are much broader). The two slender and elegant cascades are divided by a rock basin and surrounded by a landscape that is wild, rugged, and unspoiled. This is a truly romantic scene that any landscapist would adore. If you climb slightly higher, you'll see the spot from which Thomas Cole's *Falls of Kaaterskill* (Figure 7) was painted.

After you have stopped long enough to rest and take in this marvelous place, you must retrace your steps. If you have the energy to explore the second section of our artwalk, return to your car to drive up to the North Lake State Campsite, a park from which you can walk to the site of the Mountain House Inn. To reach the park from Route 23A, continue in the same direction to Haines Falls and take a right on Route 18, following signs for the North Lake State Campsite. You will arrive at a toll booth where you pay a small fee and are given a map and trail guide that shows you (more or less) how to find the site of the old Mountain House.

Continuing in your car, you now enter Catskill State Park, a woodsy region popular with campers and hikers and filled with clearly marked trails. Park at North Lake, where the road ends. Here you'll see a small sandy beach, picnic and restroom facilities, and signs telling you what is prohibited (nearly everything except hiking). To reach the Mountain House site, follow the signs up a gentle hill until you come to the commemorative

7. Thomas Cole. *Falls of Kaaterskill.* 1826

marker for the hotel. Continue toward the escarpment for what has been—and you'll find still is—one of the most impressive and vast panoramas in the East. The landscape seems to go on forever: miles of the glistening Hudson are laid out in front of you, surrounded by the lush river valley. On the horizon you can see the Taconic and Berkshire Mountain ranges.

If you walk farther along the escarpment, you'll find a path leading toward "Artist Rock" (about ½ mile away)—the third leg of our artwalk. Follow the signs to "Artist Rock," "Sunset Rock" and "Newman's Ledge," trails all quite clearly marked with blue blazes. Once you are past picnic areas and other indications of organized parkland, you find yourself on virgin, somewhat hilly terrain along the cliffs. The views are extraordinary.

It is along this trail that you can look back toward the Mountain House site to see another captivating panorama that inspired so many artists. As you walk, you'll be able to identify the site chosen by Hudson River artist Jasper Cropsey in his painting *Catskill Mountain House* in 1855 (Minneapolis Institute of Art). Another painting of the same site is Thomas Cole's *A View of the Two Lakes and Mountain House, Catskill Mountains, Morning, 1844* (Brooklyn Museum).

After a short but arduous climb on top of large boulders (fortunately not near the edge of the cliff), you reach a plateau which appears almost to be a man-made terrace, so regular is the rock surface. But this is a natural stone formation; at the top, overlooking the vista beyond is Artist Rock. The trees around it are overgrown now, but the artists of a century and a half ago could see the Mountain House from here too. You can continue along this trail to see the wonderful "Sunset Rock" and "Newman's Ledge."

If you are still able and adventuresome, go back to the hotel site and set out on the other section of the Escarpment Trail. It used to be possible to reach the falls from above, along a network of trails that still exist. This extensive trail system includes miles of fabulous views atop tall cliffs overlooking the Hudson Valley and Kaaterskill Clove. The hike from the hotel site to the falls is about four miles, but the trail along the ledges is difficult and dangerous. The section of it that actually goes to the falls was recently definitively closed as unsafe. So your walk will not reach the falls from above. Still, you will certainly not be disappointed by the spectacular views.

DIRECTIONS: From New York City, take the George Washington Bridge to the Palisades Parkway to the New York State Thruway north. Exit at Saugerties (exit 20). Take Route 32 to Palenville, and Route 23A toward Haines Falls. After about 3½ miles you'll see a small sign on the right-hand side of the road indicating the way to Kaaterskill Falls (you will also see a gorge and another waterfall). Go another ¼ mile until you reach a parking area on the left side of the road. Walk down to the sign indicating the ascent to the falls. All other sites in Catskill State Park are marked.

Of similar interest . . .
Other sites favored by Hudson River painters are described in chapter 1 at West Point, and chapter 2 at Cold Spring. A visit to Thomas Cole's house is included in chapter 37.

6

Starrucca Viaduct: Progress Amid Natural Beauty

Susquehanna Valley, Pennsylvania

Hudson River School painters brought the beauty of the American landscape to the attention of a nation that had greatly overlooked it. In their rush to build and develop the country, Americans had paid little attention to their native scenery. The first Hudson River painters spoke in religious terms of "God's hand" in the American landscape, and of the duty of all to preserve it. They were, of course, talking about the rivers and hillsides and forests unspoiled by human hands. Their paintings of these glorious views became the first "native" style of painting.

Jasper Cropsey was a leading landscapist in this mid-nineteenth century tradition. A critic at one of his exhibitions remarked:

> The axe of civilization is busy with our old forests, and artisan ingenuity is fast sweeping away the relics of our national infancy . . . Yankee enterprise has little sympathy with the picturesque, and it behooves our artists to rescue from its grasp the little that is left, before it is ever too late.

But in a curiously American twist, landscapists soon sought to find a balance between progress and natural beauty. Why not find beauty in man's creations on the landscape as well? In 1865 Cropsey painted *Starrucca Viaduct* (Figure 8), a poetic landscape of Pennsylvania's Susquehanna River, including its

8. Jasper Francis Cropsey. Starrucca Viaduct. 1865

newly constructed railroad viaduct with a rushing train. To Cropsey, a specialist in fall coloring and naturalistic scenery, the inclusion of a great engineering feat like the Starrucca Viaduct and steaming train in a landscape was an implicit celebration of American progress.

Cropsey was born in 1823 in New York State, and practiced as an architect before leaving for Europe in 1847. Over the next fifteen years he spent a great deal of time in London, where he was associated with pre-Raphaelite landscapists and the British critic John Ruskin. When he returned home after the Civil War, he continued to paint realistic landscapes, varying his style very little. His specialty was autumn foliage and Eastern scenery. This painting, perhaps more than any other of Cropsey's work, captures nineteenth century America's dual romance with nature and progress.

The Starrucca Viaduct, by the way, was a widely heralded achievement in American engineering. Constructed in 1847–1848 by the Erie Railroad, it is the oldest stone railroad bridge still in use in Pennsylvania, and a monumental sight to see. It is 1040 feet long, 100 feet high, and 25 feet wide; its massive, but artistically arched design is still striking today.

Fortunately for walkers, there is an uncommonly lovely way to see the viaduct and to spot the very site of Cropsey's painting. (Keep in mind that in those days artists still worked—or at least sketched—out of doors.) We believe that this artwalk will take you to the view that the artist saw along the Susquehanna's charming banks. The walk there, which is less than a mile long, is in itself a delight, and the sighting of the viaduct is both romantic and dramatic.

Begin your walk by leaving your car in the small shopping center behind the First Methodist Church at the intersection of Routes 92, 171 and Erie Street in the town of Susquehanna. (The painting is subtitled *In the Susquehanna Valley near Lanesboro, Pennsylvania*; you will be walking toward Lanesboro.)

Walk through the parking lot behind the stores. You will see the river and the railroad tracks. Cross the tracks carefully (they are occasionally still in use), where you will find a wonderful riverside path heading to the right (as you face the river). We took this walk in the dead of winter and it was glorious—both because the view was so clear and because it was deserted except for a few human and canine footprints in the snow. But you will enjoy the scenic river with its inlets and shoals and leaning trees in any season. You will need to walk less than a mile for your first view of the viaduct towering above the river. At a certain point—which we leave to you to discover—you will find yourself in the artist's footsteps.

After your walk, you should drive up the hill (along Route 171) for another view of the viaduct, and if you continue a mile or two farther, for a ride under its massive arches.

DIRECTIONS: From New York City, take Route 80 west to 380 North, to Route 81 North. Exit at Route 171 for the town of Susquehanna.

7

Off-Shore Art Colonies

*Appledore, Deer, and Monhegan
Islands, Maine*

Getting away to an island retreat is an enduring popular fantasy. Three enticing islands along Maine's rugged coastline—Appledore, Deer Isle and Monhegan—have particularly appealed to artists, art lovers, and nature enthusiasts over the years. All provide a pleasurable day's "escape," off the beaten track.

APPLEDORE

To visit Appledore is to relive a fascinating period in the American art scene. The ninety-five-acre island, the largest of the barren and somewhat bleak Isles of Shoals, located some nine miles off the coast of Portsmouth, New Hampshire, is the site of a beloved Victorian garden that was immortalized in many paintings and writings. One of the first seaside summer resorts on the East Coast during the mid- to late nineteenth century, Appledore has had an intriguing history. How this garden was created, how it inspired an entire generation of American artists, and what became of it, all add to the lore and appeal of the island.

As early as the sixteenth century European fishermen found the tiny cluster of islands to be rich fishing grounds and they colonized the islands. A thriving fishing industry, unrivaled in New England, brought wealth to the Isles of Shoals for a brief time. After years of neglect the islands enjoyed a renaissance when summer tourists rediscovered them in the mid-nineteenth century. They liked the romantic, rugged, moorlike beauty, windswept landscape, and ocean views they found there. Thomas Laighton, a businessman from Portsmouth, opened the Appledore House Resort in 1848 to immediate success. With him came his family, including his remarkably creative and charismatic daughter, Celia.

The reputation of Celia Thaxter (her married name) as a poet of distinction grew. She attracted the attention of many of the literary and artistic lions of her time, who became her friends and later visited in the summers at Appledore. These luminaries—the list reads like a cultural Who's Who of late nineteenth century America—included James Russell Lowell, John Greenleaf Whittier, Nathaniel Hawthorne, Harriet Beecher Stowe, Mark Twain, and the painters William Morris Hunt and Childe Hassam, to name a few. They were drawn to the island's stark, wild beauty, true, but especially to the intellectually and culturally stimulating atmosphere Celia provided, and to the enchanting flower-filled life-style they could enjoy at the hotel. They were also charmed by the fabled garden she cultivated on a terrace that sloped from her cottage toward the sea. This splendid 50′ × 15′ plot of brilliantly colored old-fashioned flowers—poppies, hollyhocks, larkspur, among many other varieties—contrasted sharply with the harsh, stark surroundings of rocks, brush, and sea, a contrast that greatly struck many of these artists.

One artist who was particularly inspired by Celia's garden was the impressionist Childe Hassam, who painted it over and over in its many configurations. He and Celia became fast friends and collaborators. When Celia wrote an account of the joys and frustrations of creating a garden in a physically difficult environment in An Island Garden, Hassam illustrated it. He joyously depicted the vitality and sparkle of her garden and other views of the Isles of Shoals in hundreds of oils, watercolors, and pastels over a period of more than thirty years. Some of his best, most vigorous work—such as his Isle of Shoals Garden or Garden in its Glory (Figure 9), which depicts Celia in her garden—were made during his time at Appledore.

Celia Thaxter died in 1894 and, with her, her offshore cultural salon and lovely garden. The hotel and her cottage burned

9. Childe Hassam. *Isle of Shoals Garden* or *The Garden in its Glory*. 1892

down in 1914, and Appledore was almost forgotten. During World War II the island housed a submarine observation post (a U.S. Army barracks was placed right on what had been Celia's garden) and, finally, in the 1960s, the Shoals Marine Laboratory, which still exists. In the process of restoring some of the old cottages and building new ones, the Laboratory directors had the imagination to reconstruct Celia Thaxter's unique garden, using her book as a guideline.

Today the garden has been restored to include more or less everything Celia grew. It can be enjoyed during the summer months by members of the scientific community, as well as day-trippers. While on Appledore you should also visit the Laighton family cemetery, a lonely, windswept spot located near her garden; it is here that Celia was buried. Day visitors may also ask for permission to tour the classrooms and labs of the Shoals Marine Laboratory, and can walk along nature trails to spot gulls, snowy egrets, black-crowned herons, or others of the one hundred or so species seen on the island during migrations.

Getting to Appledore requires some planning and money (see page 40), but we hope you will feel that being on this special site with its melancholy beauty and connections with the past will be inspiring enough to make it worth the effort.

Visitors to Appledore are first taken to nearby Star Island (also a conference center), where there are additional places of interest to see. Don't miss the lovely stone meeting house built in 1800, which Nathaniel Hawthorne greatly appreciated; or the Charles F. Vaughn Memorial Cottage with its exhibits of Celia Thaxter memorabilia. Nature lovers can walk along the island's rocky coves and cliffs and hope to spot nesting gulls. Be sure to avoid nesting areas during spring and early summer, however; gulls can be quite ferocious and will dive at those who come too close to their nests!

DEER ISLE

In the heady days of early abstractionist painting in America—beginning in the second decade of the twentieth century—such artists as Marsden Hartley, Georgia O'Keeffe, and John Marin all painted in Maine in the summertime. Just as the delicate gardens of Appledore appealed to the impressionists, the more elemental natural scenery of the Maine coast and its islands captured the attention of these painters. The dark pines, jagged rocky coast, and brilliant light inspired such artists to abstract from nature, creating new styles of landscape.

John Marin's paintings of the Maine scenery both in oil and watercolor are particularly well-known. It is hard to look at Maine's coastline and not see a Marin of the scene in the mind's eye! Marin's summer headquarters were for many years at Deer Isle, about halfway up the Maine coastline. Here at Deer Isle he made numerous sketches and paintings of the sea and the land.

Critics have found Marin's work in the twenties and thirties hard to define; they have variously described his style as related to that of Sung Dynasty landscape painting, as an outgrowth of Impressionism, and as an attempt to combine both abstractionism and realistic landscape painting. Whatever its antecedents, however, Marin's free use of loose impressionistic images and abstract patterns was very much his own and surely captured the essence of Maine's beauty.

From Deer Isle two other tiny islands off the coast can be seen. *Mark and Andrews Island from Deer Isle* (Figure 10) is a typical Marin watercolor of Maine scenery. You can see this view by crossing the bridge from Sedgewick and proceeding out to Deer Isle by car and then walking to the coast.

MONHEGAN

Monhegan Island has long been known as an art colony. Though its prominence in the world of art is in the past, it is still home to many artists and art lovers. The tiny island—little more than one square mile in area—was discovered by seafarers and explorers centuries ago, but it was not until the 1870s that the first artists made the ten-mile crossing from the mainland to paint its wild shores and stormy seas. They were not only drawn to the majestic 160-foot cliffs and dramatic ocean views, but also to the picturesque fishing community, pretty meadows, and virgin forest. (Winslow Homer was a notable exception to the long list of distinguished artists who came and stayed; after experiencing violent seasickness on the ferryboat crossing, he was forced to turn back, never to return!)

10. John Marin. *Mark and Andrews Island from Deere Isle, Maine.* 1920

Since the late nineteenth century more than three hundred artists, including many notable American painters, have worked on this island. Well-known paintings of Monhegan Island were made by Robert Henri, Edward Hopper, George Bellows, Rockwell Kent, and Jamie Wyeth. You may be particularly familiar with Rockwell Kent's jagged rock forms in his black and white woodcuts, or Robert Henri's bold canvases depicting the turbulent and angry sea crashing dramatically against the fish houses on shore. German-born Emil Hozhauer painted the enduring subjects of fishermen with their nets at sea and, more recently, Jamie Wyeth has depicted the many people and animals that have fascinated him on the island.

Today a handful of artists still live on Monhegan year-round, although their names may not be as familiar. The majority come to work during the summer months. And, happily for interested art lovers, a few set aside a day here and there for visitors to come to their studios. Inevitably, tourists and day-trippers have discovered the island as well, and come to enjoy the local art scene—the artists' studios, galleries, and occasional local art exhibits—as well as the little fishing and lobstering village and the many natural wonders. Birdwatchers might spot the 250 or so species that stop during spring and fall migrations, and nature enthusiasts can walk the seventeen-mile woodsy trails to admire the more than seven hundred different kinds of wildflowers that bloom in season.

Not surprisingly, the summer months see quite a number of day-trippers, eager to enjoy a few hours on the island before taking the ferryboat back to the mainland. Fortunately, the provident islanders have tried to preserve the natural surroundings as best they can: the atmosphere is uncommercial and tourist facilities are limited, discouraging mass tourism. You must definitely plan to reserve your place on the ferryboat ahead of time, as space is limited.

Before you set off on your day's exploration of art sites on Monhegan, you should get a map at an island shop. Note that the souvenir map showing artists' studios is not necessarily accurate or up-to-date; to visit the studios open to the public, check the bulletin boards around the village for a flyer including visiting times and locations. In some cases you might find signs next to the studios indicating they are open.

On your wanderings, don't miss the Monhegan Museum, located in the house formerly occupied by the lighthouse keeper, now designated a Historic Site. Here you'll find displays of island flora, birds, geology, and history. There is also an annual art exhibit featuring Monhegan artists.

INFORMATION: *Appledore*. The ferry for day-trippers (one hundred visitors maximum per trip) sails out of Portsmouth, New Hampshire, at 11:00 A.M., arriving first at Star Island at about noon; from there you are picked up by the Shoals Marine Laboratory launch for the short trip to Appledore. (To reserve the launch you must phone ahead: 603-862-2994.) The ferry leaves Star Island at 3:00 P.M. for the trip back to the mainland, so that those going on to Appledore have less than three hours to visit. The cost of the ferry is moderate and we thought admission to the garden was expensive.

Note: The garden is open on Wednesdays during the summer and can be seen only by guided tour.

Monhegan. The ferry to Monhegan leaves from Port Clyde or Boothbay Harbor, Maine, from mid-June to mid-October.

Phone or write: Monhegan–Thomaston Boat Line

P.O. Box 238

Port Clyde, ME 04855

(207) 372-8848

Fares are $20 round trip, $12 for children.

DIRECTIONS: From Boston to the Maine Islands take Route 95 north.

For Appledore: Take Route 95 north to Portsmouth exit, to ferry.

For Deer Isle: Route 95 to Route 3 to Route 1; take Route 15 toward Stonington. You can reach the island by car.

For Monhegan: Route 95 to Route 1 north; at Thomaston take Route 131 south to Port Clyde for ferry.

8

Grandma Moses in Rural New York

Eagle Bridge, New York

The pretty rolling landscape of the New York/southern Vermont border will remind you of the picturesque scenes painted by Grandma Moses, the chronicler of a folksy and charming rural America. And no wonder! This area around Eagle Bridge and White Creek, New York (just over the border from Bennington, Vermont), is where she lived and what she painted. She began to paint in 1937 (at the age of seventy-seven). Come with us—by bike, on foot, or even by car—on a charming tour of this unchanged and delightful scenery.

This is such picture-book country (and the images of Grandma Moses are so indelibly engraved on our minds) that we feel nature is once again imitating art. There are bright red barns and stark white houses, black and white cows everywhere, old trees and stone walls, astonishingly thick forests outlining the gentle hillsides, and everywhere vistas of Vermont's mountains in a distant lavender haze. In spring and summer the view is startlingly green with spots of yellow and white wildflowers; in fall there are the deeper gold and red tones of the foliage of sugar maple and golden oak; in winter brilliant snowy white fields contrast with black tree trunks and deep green pines.

On this outing you'll see many examples of Grandma Moses' work in a local museum (which also contains intact the very schoolhouse she attended), the house called "Mt. Nebo" in which she lived, the nearby hamlet of White Creek Center (the subject of one of her pictures), the studio of a fourth generation Moses also working in a "primitive" manner, and several specific vistas that she painted.

You can begin your Grandma Moses tour at either end of this picturesque path. If you wish to begin at the Bennington Museum just across the border in Vermont, you'll find a number of her works housed there. This is, in fact, the largest public collection of her paintings anywhere. The museum also contains many of her personal belongings, her worktable, paints and brushes, and family photos. In addition—and perhaps of particular interest to children—is the old schoolhouse she attended, which has been lifted intact from nearby Hoosick Falls and set down adjoining the front entrance to the museum.

In the museum shop be sure to buy two small reproductions of her paintings, because one, a postcard of a painting called *Autumn*, is a still-almost-accurate color picture of White Creek hamlet (which you will see on your outing), and the other, in the form of a notecard, is a color reproduction of a particularly charming site on Route 68 called *White Creek* (Figure 11).

Once you have steeped yourself in her style, you can set out, guidebook and postcards in hand. If you go on a weekday, there is the likelihood that you will pass hardly another soul or car or truck, adding to your sense of journeying into an almost forgotten American scene. (By the way, Grandma Moses' autobiography, *Grandma Moses: My Life's History*, describing her childhood in Eagle Bridge, gives a delightful picture that fits right in with the images you will see in her paintings and on this outing.)

You may wish to reverse this tour and begin on Route 22 in New York State, ending at the museum.

From Cambridge, New York (an old and rather funky town), head south on Route 22 for about 2½ miles. You'll see a sign reading "White Creek: 5 miles"; slow down, for you will take the immediate left just at a small red barn. Here, right after you turn, is the tiny hamlet of White Creek Center (not the larger town of White Creek). The painting that Grandma Moses made of this little crossroads includes the church and the houses and the chickens, but the old barn with its waterwheel is gone.

11. Grandma Moses. White Creek. n.d.

When you have wandered around the wonderful rural grave-yard, continue on the same road, and out into the farm country through which Route 68 meanders so prettily. We highly recommend biking along this route; the hills are not bad and the views sensational. About ½ mile farther from the hamlet is one such view on your left.

Some two miles along Route 68 you'll see a green sign with an arrow pointing you toward Eagle Bridge. Turn right here for another lovely tour through farm country to reach "Mt. Nebo," Grandma's last home—and now the home and gallery of the fourth generation Moses mentioned above, also a folk painter but working in a more commercial vein.

This road to Eagle Bridge, where the Moses homestead sits, is so lovely that it is a pity to find that Eagle Bridge itself (named for its bridge with a prominent eagle on the top) is a rather run-down town.

However, Mt. Nebo is a pristine place, looking as if it had stepped right out of the paintings. To find it, note the large Moses family vegetable stand on your left, just after you recross Route 22 en route to Eagle Bridge. Make a left here and very soon you'll see a sign directing you to the Moses homestead about ¼ of a mile beyond. You may enjoy a visit to the Moses Gallery, though for us it was less the high point of the tour than a reminder of how hard it is to re-create the innocence of original American folk art in today's sophisticated, commercial climate.

But the people who work at the Gallery were most helpful in directing us to Grandma's original sites, including the vista we have in hand, *White Creek*. Retrace your steps across Route 22 and back to Route 68, here also called Cobble Hill Road. This time turn right on Route 68 and continue on toward White Creek. You will pass a picture-book place called "September Farm" on your left.

Just beyond Rice Lane (a left side road), you'll see a white house on a hill also on the left. The charming view painted in *White Creek* was made from this Moses relative's home. Looking out from the front of the house over the valley and hills beyond, you'll spot the two farms in the picture (the Walker Farm—left, and the Perry Farm—right), and White Creek itself, where Grandma's grandchildren went swimming. (The creek is only visible nowadays in winter, since trees have grown up along its banks.)

Continuing on your way you will next go downhill somewhat to the very old town of White Creek, where several historical markers will date the buildings to pre-Revolutionary times. (Grandma's ancestors were among the first European settlers of White Creek.)

From here you can pick up Route 67 which will take you across the state line into North Bennington, and eventually to the museum, on Route 9 in the outskirts of town.

In Grandma Moses' autobiography she describes how she went about painting.

> Before I start painting, I get a frame, then I saw my masonite board to fit the frame. (I always thought it a good idea to build the sty before getting the pig, likewise with young men, get the home before the wedding.) Then I go over the board with linseed oil, then with three coats of flat white paint to cover up the darkness . . . now the board is ready for the scene, whatever the mind may produce, a landscape, an old bridge, a dream, or a summer or winter scene, childhood memories, but always something pleasing and cheerful, I like bright colors and activity . . .

INFORMATION: You can make this tour at any time of year. The Bennington Museum is open all year, though only on weekends during the winter months. (Telephone: 802-447-1571.)

DIRECTIONS: From New York City take the Taconic Parkway to its end, New York State Thruway to Route 22 North, to Route 7, to Bennington. From Albany, New York, take exit 23 on the New York State Thruway to Route 787 north to Troy. Take Route 7 east to Vermont where it becoms Route 9 to Bennington. If you prefer to start your outing at Hoosick Falls, follow above directions to intersection at Route 7 and Route 22 before reaching the Vermont line.

9

Cape Cod's Mecca for Artists

*Provincetown and Truro,
Massachusetts*

The uncommon natural light is the first thing the artist notices about the tip of Cape Cod. Artists first came in the late nineteenth century, when outdoor easel painting was new and was nowhere more inviting. And despite the many, many changes of every sort that have come to this extraordinary place over the last century—despite a drastically changed art world—the artists are still coming.

The wonderful clarity of the light, the brilliant colors, the dramatic scenery, the art "scene"—all of these things continue to bring hundreds of artists to Provincetown and its neighbors, Truro and Wellfleet. The qualities that brought artists and art students in droves still remain, though the Cape end's glory days as an art colony may well have passed. But with its exquisite natural beauty of sand and sea, it remains a vibrant art-filled place to visit.

You'll still find the picturesque fishing boats moored at Provincetown's wharf, the pristine peach tones of the sand dunes (now the Provincelands of the National Seashore), the ever-changing greens and blues of bay and ocean, the New England shingled houses, the startlingly white lighthouses against the deep sky, the stretches of sand flats with their miragelike spots of color in the distance at low tide.

12. Niles Spencer. *Back of the Town (Provincetown)*. 1926

The visitor who wants to experience the full bloom of the summer art scene should be prepared, however, for a honky-tonk downtown in Provincetown (where art comes in many schlock forms, as well as in a serious gallery scene) and a touristy local economy. But the serious art world of the Cape end supports the well-known Provincetown Art Association and some seven or eight galleries, while half a dozen more are thriving in Wellfleet. (All galleries welcome strangers to their openings; just walk in and start up a conversation with the nearest artist, who may well invite you to his or her studio.)

The art you will see ranges widely from the commercial seascape to constructions dripping red paint (a heartfelt show honoring AIDS victims) to examples of every current style now known to the New York art world (from which many of these artists emigrate each summer).

If you prefer a quieter visit, come in the "off-season" after Labor Day. Though your artistic choices will be somewhat narrower (some galleries—but not all—stay open year-round), the towns themselves revert to their better winter natures—cold, windy, and very beautiful.

There are several different ways to capture the ambience of Provincetown's very odd mixture of the awful and the sublime. Judging by your own tolerance or enjoyment of the awful part, you can stay in the middle of it, or in the lovely quieter East or West End's rooming houses, or just spend a day or two wandering through its historic streets while living decorously up-Cape. (The tip of the Cape is known as "down-Cape.")

But try not to miss the wonderful natural and aesthetic beauties that have brought so many artists to this spot since Charles W. Hawthorne first opened his studio a century ago. Provincetown at that time had already had its share of colorful history. (The Pilgrims, in fact, landed there in 1620 before giving up on the sandy spit of land and heading across the bay to Plymouth.) When Hawthorne opened his Cape Cod School of Painting in 1899, Provincetown was merely a collection of fishing shacks. (But its colorful life-style had already driven Truro to separate itself from its uncouth neighbor.)

P-town's fishing industry and picturesque charms were Hawthorne's (and his students') favorite subjects. A generation of young painters followed his lead, sketching out of doors (like

13. Morris Davidson. *Fishing Boats in Harbor.* 1948

their European counterparts) and living cheaply among the hospitable Portuguese fishing community.

Writers, too, including Eugene O'Neill, John Dos Passos, Sinclair Lewis, Susan Glaspell, John Reed, and Mary Heaton Vorse (among other well-known literary names), were living here in the years during, and just after, World War I. (Norman Mailer, Tennessee Williams, and Stanley Kunitz came later.) The first Provincetown Playhouse opened on an old fishing wharf in the summer of 1915.

But it became very much an artists' town. In 1914 the Provincetown Art Association was formed and is still going strong; its historic roster is a Who's Who of the American art world of the twentieth century. In the early days following the Armory Show and the beginnings of modernism, the Art Association solved the increasing divisiveness of abstraction versus traditional painting by presenting two separate shows each summer. Entries to these exhibitions were judged by a jury of well-known artists of each "school."

Cubist Karl Knaths arrived on the Cape in 1919. Artists like Edwin Dickinson, Edward Hopper, and Max Bohm came; Niles Spencer worked in Provincetown in the 1920s. Striking a compromise between realism and abstraction that he called "precisionism," Spencer looked down from the hills behind town at the geometric design of Provincetown's clustered houses and churches. "There is realism in the work of abstract artists," he wrote. "The deeper meanings of nature can only be captured in painting through disciplined form and design." An example of his style can be seen in Back of the Town (Provincetown), 1926 (Figure 12 on page 47.) (To see this view climb up the hill by the monument and look toward the harbor.)

Since then many artists have chosen to work and show in summertime on the Cape; others have settled in year-round. In the forties and fifties many of the nation's leading abstractionists opened their own studios and/or schools of painting, among them Adolph Gottlieb, Morris Davidson, Hans Hoffman, Robert Motherwell, Chaim Gross, Franz Kline, Boris Margo, Milton Avery, Victor Kandell, Helen Frankenthaler, Sam Francis, Mark Rothko—the list is an extraordinary one.

Some artists worked from the picturesque sights, abstracting shapes and forms of fishing trawlers at the pier, sand dunes,

14. Helen Frankenthaler. *Seascape with Dunes*. 1962

15. Edward Hopper. *Mouth of the Pamet River.* 1937

and ocean waves; others enjoyed the art colony's atmosphere while creating purely abstract works.

Your peregrinations in Provincetown should include the Art Association, which still has juried shows nowadays, as well as a magnificent permanent collection of about five hundred priceless works. Here you will get a taste of the great variety and diverse styles the town's artists have produced over the years. While there, pick up painter Ross Moffett's history of the Art Association in Provincetown for the complete story of this amazing mix (and nonmix) of creative people within a tiny town on the sea.

As you explore Provincetown you'll also sense the inspiration for many a painting in the sights around you, beginning with the sailboats in the harbor (a beloved subject of semiabstract and cubist painters, with their stark white triangles of sail), and the fascinating complexity of the fishing trawlers, with their orange masts, deep colored hulls, and nets and ropes and flags. Walk out to the end of the main pier where they are moored to see the inspiration for paintings like Morris Davidson's 1948 *Fishing Boats in Harbor* (Figure 13 on page 49).

In addition to the two piers with their fascinating scenes, visit the Town Hall to see Charles Hawthorne's murals of fishermen at work. Climb up Monument Hill for overviews of the town, like the Niles Spencer mentioned above, and wander the narrow streets at both East and West Ends. Walk across the breakwater and hike across the dunes to the ocean (by beginning just outside of town at the Head of the Meadows) for the panoramic views. This is another subject that artists of many different styles have painted, including abstractionist Helen Frankenthaler in her 1969 painting called *Seascape with Dunes* (Figure 14 on page 51).

Stroll out on the sand flats at low tide or visit the "back beach" (the ocean side) where you'll catch the aura of Milton Avery's beach scenes. The jumble of signs and buildings on Commercial Street, downtown, the strange formations of seaweed at high tide, the curious vegetation in the sand out by the beaches of Race Point or High Head—these are all images that have fascinated artists of many generations working in a great variety of styles.

Some artists have always preferred the peaceful landscape of Truro to the bustle of Provincetown. Among them was Edward Hopper, who painted many scenes of the ocean front, including Highland Light (North Truro) and views of the gentler Pamet River area of Truro on the bay side; his 1937 watercolor is called *Mouth of the Pamet River* (Figure 15 on page 52). To see this view, turn right from Route 6 (at the Pamet sign) as you head toward Wellfleet from Provincetown.

And, of course, visit the galleries. Despite the passing of Provincetown's glory days as the center of the nation's new art, there is still lots to see, and you may well discover a painter or sculptor whose work captures for you the very ambience of the Cape and its long artistic history. Only a few major galleries remain in Provincetown; three are in the East End (as is the Art Association). Wellfleet now has a number of top-notch galleries, most within a block or two of one another. Don't miss the distinctive new art being shown there during the summer.

INFORMATION: The Provincetown Art Association is at 400 Commercial Street. (Telephone: 508-487-1750.) While the height of the summer season is when most galleries are open, many people prefer the off-season for visiting the Cape.

DIRECTIONS: From Boston take Route 93 south to Route 3 to the Cape Cod Canal; take Route 6 to Truro and Provincetown at the tip of the Cape.

10

William Sidney Mount, Long Island's Genre Painter

Setauket, New York

William Sidney Mount was a genre painter and portraitist who cheerfully chronicled rural life in the far reaches of Long Island. A truly nineteenth century American jack-of-all trades, Mount made paintings, wrote music and played the violin, thought up inventions including a new kind of fiddle, lived his entire life in the midst of his apparently jolly family, and left numerous diaries and letters, musical compositions, designs, and—of major interest nowadays—paintings. A visit to his homestead and the surroundings that he painted might give you a taste of a simpler, more contented time, as seen by a talented and pleasing artist.

By the mid-nineteenth century genre painting—the first truly popular style of art in the United States—had replaced the heroic historical panoramas of earlier Americana. Appealing storytelling scenes of farm life, domestic events, and character studies captured the tenor of American life and beginning in the 1830s were popular with all kinds of just plain folks. Genre artists painted what they knew and saw around them, sometimes adding a touch of whimsy or morality to appeal to the current taste.

But a few of them, like Mount, brought to their work more than sentimental anecdote or sappy romance; in Mount's paintings there is both joy and artistic sophistication. Seeing a collection of Mount's canvases all together (which you will be able to do on this outing) is to experience a full and charming picture of a particular time and way of life.

To Mount, Stony Brook and Setauket, where he lived—and from which he rarely ventured—were not just pretty landscapes. They were places in which real people lived, fished, hunted, danced, and fiddled. Ordinary people were Mount's subjects. "I must paint pictures as speak at once to the spectator, scenes that are most popular, that will be understood on the instant," he wrote. On the other hand, he rejected popularity for its own sake. "I must endeavor to follow the bent of my inclinations. To paint portraits or pictures, large or small, grave or gay, as I please, and not be dictated by others. Every artist should know his own powers best and act accordingly." From these thoughts, we must conclude that he painted what he most enjoyed, and that good humor is evident in his work.

No grand ladies in gilded drawing rooms attracted Mount's brush. Instead, farmers "nooning," or checking the growing corn, or making cider, young folks dancing to a jolly fiddler's tunes, neighbors reading the morning *Herald,* or holding up a newly trapped rabbit—these were the small daily parts of Mount's warm and wholesome experience. Many of his paintings gracefully include African-Americans farming and fiddling and, in one of his best-known portraits, playing the banjo; Mount's were among the first American paintings to do so.

Just as Mount lived his entire life in the same region, the greater part of his paintings, journals, inventions, and letters are also still together in one place. In fact, a visit to the museums at Stony Brook will afford a fine sampling of his oils; here you can see more of the memorabilia relating to his family, who were quite an extraordinary group. If you find yourself thoroughly intrigued by the subject, speak to the curator who is both available and enthusiastic; a great deal of research has been done on the Mount family, and much of it is published. To some historians the artist and his well-documented life seem to be a shining example of Yankee charm and ingenuity, combined with a successful career as an artist.

Mount was part of a large and cohesive family, many of whom were artists of some sort. His father was an innkeeper. One brother was a sign painter who discovered William's talent and sent him for his only formal training—two years at the

16. William Sidney Mount. Dance of the Haymakers. 1845

National Academy of Design. Another brother, Shepard Alonzo Mount, was also a well-regarded portraitist; his sister painted flower pieces. Yet another brother was an itinerant dancing master, to whom William sent tunes and advice; and there were various in-laws and nephews and nieces.

Correspondence with all of these people has been published in a large book on Mount, and, like his painting, shows Mount's warmth and modest disposition. "I yearned to be a painter," he wrote. "I asked God in my humble way to strengthen my love for art; and in His goodness He directed me to a closer observation of nature and I gained strength in art."

Still standing and newly renovated by preservationists is the Hawkins–Mount Homestead, the house in which Mount lived a great part of his life. You can visit the Homestead (be sure to see the painting Mount did of it first) and the barns immortalized in so many of Mount's paintings (see his 1845 *Dance of the Haymakers*, [Figure 16], and *The Power of Music* and *Dancing on the Barn Floor*).

You may also want to drive out to West Meadow Beach to see the view of Crane's Neck, another subject of a Mount painting on view at the museum. The picturesque Mill Dam in Stony Brook was also a favorite Mount site. The mill and large water wheel on the dam can still be viewed on a nice walk, though the mill itself has been enlarged considerably since Mount painted it. (See directions for all sites below.)

INFORMATION: The museums at Stony Brook are open Monday, Wednesday-Saturday 10:00 A.M.-5:00 P.M., Sunday noon-5:00 P.M., closed Tuesday. There is an inexpensive entrance fee. Telephone: 516-751-0066.

DIRECTIONS: The museums at Stony Brook are at 1208 Route 25A, Stony Brook, Long Island. From New York City take the Midtown Tunnel to the Long Island Expressway (Route 495) to exit 62. Proceed north on County Road 97 (Nicolls Road) to its end, turn left onto Route 25A for 1½ miles to the intersection of 25A and Main Street in Stony Brook. Stony Brook is also on the Long Island Railroad. (The Art Museum is part of a collection of museum buildings housing a well-known Carriage Museum, costumes, and other collections; the Art Museum is the white columned building on the hill.)

To the Hawkins–Mount Homestead: After leaving the Art Museum, turn left at the bottom of the driveway and go about ½ mile to a fork. At the intersection of the fork, you'll see Mount's house and barns, immediately on your left.

To West Meadow Beach: Continue on 25A into the village of Setauket. Take Old Field Road (left) to West Meadow Road, and continue to the Beach, from which you can view Crane's Neck as Mount did.

To the Mill at Stony Brook: Continue on Main Street in Stony Brook from the museums and you will see it on your left before you reach town.

Unusual Visions of Landscapes: Environmental Art and Archaeology

11

Monument to the Coal Miners

Frostburg, Maryland

Here in mountainous Allegheny County of Western Maryland the term "environmental art" takes on a new meaning. Deep in the heart of coal mining country, the artist Andrew Leicester has created a memorial to miners that is truly "environmental."

Western Maryland was the site of the first bituminous coal mines in the country, and the state's Arts Council decided to commemorate this part of its history with a sculpture on the Frostburg State University campus. Leicester had grander ideas; his work combines sculpture, architecture, painting, and, of course, the environment. It celebrates the uses of the earth, the glories of the natural setting, and the hard life of the miners who worked there. But this is not merely a reconstructed piece of the past; made in 1982, *Prospect V-III* is a contemporary work of art in every sense.

The choice of Frostburg's campus was not an accident. Here, where the miners actually worked, land was purchased in the late nineteenth century for a normal school, with the help of miners' donations as they left the pits each day. Near the campus is a modern and mechanized strip mine, which replaced the shafts and pits used in the past. The contributions and assistance of retired miners in the area are evident throughout Leicester's work; the memorial was a deeply felt tribute to the community, which responded with enthusiasm.

Prospect V-III is primarily a wooden structure that is twenty-seven feet high and more than 120 feet long. At the center, it descends in a shaft deep into the ground. It is designed to bring to mind the architecture of mining shafts and company towns. Its spectacular setting on a steep hillside overlooking the picturesque George's Creek is emphasized by a viewing platform at the edge of the construction. (George's Creek basin was the historical center of early coal mining operations.)

There are three individual chambers, a hexagonal rotunda, and—at the center of the construction—a realistic, narrow mine shaft that plunges into the earth to a real coal seam. Each section of this work has its own significance; by utilizing both realistic trappings and conceptual forms, the artist has made an extraordinary monument to an entire industry and its workers.

In the first chamber there are railroad tracks leading to the shaft. On them sits a coal cart that doubles as a cradle. The symbolic painted butterflies on the walls ironically turn into black lungs, in a reference to the scourge of "miner's disease."

The second chamber is tomblike, representing the miners' deathlike surroundings while they work.

A fascinating collection of memorabilia donated by local miners and their families, from lunch pails to picks and shovels, to old photographs and documents, adorns the third chamber. This is a most evocative part of the memorial.

The domed rotunda separates the mine shaft from these three chambers. Its skylit ceiling—a surprise after the dark rooms—contains suspended miners' clothing. This display represents the changing rooms, where the workers put on their black overalls to begin their descent into the earth.

The walls of the rotunda bear words and symbols ranging from hieroglyphs from the Egyptian Book of the Dead to English mining terms. Half buried in the hillside, the rotunda—with its light ceiling but dark opening toward the shaft itself—accentuates the miner's tomblike experience. Finally, there is the entrance to the shaft, where the tracks vanish into the dark.

Leicester's memorial brings ideas of contemporary art to the public in a strikingly understandable and purposeful way; its subject was dear to the community, and the work obviously was designed to communicate on many different levels. In the case of this environmental art, there is little question of relevance!

INFORMATION: This site may be visited by appointment only. It is only open in spring and fall. Telephone: 301-689-4797 (the University's Visual Arts Department) to arrange your visit.

DIRECTIONS: From Baltimore take Route 70 West, which becomes Route 40, to Cumberland; from Cumberland take I-68 west. Take the Frostburg exit (exit 33) and follow signs to Frostburg State University.

12

Opus 40,
A Bluestone Environment

Woodstock, New York

If you have ever visited an abandoned stone quarry, you know what a dramatic and beautiful sight it is. Perhaps you have made a comment about nature imitating art, for the picturesque quality of light and shadow on stone and water has long been a favorite subject for artists. A visit and walk about *Opus 40* will blur the traditional lines of art and nature still further. This abandoned bluestone quarry is an extraordinary example of environmental art in which both art and nature are so intertwined that you will no longer distinguish between them.

Opus 40 is the lifelong enterprise of environmental sculptor Harvey Fite. Fite bought the six-acre site where bluestone had been quarried, and over a thirty-seven-year period he transformed it into a monumental environmental sculpture. Originally Fite conceived of the quarry as a dramatic sculpture park for his works, but he found the natural surroundings of the abandoned quarry overpowering for his individual carvings. He removed them to the grassy areas bordering the quarry and set to work to make the quarry itself into his major work of art.

Opus 40 is made of thousands of tons of stone laid out into pathways, walls, convex and concave shapes, circular formations around quarry springs and trees, and abstract monuments. You can walk through it and around it, climb on it, enjoy different angles and views of nearby Overlook Mountain, and in general lose yourself within this total art environment.

In the center, and at the summit of *Opus 40* you'll find Fite's monolith, a nine ton stone column from which the patterns of the sculpture radiate. It is here at the center that some visitors choose to sit and meditate, and where jazz and folk music concerts and other events are held on summer afternoons.

In addition to the quarry area, you can also walk on nicely wooded paths around the acreage or loll on the grassy areas where Fite's more traditional sculptures are set. In summer several (nonswimming) pools and fountains that are part of the environmental site are filled with water, making this a pleasant outing on a hot day.

There is also a museum called the Quarryman's Museum on the property. Fite built it to house his collection of tools and artifacts used by quarrymen, and to honor and explain the tradition of quarrying and stoneworking. Hand-forged folk tools and a slide show on the construction of *Opus 40* are among the museum's offerings.

The carefully conceived and rather formalistic patterns of *Opus 40* make this one of the more interesting environmental art sites we have visited. Nevertheless, you may wonder—as do many critics of environmental art—whether the natural state of an abandoned quarry is not equally inspiring or aesthetically interesting, with its accidental piles of fallen rock and haphazard design around a central space. Whatever your view, you'll find Fite's transformation of this giant art site extraordinary, and a visit there a rewarding and thought-provoking experience.

INFORMATION: *Opus 40* is located at 7480 Fite Road, Saugerties. Telephone: 914-246-3400. It is open May through October weekdays except Tuesday, from 10:00 A.M.-4:00 P.M., Sunday noon-5:00 P.M. There is an inexpensive admission fee to visit *Opus 40* and the Quarryman's Museum, but children under twelve are admitted free. Group tours are available. Rubber-soled shoes are recommended.

DIRECTIONS: From New York, take the New York State Thruway north to Saugerties exit. Take Route 212 west through Woodstock. Follow signs along the road.

In the vicinity . . .
Woodstock, the small village nearby, has long been known as an artists' colony (though its name is now linked with the music

festival which actually took place many miles away). Woodstock has summer exhibitions and a variety of craft and studio workshops.

13

Mystery Hill,
An Archaeological Puzzle

North Salem, New Hampshire

You need not travel to exotic places to find prehistoric sites. Or so claim certain scholars when they speak of "Mystery Hill," near North Salem, New Hampshire. Set atop a wooded hillside amid acres of pristine forest, this curious stone complex of standing megaliths, granite walls, tunnels, and chambers is the focus of an ongoing controversy.

Some archaeologists believe that "America's Stonehenge" —as it is sometimes called—points to a significant civilization that long preceded Columbus and the earliest European explorers. (Other similar, although much smaller sites, are scattered about in the East.) Some scholars think that it dates to the colonial period, when farmers could have created the structures for storage or fashioned large boulders in good fun, imagining that future generations would find them enigmatic. But according to much current opinion, Mystery Hill was—like Stonehenge—a megalithic calendar site, a sacred place built to determine solar and lunar movements with great accuracy and to celebrate these events with rituals. These archaeologists speak of its similarity in setup and construction to prehistoric sites found in Spain and Malta. They have worked at deciphering stone markings thought to be in languages used by the ancient Celts who traveled to the Mediterranean. To authenticate the age of the site more fully they have conducted radiocarbon testing and concluded that Mystery Hill might be 3,500 years old. Could seafarers from the Old World have come here at that time? And why?

If you like a good mystery you are bound to be intrigued by Mystery Hill. But you don't have to involve yourself in these scholarly debates to appreciate the site. You can think of it as a giant environmental work of artistic interest and can enjoy walking in the woods through the unique "sculptural" complex. The intricate stone wall constructions (Figure 17) and meandering tunnels and passageways contrast visually with the sharply defined vertical megaliths located within and on the edges of the site, creating a counterpoint of different shapes set off by the soft surrounding woods.

Fortunately, Mystery Hill is not the typical commercial tourist trap, despite the road signs announcing it as you approach. There is a small, unpretentious, somewhat folksy visitors' center where you buy your tickets and can also read up on the pros and cons of the Mystery Hill debate. You'll find yellowed newspaper clippings posted on the walls, as well as displays of stone inscriptions and archaeological finds pertaining to the site. You can learn about the history of Mystery Hill and of its first modern owners, Jonathan Patee and family, who lived on the grounds from 1823–1849. Researchers think that during this time many of the ancient stone slabs were carted off and used in building sewers and curbstones in nearby Lawrence and Lowell, Massachusetts, destroying much of the complex. Patee's house burned down in 1855 (you can still see some leftover bricks from his hearth on the site), and the place became a local curiosity. It was finally opened to the public in 1958, and research and excavations are still under way.

Before setting forth on your exploration of the site, pick up a map for your self-guided walk. (Guides are available by appointment for those who prefer to be accompanied.) The path is well marked, as are the thirty or so points of interest, mostly located within a carefully tended area surrounded by a not particularly attractive chain-link fence. Individual points of interest are labeled with numbers or letters and occasional rock markings and incisions are outlined in white paint for easier identification. You can wander around the chambers and passageways (some of which have been restored), up and down stone steps, and imagine the ancient uses of these structures.

17. Mystery Hill, North Salem, New Hampshire

A massive stone slab weighing some four-and-a-half tons—thought to have been a sacrificial table—can be viewed from above and is considered to be one of the more controversial pieces here. One can only imagine what went on at this spot. You'll also see a number of large stone slabs scattered about the grounds, many of which were probably upright at one time.

From the astronomical viewing platform at the top of a hill (a modern wooden structure) you can observe the major astronomical alignment stones. These triangular monoliths that are up to five feet long and three feet wide appear to have been solar-aligned for solstice and equinox sunsets and sunrises. The tour guide map gives a detailed accounting of astronomical alignments, and you can follow the trails that lead to these monoliths. Some trees and shrubs have been cleared around them so that they can be identified with ease. Apparently the staff at Mystery Hill still performs some sort of services during solstice and equinox risings, and it is possible to get permission to attend these events.

INFORMATION: Mystery Hill is open daily 10:00 A.M.-5:00 P.M. (or until dusk) from May to October, and on weekends during April and November. There is a moderate admission fee (Note: you pay less if you're a member of AAA). Telephone: 603-893-8300 for further information and for guided tours.

DIRECTIONS: From Boston: Route 93 to exit 3 (Windham), take Route 111 east for about five miles; follow the signs for "America's Stonehenge."

14

The Stone Boat of Jamesville Quarry

Jamesville, New York

While you expect to find environmental art in parks and other public places, you might be surprised to discover one such piece at the bottom of a working quarry. At the quarry at Jamesville, known as Barrett Paving Materials Quarry (just south of Syracuse), sculptor William Bennett is in the process of creating a massive environmental artwork. Known as the "Jamesville Quarry Sculpture," it is a work very definitely in progress. The artist has been chipping away since 1976 on a sporadic basis, during the summer months only. (The working section of the quarry is nearby; its owners are obviously art enthusiasts.)

Bennett, who has long thought of quarries as powerful spaces, is using the limestone of this site to create *Wedge* (*Stone Boat*). True to its name, it is a long (80' × 10' × 6') triangular wedge that begins at ground level and goes down to six feet. Opposite *Wedge* he is proposing to dig down to twenty feet to create *Inverted Pyramid*, which is to measure 160' × 160' when completed.

If you are intrigued with the idea of seeing art within this rugged setting, or are interested in seeing the creative process as well as the completed forms of environmental art, or are just partial to quarries—this site is worth a visit.

INFORMATION: Barrett Paving Materials is in Jamesville, New York. It is open Monday through Friday from 7:00 A.M. to 3:00 P.M. For more information telephone 315-492-4030.

DIRECTIONS: From Syracuse take Route 481 to exit 2 (the James-ville exit); follow signs for General Crushed Stone, then for Barrett Paving Materials.

In the vicinity . . .
The Everson Museum in Syracuse and Cornell University in Ithaca have outstanding art collections. (See page 261.)

You might also wish to combine this outing with a visit to the studio of John McQueen in Trumansburg, New York, less than two hours away (see page 132).

Of similar interest . . .
For another visit to a quarry art site see *Opus 40*, Woodstock, New York (see chapter 12).

Architectural Pleasures: Unique Communities and Eccentric Monuments, Old and New

15

Cobblestones and Brick
in a Historic River Town

New Castle, Delaware

A visit to New Castle, Delaware, is a step into a genteel world of eighteenth century grace. This rare historic village of mostly red brick Georgian houses on quiet tree-lined streets combines architectural charm with an enchanting setting along the shores of the Delaware River. One of the oldest settlements in the Delaware Valley, New Castle offers an impressive number of public buildings and homes of architectural interest, spanning some two hundred years. While you will see many in the dignified Georgian style, you'll also find Colonial, Federal, Queen Anne, Victorian, and Gothic Revival examples. A visit to this historic spot is a delightful sampling of American architecture.

Fortunately New Castle has not been commercialized or otherwise spoiled by the onslaught of tourism. There are few shops and commercial establishments within the historic district—and those we saw seemed tasteful and discreet. You are left to enjoy the quiet atmosphere of a well-kept secret. New Castle remains a carefully preserved, yet vibrant living community with none of the contrived atmosphere of some historic places, where people might parade about in colonial garb for the gratification of visitors. The majority of historic houses continue to be lived in and have not been converted to museums or other establishments. Much of New Castle's healthy state of affairs is due to its active preservation society, which has seen to it that buildings retain their historic character and that they are tended carefully in old age. But the village's odd history has also conspired to keep it intact, with few new buildings replacing earlier sites (Figure 18).

New Castle (first called Fort Casimir) was founded in 1651 by Peter Stuyvesant of Manhattan fame, then governor of the Dutch West India Company's American enterprise. Its strategic setting gave the Dutch an advantage in Delaware River traffic until 1664, when the fort was captured by the English. New Castle's importance culminated in the early eighteenth century, when it was made the colonial capital of Delaware, and then briefly the state capital. The town enjoyed its role as transfer point for those traveling to and from Washington, D.C., Baltimore, and other spots along the coast. But it eventually was bypassed, as development of modern transportation by rail and highway made its harbor outmoded. Its neighbors, Wilmington and Philadelphia, grew to become large cities, but New Castle remained a small town with no need to expand or replace its old buildings.

A walk through today's New Castle will appeal to anyone interested in architecture. The houses, churches and other public buildings reflect the styles of the past two hundred years, and even earlier—for there are quite a number of pre-Revolutionary buildings. Some of the early houses have been added on to, and it is sometimes difficult to determine an exact date. The overall effect is one of architectural harmony, as even the ninteenth and twentieth century buildings and additions blend in well with the old.

You will probably want to wander around on your own and explore at will the several blocks that make up the historic district, although there are weekly guided tours for those so inclined. (These tours usually take place on Saturdays at 1:30 P.M., weather permitting.) For your self-guided walk, we recommend you first stop at the Court House right in the center of town, on Delaware Street. There you can pick up a map that will indicate points of interest, as well as other information. You can also start your tour by visiting the Court House itself, one of the must-see spots.

18. New Castle, Delaware

This fine Georgian building (1732), surrounded by the historic Green, was built on the burned remains of an earlier seventeenth century courthouse. It was the meeting place of the Colonial Assembly for many years before the Revolution, then the site of the drafting of the Constitution of Delaware. It became a county courthouse and later was even used for commercial activities, falling into some disrepair. Restoration since the late 1950s has brought it back to its earlier appearance. You'll want to linger in the wonderful courtroom, recently refurbished in the style of Delaware's colonial days.

Now, with walking map in hand, you can begin your exploration of the town. There are over ninety historic houses, buildings, or sites of interest within this small area (described in a booklet available at the Court House). Though many are private and can only be seen from the outside, they help create the rare architectural harmony of New Castle.

The Immanuel Episcopal Church on the Green near the Court House is one of the oldest and most august buildings in New Castle. Begun in 1703, it was partially damaged by fire and later rebuilt; but the walls and tower fortunately survived and the rest of the structure has been carefully restored. The old churchyard will please those of you who like to wander around such places; it is filled with eighteenth and nineteenth century markers, including those of signers of the Declaration of Independence, framers of the Constitution, judges of the Supreme Court, and Delaware governors. As you walk around and read the epitaphs you feel like a witness to an important period in American history.

On the south side of the Green you'll find the New Castle Presbyterian Church (at 25 Second Street); built in 1707, it is one of the oldest buildings in town.

Facing the church is the Old Library Museum at 40 East Third Street, an unusual hexagonal building dating only from 1892. In the past it has had a variety of uses—once even as a sculpture studio—but is now a museum that displays historic memorabilia concerning New Castle and surroundings.

Along Third Street, facing the Green, is a charming row of eighteenth and nineteenth century brick houses. Among them is the Old Dutch House (at 32 East Third Street) which, fortunately, can be visited inside and out. Built in the early eighteenth century, it has the deeply pitched roof and overhanging eaves typical of the Dutch style. It is now also a museum, in this case of early eighteenth century Dutch furnishings and artifacts. Surrounding it is a little garden that has recently been restored.

The Amstel House on the corner of Fourth and Delaware streets is a wonderful eighteenth century Georgian house that is also open to visitors. Built in 1738, it was (or so they claim) the site of a wedding attended by the ubiquitous George Washington. Not to be missed are its carved cornices and other special architectural details.

The George Read II House and garden on "The Strand" is no doubt New Castle's most elegant house. It was built between 1797 and 1804 by George Read II, the son of a signer of the Declaration of Independence. He wanted it to be a proper Philadelphia-style house, with high ceilings, marble fireplaces, plaster ornamentation, finely carved woodwork, and gilded fanlights. The result is a grand house with an appropriately stately garden, both of which can be visited.

The George Read II House is only a block from the Delaware River, so you must not miss a walk to the banks to enjoy the view. Unfortunately, the once bustling wharf is no more—but you'll find the river setting charming.

INFORMATION: For information concerning times that various houses are open, tours, fees, or other, we suggest you telephone the New Castle Visitors Bureau at 302-322-8411.

DIRECTIONS: New Castle is six miles from Wilmington, Delaware, on Route 9, and a quick trip from the New Jersey Turnpike, at exit 1.

In the vicinity . . .
While in the area you might want to drive into the Brandywine Valley, only a short distance away where there are museums relating to the du Pont family and the Wyeth family of artists. This area is very popular with tourists (so you should expect a different atmosphere from that at New Castle), but you'll find famous mansions and gardens well worth a visit such as Winterthur (see page 247), Nemours Mansion (see page 247) and Longwood Gardens (see page 263).

16

Pyramids, Gothic Arches, and Classic Temples at West Laurel Hill Cemetery

Bala-Cynwyd, Pennsylvania

It may surprise you to find a cemetery as a site for an art or architecture walk, but this is not an ordinary cemetery. A walk through West Laurel Hill, in Bala-Cynwyd, near South Philadelphia, is like a fantastic tour through the history of architecture. Not only is the natural scenery spectacular—there are more than 150 species of trees, many of which blossom in season—but there are mausoleums in styles ranging from Egyptian pyramids to Greek temples to miniature Gothic chapels.

A walk around this very large area is filled with intriguing sights, beautiful views, and food for thought; who were these people who were buried like kings in nineteenth century America? Where did they get such curious ideas of art and architecture—combining Egyptian or classical Greek tomb style with the brilliant colors of art nouveau stained glass or the whimsical design of Moorish ironwork? (Postmodernism seems to have been preinvented at West Laurel Hill!) Why does the ornamentation include so many references to ancient Egyptian and classical myth in these nominally Christian tombs?

Many of the mausoleums are dramatic, imposing, and grand, yet they are still miniatures; two of them are replicas of the Parthenon. As you walk through the graceful landscape you feel almost as though you are Gulliver in a small mythical city.

In fact, the sense of being in another time and place is pervasive; there are few visitors (we were there on weekdays), nothing to read—there are almost no inscriptions beyond the names of the honored dead—and the stillness is broken only by the sound of the wind in the giant old trees. You can walk up to the "entrances" of many of the tombs (which, of course, are never entered) and peer into their empty interiors to see the colorful stained glass light, or sit on one of the numerous walls or stone stairways to draw or contemplate your surroundings without interruption.

West Laurel Hill Cemetery was originally a country estate in the outskirts of Philadelphia, about four miles from the city. In 1869 the hilly spot was purchased by some leading citizens for use as a cemetery; it was to provide a safely removed and inspirational spot for contemplation of nature and God. (Cemeteries like West Laurel Hill became models—with their design of pathways, plantings and open space—for the great public parks that appeared in the nation's cities in the nineteenth century.)

Because of the cemetery's situation beyond the city's limits, transportation there was difficult in the early days. Funerals took all day, with excursions by steamboat on the Schuykill River or by carriage up to the high bluffs of the cemetery. Eventually railway cars were employed to carry funeral corteges. As you will see from the names on the tombs, leading citizens of Philadelphia's business and social world chose this cemetery as their last resting place. By the turn of the century it had become a testament not only to worldly success, but to the Victorian fascination with grandeur—both in art and nature.

A walk through the grounds poses some problems. The area is very large, and you will necessarily have to leave out some of the walkways unless you have a great deal of time. The old carriage roads cover more than one hundred acres of hill and dale. It is possible to drive through most of the cemetery if you wish, but you will be unable to leave your car along the way, so we recommend parking at the office lot in the center of the grounds. You can then follow our route to see the tombs we thought most interesting—or if you prefer, wander at random

As you walk, you may note—in addition to the particular sites described—some sixty-two obelisks, numerous marble statues and urns covered with ivy, several sets of classical columns unattached to buildings, and a recurrent architectural detail at the top of the facade of many temples: the Egyptian winged sun disk or Winged Ba (representing the soul), occasionally intertwined with snakes. You will also spot Doric, Ionic, and Corinthian columns, Gothic arches and spires, and a marvelous collection of doors. These portals to the tombs are in every conceivable style, some echoing the design of the windows within, others in ironwork of Moorish or art deco design. Be sure to go up the steps to look in beyond the doors at the vast variety of stained glass within many of the mausoleums. While most tombs are built of marble, you will also find sandstone and granite; the overall impression is of sparkling white buildings set against an extraordinarily green landscape.

One additional note before you begin: Don't overlook the trees and shrubbery. The natural beauty of the 187 acres is astounding. Many of the trees were planted more than one hundred years ago. Among the one hundred and fifty species are a sixty-five-foot-tall magnolia shadowing a grave marked "Carpenter," flowering dogwood, cherry, weeping beech, sweet gum, oak, birch, euonymous, sugar maple, fern maple, and copper beech; you'll also find flowering shrubs in season, from mauve hydrangea, azalea, rhododendron, to (of course) a profusion of laurel. Colors are particularly grand in spring and fall.

As you drive into the gate, you will see painted arrows on the roadway directing you to the office. Follow them by car and park in the lot in front of the beautiful ivied tower and the brick office building. At the office you can buy a history of the famous people buried in the cemetery and pick up a detailed map (which, however, includes no names or guide points). As you park you will be facing our first stop.

Directly bordering the parking area are two side-by-side graves marked "Soulas" and "Pidgeon." We begin with these two graves because they typify the neoclassical style, an emphasis that you will see time and again on this walk. Each is distinctive for the classical mourning female figures behind glass-topped graves. (The tombs appear empty when you look into their fifteen-foot depth.)

Turn to your left to find the first large mausoleum of our walk. It is a monument to Frederick August Poth, a very successful

German-born brewer. This classical revival structure is marble with symmetrical Corinthian columns, flanges and urns. It is massive and impressive and dates to 1905.

If you continue on the pathway to the left of the Poth tomb you will come to a row of some of the most interesting mausoleums. Here you'll find the Greek revival style in a number of forms, most including stained glass in an art nouveau mode. Be sure to go up the steps of each and peek in to see the widely divergent styles of the glass and the doorways.

In addition to the Greek revival designs along this row, there are also two interesting mausoleums showing Moorish influence. One of them is the John Lang monument, a curious blend of Moorish and classical design; note the carved decoration. Across from it (and slightly farther along) is the Coane monument. This one, which contrasts with its neoclassical neighbors, looks rather like a beehive.

Just behind the Coane monument is a grave marked "Stetson." Though it is not of particular architectural interest, you may like to know where the founder of Stetson hats is buried!

Also on the right side of this roadway—but somewhat behind this row—is a very distinctive tomb for Matthew Simpson (1811–1884). He was a bishop of the Methodist Episcopal Church. His mausoleum is a replica of a Gothic chapel complete with a Gothic arch, trefoil (intersecting circles symbolizing the Trinity), and Latin Cross. Note the fine stained glass windows, which include a New Testament scene, a fleur de lis, and a Star of David.

If you return to the same pathway, opposite and somewhat farther along, you'll find the Eisenlohr monument, one of the finest of the Greek revival examples. It is not only distinguished in its architectural detail; it also has unusually nice stained glass in the art nouveau style within.

At the end of this section of roadway is a major monument marked "Harrah." Charles J. Harrah (1817–1890) was a steel and railway magnate and humanitarian who personified the successful nineteenth century industrialist. His career took him to Brazil, where he developed railways and shipyards, as well as the first public school. His mausoleum is appropriately grand, with its Victorian Gothic spires and ornamentation. Its design is based upon a series of rounded and pointed arches culminating in a spire with a cross at the top. It has been likened to the Prince Albert Memorial in London, and is what used to be known as "an architectural confection."

Returning to the intersecting paths at the Harrah memorial, take the narrow path and climb up the hill. At the top, to your right, you'll come upon several interesting mausoleums overlooking lower areas of the cemetery. First, you'll see the Alter monument, whose unusual stained glass windows pick up the intricate Moorish design of the wrought iron door.

Surrounding this tomb are two oddities: large white marble chairs that look like bizarre monuments themselves. They were placed on private lots by some long-forgotten grave site owners to provide a view of the hillside and, presumably, a place for meditation and prayer. In their peculiar juxtaposition with the varied tombs and monuments, however, they seem like works of art placed by some twentieth century sculptor in an unlikely place. There are several other such monuments at West Laurel Hill.

On the same path is a distinctive and very ornate art nouveau tomb dedicated to John P. Mathieu. Note the St. John the Baptist windows, the curlicues on the roof, the stylish arched door, and the matching decorative flowerpots.

Go back to the intersection and continue in the same direction until you come to the Berwind Memorial. Another well-known capitalist, Edward J. Berwind was a naval aide to President Grant and became one of the largest individual owners of coal mines in the country. Berwind's mausoleum is notable; it was designed by the famous architect Horace Trumbauer (who is also buried at West Laurel Hill). It is a striking, tall, octagonal tower, with neoclassical winged figures in a bas relief circling the eight sides.

In a parallel row nearby is one of two monuments to the Pew family. The mausoleum of Joseph Newton Pew, the founder of the Sun Company, resembles a large neoclassical temple, with graceful proportions and elegant surfaces.

Just around the bend is another Pew monument, this one—though there is no miniature temple—is nevertheless another evocation of ancient Greece. It consists of linked marble columns set in a lovely site, surrounded with greenery.

Following the map, climb to one of the highest and most beautiful spots at West Laurel Hill. Here the founder of the Campbell Soup Company, John T. Dorrance, is honored with a neoclassical temple of Ionic columns and a flat roof. Its imposing entranceway between the columns was placed on the long side of its oblong shape, giving it a massive facade. Dorrance, one of the world's richest people during his lifetime (1919–1989), was a patron of the Philadelphia Museum of Art and an art collector himself. Next to the Dorrance mausoleum on the hilltop is another tomb belonging to the same family.

Continue along this roadway to get a quick glimpse of one of the largest (but not particularly interesting architecturally) tombs on the tour. This huge building honors a public utility magnate named Clarence H. Geist. His mausoleum is a massive, white, somber cube.

Beyond the Geist memorial, on a pathway to your left, is a row with three tombs of interest. The first (on your right) is an Ionic-style temple that is a miniature replica of the Parthenon, though it is hardly miniature. This grand mausoleum is dedicated to Edward M. Story.

A bit farther along, on your left, is the J. Howell Cummings mausoleum, a particularly nice example of stylish 1920s architecture with its soft peach and gray facade and elegant doors decorated with sheaves of wheat.

Next you'll come to a curiosity: Algernon Sidney Logan's obelisk and temple. Logan was a poet and novelist (1849–1925), and the titles of his books are carved into the side of the marble obelisk, along with a clock face, whose hands are set at three o'clock—the time he died. This is one of many obelisks throughout the cemetery. Note the variety of styles, particularly at the topmost points.

Finally in this region you'll come upon a sandstone castle-style mausoleum with a wrought iron gate. This is quite unlike the pale toned tombs that fill most of the grounds. Instead, this one—dedicated to George Miller—is distinctive for its deep sand color and its somewhat medieval appearance.

From here walk up to the left path to a three-way intersection. Here you'll come to one of our favorite architectural examples: the Henry M. Schadewald mausoleum on the left. This unusual building is a Moorish design which seems to have been inspired by the Arabian Nights. Its beautiful doorway is a series of art deco arabesques made of iron. Don't miss this one.

Opposite, just across the intersection, is one of the most intriguing of all the mausoleums at West Laurel Hill Cemetery. The Drake family (two of whose members survived the sinking of the Titanic) are interred here in an Egyptian-style temple set on a small knoll. This strange structure boasts a number of apparent Egyptian symbols, including the four statues at the corners of the roof, lotus flowers carved into the facade, and the winged sun disk over the entrance. In addition to the Egyptian theme, the architect added some ancient Greek symbols for good measure; the four statues that seem to be Egyptian sphinxes (male lions with human heads) are, in fact, winged female lionesses, a Greek adaptation of a Near Eastern motif. This odd mausoleum was moved from the city cemetery, bodies and all, and reconstructed at its present site.

On the same side of the roadway, on your left, is another Egyptian-influenced mausoleum, dedicated to John Kenworthy. This one also bears Egyptian symbols and ornamentation.

A bit farther on the same path is one of the oddest of all the mausoleums at West Laurel Hill. This Theban-style tomb is in the shape of a flat-topped pyramid, a rather ungainly curiosity. It bears the name Charles E. Ellis, a streetcar tycoon.

Follow the curving path to a curious mausoleum just down some little stone steps from the Harrah monument. Here you'll find an eccentric tomb with the name Avery D. Harrington. This little building bears medieval symbols in an almost modernistic setting. The geometric, horizontal pattern of the door is reflected in the design of the stained glass window within.

Following this path you will head back toward the office complex. But shortly before you reach it, stop to see the Dingee tomb, an extremely graceful neoclassical example; it is another replica of the Parthenon.

From here turn right at the next intersection, toward the giant green-domed mausoleum dominating the vista just ahead. It is one of the largest and most imposing mausoleums of the entire cemetery. This is the tomb of John F. Betz, a beer company magnate. It is a beautifully proportioned and massive building in the grand nineteenth century French style. It reminded us of the wonderful buildings in Paris on the Boulevard Hauss-mann—in miniature, of course—with its solemn symmetry, neoclassical columns, and lovely domed roof topped with a winged figure. Be sure to walk all the way around it.

Not far from it you'll spot two curiosities, a pair of graves marked "Jones" and "Platt." Both are stone markers in the shape of tree trunks, and are quite realistically carved and surrounded by smaller stones. Another such tree monument is the Kugler monument, a large granite tree trunk fronted with four granite logs. All of these markers struck us as very odd and rather modern in concept, though we understand that there is an old tradition of using tree trunk forms as memorials.

Nearby and slightly up the hill is another peculiar tomb, also reminiscent of France. This is the Cornelius Harrigan monument. It is a tomb in the French Empire style, shaped like Napoleon's in the Hôtel des Invalides in Paris.

Returning to the pathway, continue toward the office (which can be seen in the distance). But take the road that goes behind it. Go down the hill to spot an interesting monument to a family of sculptors. Slightly off the path is a Celtic Cross honoring the Calder family. Though the mobile maker, Alexander Calder, is not buried here, both his father, Alexander Sterling Calder, and his grandfather, Alexander Milne Calder, are. They were well-known artists whose works grace both Philadelphia's and New York's public spaces. The cross, which bears the names of various other Calders as well, is notable for the carving in its Scottish granite. The cross has a distinctive intertwined pattern of rosettes, as well as the traditional circle intersecting the arms of the cross. Be sure to walk fully around this monument and not to miss the Celtic writing on the front.

If you haven't had enough walking, you might like to search out the graves of a few other prominent Philadelphians: Jean August Girard (the founder of Girard College)—a glass-enclosed bust on a pedestal; Dave Garroway (the radio and television host); Raymond Pace Alexander (a noted African-American judge); Cyrus Curtis (founder of the Curtis magazine empire); Catherine Drinker Bowen (biographer and historian); Loren C. Eiseley (a philosopher and anthropologist); Robert C. Grier (a Supreme Court Justice during the Civil War); Herman Haupt (a Civil War general); Anna M. Jarvis (the founder of Mother's Day in 1908); Frank Maguire Mayo (one of the most famous actors of the late nineteenth century); Alfred James Reach (a founding father of baseball); Fritz Scheel (conductor and founder of the Philadelphia Orchestra); Justus Strawbridge and Isaac Clothier (of the department store); and Horace Trumbauer (the architect of many of the great public buildings of Philadelphia, including the Art Museum). If you particularly wish to find any of these grave sites, the helpful folks in the office will look them up for you and direct you to them. (In fact, they will mark their map for you with any of the tombs listed above.)

INFORMATION: West Laurel Hill Cemetery is open Monday-Saturday, 8:00 A.M.-4:00 P.M.; Sunday and holidays, 9:00 A.M.-4:00 P.M. For information telephone 215-664-1591.

DIRECTIONS: From Philadelphia, take Route 76 West (from the Walt Whitman Bridge). About seven miles from the bridge take exit 31 (City Avenue); continue on City Avenue to Belmont Avenue and turn right. After the second intersection, look for the entrance gate on the right.

In the vicinity . . .
For other art sites in the Philadelphia region, see chapter 40.

17

Frank Lloyd Wright's "Usonia": A Planned Community

Pleasantville, New York

Usonia is no ordinary community. Nestled in rural Pleasantville, in the rolling hills of Westchester County, this unique enclave of some forty-eight modern houses set amid nearly one hundred acres of wooded land is distinctive in its architecture and philosophic raison d'être. The creative spirit behind Usonia was the great architect Frank Lloyd Wright, who designed its site plan, as well as three of its homes. To visit this community is to enter the fascinating world of this twentieth century master and to see firsthand a realization of his aesthetic ideals and philosophical concepts. A walk in this pretty area is also very pleasant, with hilly, wooded roads throughout.

The term "Usonia"—an acronym of United States of North America (with an added "i" for euphony)—was used by Wright to describe architecture for the "average U.S. citizen" (but also based on the writer Samuel Butler's "Utopia"). The term "Usonian house" applies not only to the specific houses in Usonia but to a type of house Wright designed in the 1930s and 1940s; it was meant for the average middle-income American. Intended to be simple in construction and proportion and, therefore, affordable, it was nonetheless anything but "average." Rooted in Wright's radical concept of organic unity, a Usonian house was totally linked to its environment. It was to be "a natural performance, one that is integral to site, to environment, to the life of the inhabitant. Into this new integrity, once there," wrote Wright, "those who live in it will take root and grow." Houses were made of natural materials—usually wood and stone—with large expanses of glass to relate the outdoors with the indoors; structures were low, with cantilevered rooflines, so they would blend in better with their natural surroundings.

In 1944 a group of Wright's admirers, seeking affordable housing in a cooperative setup in the country, retained Wright to design Usonia. The main instigator of the project was David Henken, a mechanical engineer who had seen an exhibit of Wright's, a project called Broadacre City, at the Museum of Modern Art. He had been so impressed that he then went to study with Wright for two years at his headquarters in Taliesin, Wisconsin. The idealistic Henken envisioned a Utopian community where responsibility and costs would be shared, ownership of property would be communal, and where everyone would live in harmony. (This utopian ideal has a long history in the United States, particularly in the nineteenth century, but Usonia was unusual for its time—the 1940s and 1950s—when individual rather than communal ownership was a goal of the "American dream.") He organized a nucleus of twelve families, all enthusiastic about the idea of cooperative living in the country. They pooled their financial resources—at first, $10 a week from each family for the cooperative. They found the ideal piece of land in Pleasantville for a mere $23,000. Wright—who had only agreed to building five of the proposed fifty-five houses plus the community buildings—began drawing up the site plans for Usonia. In the end, he built only three houses (in the late 1940s and early 1950s): the Serlin, Reisley, and Friedman houses, all of which can still be seen. Other architects with similar aesthetic ideas were engaged to design the remaining houses: Ulrich Franzen, Kaneji Domoto, Aaron Resnick, Ted Bower, and David Henken himself.

Wright designed circular, rather than traditional, rectangular, site plans. In this way there would be common land between each one-acre circle and the land would flow freely without the arbitrary divisions usually imposed in a traditional subdivision. There were to be no backyards or frontyards, and the houses were sited so that they would blend into the surrounding landscape, rather than disturbing the natural beauty of the area. The shapes of the houses were odd and irregular (the Friedman house is circular) to accommodate their surroundings. Even though there was a common theme that united the houses in Usonia and they were to be built in groups and not individually, each was designed to be distinctive.

By the early 1950s, practical problems plagued the cooperative. More money was needed to finance additional houses (a total of fourteen houses were built cooperatively), but banks were unwilling to grant mortgages to such a nontraditional group. There were also the inevitable problems concerning materials, schedules, and prices (the homes ended up costing more money than anticipated). Tensions and disagreements arose within the community. By 1955 individual owners—rather than the cooperative—had taken possession of their own homes and only the forty or so acres of recreational land were left for cooperative control. A similar fate engulfed most of the other cooperative communities that preceded this one (indicating perhaps that human nature may be more idealistic in the abstract).

Today the cooperative continues to maintain the roads, water system, and tennis court, and there is still a very strong feeling of community (very few of the original owners have moved away or sold their homes). The original utopian dream may have faded, but its legacy lives on, as you will see on your walk through Usonia. Though you will find only three houses Frank Lloyd Wright designed himself, all forty-seven structures adhere to Wrightian architectural ideas and each is interesting in its variations on the Wrightian plan.

This is a moderately hilly walk through lovely rock and tree-filled terrain, which would be enjoyable even without the added interest of the architecture. The site chosen for Usonia has a natural beauty all its own, like many Hudson Valley areas, and it has remained totally unspoiled.

Leave your car just off Bear Ridge Road at the intersection with Usonia Road. If you would like to know more about the origins and specific architectural details of what you will see before taking this artwalk, we suggest you write or call Roland Reisley before going (see details on page 95). The directions that follow will, however, enable you to spot the major houses and sites.

As you begin your walk heading up Usonia Road you will see a modernish white house in what Wrightians somewhat satirically call the "international style" on a hill to your right. (It is not a FLW house.) But as you continue along Usonia Road, you will overlook to your left several contemporary homes below the road level. These are Usonia tract homes, though not of specific Wright design. If they interest you enough for you to want a closer look, take Tulip Tree Road, the first left you will come to, and walk down before returning to Usonia Road.

Continue along Usonia Road, where it overlooks a lovely valley and turn left on Orchard Brook Drive. Very soon you will spot a distinctive house wonderfully set on a hilly overlook. It is unmistakably by Frank Lloyd Wright. The master's touch is evident in the round portion of the structure and its distinctive interaction with the natural beauty surrounding the building. This is the Friedman house, one of three original designs for the site. Mr. Friedman was a toymaker, and Wright decided to design an appropriately playful house for him. (He later called it "House for a Toymaker.") You can take a detour here to see it from another angle if you wish, by walking along the road to its end.

The Friedman house is in the vein of Wright's prairie-style houses, characterized by horizontal wood siding, deep eaves, and a great deal of stone and glass. But it is particularly innovative in its use of round forms. The structure is designed on a plan of two intersecting circles, on which building cylinders rise and are capped by hat-shaped roofs. The view is unobscured by solid walls; the generous use of glass brings sky and forest to view throughout the house. Even the low stone wall surrounding the house is part of the design, creating a level for the cylinders to sit on. Wright described the Friedman house himself: "There will probably never be another Friedman house nor any closely resembling it. It is of the hill not on it, and I believe the Friedmans are loving it more and more."

If you continue along this road, bearing somewhat to the right, at the very end you will find the second Wright house of Usonia, the Serlin house. This one is less easily seen from the road, though you can view it from beyond the driveway without intruding on the privacy of its owners. The Serlin house is even more clearly based on the prairie house design, being low and horizontal. It too is set on a knoll with a wonderful view of surrounding hillsides and forest. Its rectangular forms, divided by areas of glass and horizontal wood siding, deep eaves, and the acute angles associated with Wright's designs make it a quite typical example.

Retrace your steps back to Usonia Road, passing some less spectacular, but nonetheless interesting, Usonia houses. Back on Usonia Road you will soon come to Wright's Way, a right hand turn. At a short distance on this little road is David Henken's own complex of houses and studios. The Henken family still uses this intricate compound of buildings. Though Henken designed this group, it seems thoroughly Wrightian. One of Henken's children, who grew up in one of these houses in Usonia, recalled the tremendous amount of glass and light: "In winter, I used to lie on the warm floor and look outside to the birds in the sun . . . the light coming in, with all the different angles in the house, was always shifting." It seemed to be the perfect setting for a creative family compound.

You will pass several other Usonia houses before coming to Bayberry Road. Turn right onto this road to make a loop passing by several interesting houses. Soon you will come back to Usonia Road near its end. Here you should turn left, reversing your direction on the main road. On your right almost at once you will find what is often considered Wright's best Usonia house.

The Reisley house was built for its current occupant, who now finds himself somewhat of the local historian on the subject of Usonia. Mr. Reisley will tell you many interesting details about the founding and building of the community if you make an appointment with him. (Please do not just "stop by," however, for people who live in original homes still deserve their privacy!)

The Reisley house, designed by Wright and partially completed by 1953, was quintessentially Wrightian both inside and out. It should be viewed from several angles. Your first look at it will be from below as the road rises up the hill. Keep walking up the road to get another, quite different, impression. It too was designed as a prairie house, with low, rectangular forms and acute angles. It has the combination of fieldstone and wood that Wright preferred, and small cabinlike windows along the horizontal wing.

Like the other Wright homes, the Reisley house was designed to blend in with nature; for example, its low stone walls look like a natural rocky ledge. Among its features are a balcony overlooking the wooded terrain and a twenty-foot cantilevered living room. Some of the furniture was designed by Wright and was built-in. The interior contains a dramatic, irregularly shaped central room with lovely views of the hillside, and small angled bedrooms. A stone fireplace, also set at an angle, is the centerpiece of the living room.

As you walk back toward your car, you will have a new sight of each contemporary house along the way. You also will spot the amusing metal sculpture garden of one artist along Usonia Road (just to the left after the Reisley house).

If you have found the Usonia idea intriguing and want more information on it, you might be interested to look up a 1958 exhibition catalog devoted to Usonia from the Hudson River Museum in Yonkers, New York (telephone: 914-963-4550). In addition, some of Wright's ideas for utopian communities were expressed in his exhibition for Broadacre City (a 1940 exhibition at the Museum of Modern Art); the catalog can be found in a good library.

INFORMATION: To contact Roland Reisley, telephone 914-769-2926.

DIRECTIONS: From New York City, take the Henry Hudson Parkway to the Saw Mill River Parkway to Hawthorne Circle. Take Route 141 North to Pleasantville. Turn right on Lake Street and right again on Bear Ridge Road, to intersection with Usonia Road.

Of similar interest . . .
Three other examples of Frank Lloyd Wright houses in our region are:

Mill Run, Pennsylvania. Fallingwater (telephone: 412-329-8501). One of Frank Lloyd Wright's most important private house designs, Fallingwater is open to the public by appointment. The house, built in 1936, was constructed over a waterfall with cantilevered concrete slabs and stone chimneys; it was perhaps the first "modern" house to be described as romantic. Sculpture in the house by twentieth century masters includes works by Lipchitz, Arp, Picasso, and Rivera.

Manchester, New Hampshire. Isadore J. and Lucille Zimmerman House (telephone: 603-669-6144) is a Frank Lloyd Wright house that can be visited by the public. Combining Wright's prairie house style and his Usonia style, the Zimmerman House was built in 1950. It is a small house of less than two thousand square feet, but its varying ceiling heights and built-in furniture make it seem spacious. It is being restored.

Millstone, New Jersey. The Bachman–Wilson House (1423 Main Street, Millstone). This private residence was designed by Wright in 1954; it has the overhanging eaves and cypress and cinderblock construction favored by the architect.

18

Columns and Clapboard in a New England Whaling Village

Stonington, Connecticut

The village of Stonington, on the Connecticut shores of Long Island Sound, is a rare combination of unspoiled New England charm and picture-perfect waterfront setting. Its quaint streets and fine water views make it an ideal spot for a stroll. But what distinguishes Stonington even more is its wonderful architecture. Here you will find—in well-preserved condition—a wide variety of architectural styles reflecting the town's long history—from early seventeenth and eighteenth century Colonial up to late nineteenth century Victorian—all harmoniously integrated in the small area. And, while anyone would enjoy a visit here—from the history buff to the nature enthusiast to the browser (for there are quite a few nice shops to poke around in)—those interested in architecture will be especially rewarded. Stonington is, indeed, an architectural gem.

A first overview of the village tells you at once that its life has always been linked to the sea. Strategically situated on a jut of land, this peninsular port town was home to seafarers, sailors, whalers, sealers, and shipbuilders from its earliest origins in the seventeenth century. Local traders traveled great distances to the most remote parts of the globe, bringing back many treasures (some of which can still be found in the local homes). The legendary Nathaniel Palmer, a Stonington man who discovered Antarctica at age twenty-one and later became involved in the China trade, is one of many whose sea lore enrich the town's history.

Stonington prospered through the nineteenth century as a shipping and transportation center. Railroad trains from Boston stopped here to pick up steamboat passengers from New York; a large hotel was built to accommodate them (the Wadawanuck, which still dominates the square bearing its name and is now the town library); and the inevitable hustle and bustle of people coming and going ensued.

Eventually the town was bypassed by the railroad, and it settled down into being the agreeably peaceful and quiet spot it is today. Its history of prosperity is still very much in evidence. Its homes—from the more modest to the most stately (of which there are a fair number)—are well laid out and lovingly tended, showing none of the usual signs of years of neglect. And even though this is a town that looks at its historic and architectural past as a source of inspiration, there is nothing melancholic about it. Rather, it is a vibrant and active community, intent upon safekeeping its remarkable assets.

As you walk around Stonington and admire its architecture, you will note the different styles that grace its elegant streets: Colonial, Georgian, Federal, Greek Revival, Gothic, and Victorian. The earliest—the typical New England Colonial style, with its simple structure, clapboard siding, more-often-than-not weathered gray shingles—is well represented here. This no-frills style was primarily functional, as befitted the early seaside community of hardworking people.

As prosperity set in, the more gracious Georgian style took over, with its elaborate entrances, multiple chimneys, pediments, and pilasters. At the end of the eighteenth century the even more refined Federal style became popular. Palladian windows, balustrades often hiding rooflines, fan-shaped windows over the front door, and graceful wrought iron handrails, added sophistication and elegance to these buildings.

During the nineteenth century, as Stonington's population traveled and imported new cultural ideals, more exotic architectural styles were espoused. The Greek Revival (of which there are several examples here) featured a templelike facade with columns, cornices, and classical pediments. The romantic

Gothic style, an outgrowth of European medieval styles, included pointed arch windows, steep pitched roofs, ornamented verandas, and other picturesque motifs. The Victorian "catch-all" style combined many elements from other styles in an often eclectic and imaginative way; but you will see only a few examples of Gothic or Victorian architecture in Stonington; the majority of houses reflect the earlier, typically New England styles.

Before setting out on your walk you might want to pick up a small brochure put out by the Stonington Historical Society (and available in most shops), which plots a suggested route. Or, if you want to know about Stonington architecture in greater detail, you might stop at the library (located on Wadawanuck Square) where you can browse through some informative material. Bear in mind that you can go about your walk in a less systematic way and still enjoy it, as many of the historic houses of interest are marked and dated.

Begin your walk at Wadawanuck Square, where High, Main, Broad, and Water streets converge. In the middle of the square park is the Stonington Free Library, a marble structure surrounded by triangles of grass and high trees. You will start by walking south along Water Street, a narrow, picturesque street that runs through the entire town. At the end you come to the Point, the spectacular and scenic outermost spit of land. Along the way you will see an attractive collection of eighteenth and nineteenth century homes, antique shops, and boutiques.

At the intersection with Union Street you can enjoy a fine view of the picturesque harbor and public pier (also enjoyable for walking and taking in local color). On the west side of Water Street and somewhat south of Harmony you'll find the Peleg Brown House (1786), a charming example of Late Colonial architecture. Originally the home of a shipowner and merchant, it eventually belonged to the world traveling Nat Palmer, mentioned above.

Just after Wall Street (on your right) you'll see the Arcade, an 1830s Greek Revival building with colonnade, now owned by the Historical Society. Cannon Square just beyond is a main point of interest. Here are proudly exhibited the two eighteen-pound cannons that were used in repelling a three-day British naval attack during the War of 1812. This small square is lined with a typically odd group of buildings: an imposing neoclassical bank building (now Ocean Bank), several houses in the Federalist style, and a fine old granite house. The bank, with its Doric columns and classical pediment, is a replica of the Athenian Treasury at Delphi, Greece. Inside you'll find the unique American flag made in 1796 with only sixteen stars and stripes. It flew during the Battle of Stonington in the 1812 attack.

The unusual octagonal granite lighthouse near the Point, at 7 Water Street, is a landmark not to be missed. The oldest lighthouse in Connecticut, it ceased to function as such in 1889 and is now a museum run by the Stonington Historical Society. Here you'll find a motley collection of items from the inevitable curios involving sea life (ship models and whaling gear) to farm tools, children's dollhouses, cannonballs (used in the Battle of Stonington), stoneware, and firearms. Climb the circular stone stairs to the top to enjoy panoramic views of the harbor, Wave Hill (Rhode Island), and Fisher's Island, New York, in Long Island Sound.

Walk east on Omega, turn left on Hancock and left again on Diving, making your way to Main Street. Like Water Street, this long street is lined with buildings of historical and architectural interest. Don't miss the 1790s cottage of a ropemaker, on the corner of Ash and Main; the Old Customs House (1827); the Colonel Amos Palmer House (1780) with its elegant double staircase. Two famous Americans occupied this house at different times: artist James McNeill Whistler (who lived here as a child) and poet Stephen Vincent Benet. (You can also visit Whistler's birthplace in Lowell, Massachusetts. See p. 000.) It is considered to be one of the finest houses in this part of the state, with well-preserved paneling and attractive mantels.

Farther along Main Street you'll find the curious Clubhouse of the Holy Ghost Society, which was originally built for Portuguese whalers who worked alongside Stonington whalers near the Azores; several Greek Revival mansions built by prominent shipowners and sailmakers; an imposing white Victorian mansion; and many other spots of interest. Don't neglect the small side streets that take you to surprising water views (all worth a detour). Eventually you'll reach your starting point, having made a circle.

INFORMATION: *Stonington Historical Society*: telephone: 203-535-111
Open: Wednesday 1: 00-5: 00 P.M. or by appointment; (telephone: 203-672-8441)
Lighthouse Museum (owned and operated by the Historical Society). Open "from time to time" or by appointment: 535-1440. For further information: 203-535-1385 or 203-535-0888

DIRECTIONS: From New York City take the Major Deegan to I-95 east to exit 91; turn south and follow signs to Stonington Borough or Stonington Village, about 2¼ miles.

In the vicinity . . .
Whitehall Mansion (Route 27, north of I-95; telephone: 203-536-2428). Now the headquarters of the Stonington Historical Society, this handsome 1775 house has recently been restored. Gambrel-roofed with three-foot cedar shingles (painted dark red), the house has its original paneling, broad windows, and an enormous kitchen fireplace typical of that era.
Denison Homestead (on Pequotsepos Road; telephone: 203-536-9248). This 1717 shingled home was also recently restored, taking into account the five eras in which different parts of the house were built: Colonial, Revolutionary, Federal, Civil War, and early 1900s. The Homestead is open daily 1:00-5:00 P.M. from May-October.
Mystic Seaport (Route 27, between I-95 and U.S. 1). Where Stonington is uncommercial, unspoiled, and quiet, this neighboring town is the opposite. But it is popular with children and others, who enjoy seeing its recreation of a nineteenth century port with sailing vessels, old homes, and cobblestone streets. You can visit period buildings to see artisans at work in an authentic-looking, but definitely contrived, ambience.

Works in Process: Studios, Foundries, and Workshops

19

Studio Visits in a Contemporary Art Colony

East Hampton and Environs, New York

The fabled "Hamptons" of the Long Island coast conjure up ocean vistas, wide, unspoiled beaches, soft sea breezes, and broad, encompassing skies. This elegant string of colonial shore villages, once surrounded by vast potato fields (few of which remain) has long delighted visitors. Celebrities, whose dramatic beachside homes and legendary parties are routinely chronicled in gossip columns and glossy magazines, summer here; day-trippers come for the pleasures of sea, sun, and people watching; and others are simply here to enjoy a spot of great natural beauty in what can also be a quiet, peaceful environment.

But the Hamptons are more than a glorious playground for weekend and summer pleasure seekers. Artists have long been seduced by the timeless views that can still be enjoyed at every turn. They have lived and worked here—in East Hampton, Southampton, Bridgehampton, and their environs—since the mid-nineteenth century. The list is long and impressive. Thomas Moran, the great American landscapist, was one of the first to paint here. Childe Hassam followed at the turn of the century, as did William Merritt Chase, his contemporary; the painter Lucia Cox, a protégée of F. Scott Fitzgerald's friends, Gerald and Sara Murphy, brought Fernand Léger and Max

Ernst; and Peggy Guggenheim and a coterie of surrealists arrived during the last war.

The notable abstract expressionist Jackson Pollock and his wife, Lee Krasner, moved to the Springs, near East Hampton, in the mid-1940s. They were soon joined in the area by other abstract expressionists, including such seminal figures as Elaine and Willem de Kooning, Robert Motherwell, David Hare, and Harold and May Rosenberg; the newly revitalized Hamptons became one of the country's premier art colonies. Today little remains to be seen of the expressionists' heyday, with the exception of the Pollock–Krasner House and studio, now a cultural center filled with art and memorabilia and open to the public.

But though the heady era of the abstract expressionists is long past, the area has continued to attract artists and patrons. There are as many as five hundred artists working in every imaginable style listed by the Jimmy Ernst Artist's Alliance, and the Guild Hall in East Hampton has large annual shows. Fortunately for the visitor to the area, a number of painters and sculptors open their studios by appointment. In this outing we take you along to see seven of them at work. With a bit of planning you can see these studios, as well as the Pollock–Krasner House and other art sites of interest, and possibly still find time for a stroll on the beach or along some of the enchanting country lanes that weave in and around the shore. You might also want some time to explore on foot the delightful village of East Hampton, which has retained much of its colonial character. Its often photographed windmills, stately old homes, and town pond add to its picturesque charms. Finally, at the end of the day you might be amused to ride past some of the lavish, modern, oceanfront homes that have made Southampton (in particular) a major center of contemporary architecture.

The best time to plan your visit is during the summer months, when the artists are more likely to be available (not all are in residence year-round). Of course, summer is also the time that the Hamptons are abuzz with frenetic activity; the traffic within the towns can be daunting and parking more of a challenge than you might wish (particularly in East Hampton). One pleasant way to avoid this aggravation is to park your car away from the main congestion, unload your bike (or rent one in town), and pedal your way from one art site to the next. You'll find the scenery, setting, and flat roads perfectly suited to biking.

You must telephone the artists to make an appointment before visiting them. (Telephone numbers of each artist are listed at the end.) Please note that the artists included represent only a tiny percentage of the many who live here; you might well discover others during your own ramblings. We found these artists to be particularly interesting and worth visiting; their styles are all different from one another and you will find them working on anything from fairly traditional figurative paintings to bold, avant-garde creations.

Your first stop is at the studio of the artist Christine Chew Smith in Bridgehampton. Smith works in many different media, from pastel, acrylic, and oil, to watercolor, drawing and collage. We were particularly drawn to her charming collages and large oil landscapes. Her studio opens out onto a pleasant, intimate garden, where she also paints. You will find Smith an engaging person who is happy to talk about her work and about the general art scene.

For a radical change in pace we take you next to the studio of Mihai Popa, also in Bridgehampton. You'll be amazed at the extraordinary elliptical house where he lives and works, and will think you are seeing something out of science fiction—or is it a futuristic vision of Noah's ark? Popa's studio and home, without question the most unconventional on our tour, seems to soar like a spaceship, hardly touching the ground. (In fact, its foundation is tiny compared to most, as the artist did not want to impose more than a slight footprint on the land.) Converted from an old barn and built with recycled wood, this rare structure also suggests the rounded organic forms of an ancient past. Its integration of sculpture with architecture is evident both inside and out; as you wander through the interior you might well imagine being inside a wooden sculpture rather than a studio. There is little distinction between utilitarian and art objects within these curved wood, steel, and canvas rooms that flow together. Doors look like sculptures and vice versa. Neon forms, wood and steel sculptures, and models of futuristic cosmic cities (a special project of Popa's) are on display, as are the doors, furniture, passageways, and windows. The Romanian-born artist is given to expansive philosophic discussions about the integration of art, nature, and the universe, as embodied in his work. A visit here can become an extended philosophic discussion on varied subjects and is sure to be an unusual experience.

Our third stop is at the studio of the painter Werner O. Portmann, just down the road. Portmann's suburban-looking home might seem an unlikely spot for an artist's studio; the fairly small, tidy rooms may not be what you normally expect. Nonetheless, Portmann, a courtly, pleasant gentleman from Basel, Switzerland, has been painting here for many years, as well as in New York City, where he also has a studio. His works are often landscapes depicting European cities, or figure studies. He uses the brilliant color combinations reminiscent of the Fauves and works in oils, tempera, and lithograph.

Your fourth stop is the studio of Harold Krisel. You may well have seen the works of this artist elsewhere, for he is well represented in the permanent collections of several of New York's major museums, as well as in public spaces. Krisel's works are in mixed media and you will enjoy his imaginative constructions of small, brightly colored shapes mounted onto wood and metal. Many take the form of small mosaiclike objects that come in a variety of abstract shapes and sizes.

The next studio visit is to the rather glamorous studio of David Porter in Wainscott. Porter's place is truly an artist's dream: a spacious atelier filled with light and surrounded by comfortable, elegant living areas and a pretty garden. Clearly this is an artist who has enjoyed wide recognition throughout a long career. His studio (a downstairs studio as well as one upstairs, which can be reached via an intriguing, spiral staircase) is rich with paintings, sculptures, constructions, and sundry objects. You will find a variety of styles and colors: brilliant hues, as well as white on white; quiet geometric Plexiglas forms, as well as bold abstractions. Porter's fascination with Islamic culture comes through in his soaring calligraphic sculptures, canvases with arabesque shapes, and collaged paintings made with bits of exotic terra-cotta tiles.

Our next artist, Nan Orshefsky, lives nearby. Orshefsky's pleasant and fairly intimate studio reflects her wide interests.

You will see multimedia constructions of found, natural objects (yarn, shells, wood), collages, and Japanese-style fish prints. She has lived abroad and studied the art forms of other cultures, from tempera technique in Paris to Chinese brushwork in Hong Kong. A collection of works on fine Japanese rice papers caught our eye. The gregarious artist will willingly discuss her techniques and work.

By now you are probably ready for a change of pace, if not a lunch break. Make your way to the center of East Hampton for a bit of sightseeing and a snack. Not surprisingly, boutiques and art galleries are everywhere. One that is worth a stop is the East Hampton Center for Contemporary Art, at 16R Newton Lane, where artists from Long Island and New York City are shown. But not to be missed in any event is the Guild Hall, the town's cultural center, right on Main Street. Here the works of Long Island artists, past and present, are on display. Since some of these are well-known, shows here invariably have more than regional appeal. Such noted figures as Audrey Flack, James Brooks, and Larry Rivers live and work in the area. Changing summer exhibits—including a summer sculpture show in the garden—feature the work of living area artists. (You might well see works by some of the artists you have visited earlier.) The permanent collection, shown from October 1 to May 31, displays not only work by contemporary local artists but also that of older masters who painted here, such as Thomas Moran, Childe Hassam, and Jackson Pollock.

From here head east on Main Street, bearing left just below the windmill onto North Main Street. Take the right-hand fork marked "Springs Fireplace" to Springs Fireplace Road. Continue for a couple of miles on this pleasant, tree-lined street, to the studio of Ibram Lassaw. You'll find the artist's atelier down a little lane in the back. A highly regarded contemporary sculptor, Egyptian-born Lassaw was an original member of the early group of abstractionists. His works are well represented nationwide and abroad. You may have seen his *Pantheon* in the walkway of the Celanese Building between 47th and 48th streets and the Avenue of the Americas in Manhattan. This bold sculpture dramatically expresses the contemporary urban scene in a city setting, in sharp contrast to this quiet, country spot where you can watch the artist work.

Another mile or so down Fireplace Road will take you to our next art site, the Pollock–Krasner House and Study Center at 830 Fireplace Road. In 1945 Jackson Pollock and his wife, Lee Krasner, moved to this small, unpretentious nineteenth century white clapboard farmhouse in the fishing community known as "The Springs." It was here—in this idyllic setting overlooking the Accabonac Creek and Gardiners Bay—that Pollock created the famous masterworks that so changed the direction of contemporary art.

In 1987 the Center was created as a museum and research facility. The museum includes Pollock's studio as well as the main house, all beautifully situated in a charming garden. The studio, a converted barn, displays a collection of vintage photos that document the lives and working methods of both Pollock and Krasner (Figure 19). Their working materials have been kept intact just as they were when last used, in a somewhat shrinelike manner. You can walk across Pollock's famous paint-splattered floor. In the main house the Pollock–Krasner living quarters are kept as they were in the 1950s, filled with Victorian furniture and a vast collection of books and jazz recordings. Also in the house is the study center and an art reference library dedicated to the study of abstract expressionism. It includes personal papers, art catalogues, and an oral history library on videotape. Visitors are taken on a guided tour through the House and Center and must phone in advance to make an appointment.

You may now be ready for a taste of contemporary architecture. Leave East Hampton and head to Southampton (take 27A to Main Street, turn left at the end of South Main Street and right onto Dune Road and Meadow Lane). Here you will be at the ocean's edge. Those seaside homes which have survived recent calamitous storms are among the most eye-catching contemporary architectural designs in the country. This row of waterfront homes will fascinate architecture buffs. Long a showplace for twentieth century architects, Dune Road is a smorgasbord of modern home styles, with odd contours, startling angles, and circular forms, which contrast with the quiet sandy landscape and soft Long Island sky. Paul Goldberger of *The New York Times* described this road of contemporary houses as "architecture of shrill egotism—whose arrogance

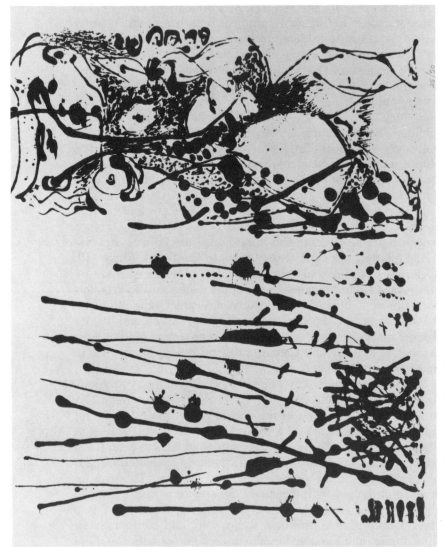

25/50

Pollock, Untitled (After Number 7, 1951), 1951/1964

says as much about its owners' aesthetic tastes as about the extent of their responsibilities to the land on which they have settled." You'll enjoy this as a bike ride. (It's a dead end road, so remember you'll have to return the way you came.) It will complete your exposure to the Hamptons' version of contemporary art and architecture.

INFORMATION: Following are the telephone numbers of the artists listed above. Remember you must phone in advance of any visits.

Christine Chew Smith: 516-537-3310
Mihai Popa: 516-537-0061
Werner O. Portmann: 516-537-2810
Harold Krisel: 516-537-3578
David Porter: 516-537-0854
Nan Orshefsky: 516-537-1077
Ibram Lassaw: 516-324-4575
Guild Hall: Open daily, 10:00 A.M.-5:00 P.M.; no admission; telephone: 516-324-0806
Pollock–Krasner House and Study Center: open Thursday-Saturday, 11:00 A.M.-4:00 P.M. from May 1-October 31; telephone: 516-324-4929

DIRECTIONS: From New York City to East Hampton: take the Long Island Expressway, then Route 111 onto Route 27 East, to East Hampton

In the vicinity . . .
Visit the Parrish Art Museum at 25 Jobs Lane, Southampton, with its superb collection of nineteenth and twentieth century American paintings and prints, as well as Renaissance works. Don't miss the sculpture garden, which is also noted for its unusual tree specimens. Admission is free. Hours: Monday, Wednesday-Saturday, 10:00 A.M.-5:00 P.M. (April-October); closed on Wednesdays from November-March; telephone: 516-283-2118.

Johnson Atelier: Superrealistic Sculpture Taking Shape

Mercerville, New Jersey

As artwalkers we have probably all seen J. Seward Johnson's lifelike sculptures of ordinary people seated on park benches or eating their lunches out of realistically dented paper bags. Johnson's sculptures bring realism to such photographic verisimilitude that it's hard to believe they are actually made of bronze.

Some years ago Johnson decided to set up his own foundry to facilitate the production of these works. The Johnson Atelier does just that, as well as providing a commercial studio to do other sculptors' casting and a school and apprenticeship program for young artists. Fortunately for the art lover (and the art-curious) the foundry can be visited. And what a fascinating visit it is! A walk through the Johnson Atelier will exercise both your feet (the whole place occupies fifty-five thousand square feet) and your mind, for visiting a large foundry where sculptures like Johnson's begin as small clay figures and turn into life-size bronze works of art is extremely interesting.

The process is explained to you as you walk, and if you don't catch all the details of the lost-wax process or the bronzing of clothing, you can ask questions or simply take in the busy and intense atmosphere of dozens of artists at work. Curiously, despite the modern works it turns out, this scene impressed us as perhaps the most traditional environment we've visited; the many people at work on the same pieces of art brought to mind the workshops and apprenticeships of the Renaissance.

The Johnson Atelier is very much a working institution, though there are several attractive galleries for finished sculpture near the entrance. After you have seen the exhibitions in the gallery space, you begin an informal tour through the labyrinth of studio workshops. This will take you to the various production units of the foundry.

In the first you'll see people modeling in clay and enlarging models; some of them will be using a pantograph—a device that scientifically measures small to large figures as the sculptors work. You'll see people working with resins and making molds for use in casting. Next you come to the lost-wax process, where an ancient form of molding from clay to metals proceeds. Here the ceramic shells for monumental sculptures are prepared. Then you see the foundry itself with its giant furnaces. The finishing processes of metal chasing, sandblasting and polishing are done in yet another large area, followed by the welding and bronzing and surface decoration. In each space the workers are apparently undisturbed by occasional visitors picking their way through the atelier, which makes it all the more enjoyable to watch them at work.

In fact, the complicated processes are all made much more interesting by the "works in progress" that you can see as you walk among the artists. And of particular fascination are Johnson's original sculptures in various stages of development—from the bronzing of the "alligator" polo shirt for one of his group statues to the final patina being rubbed onto the bronze surface of another part of the same group. We discovered many odd things about how the work is split up from studio to studio. (One of our favorite sidelights was the employment of a worker whose job it was to purchase for Johnson's statues real pieces of clothing—which are then placed on the molded figures and bronzed.)

Johnson is not by any means the only noted sculptor whose work you will see in process here. Among the other artists who use the Johnson Atelier are George Segal, Mel Kendrick, Julian Schnabel, Marisol (Escobar), Joel Shapiro and John Newman.

For the art lover who is interested in seeing how sculpture is made—beyond the small clay figures we all understand—a visit to this atelier is recommended. Wear flat shoes, by the way, for you'll be going through some messy footing; this is not an antiseptic tourist spot, but a real, pleasantly messy workshop. And we do not recommend this outing if you have respiratory problems, as there is a good deal of blasting and dust. The Atelier provides safety spectacles for all visitors who aren't already wearing glasses.

INFORMATION: Johnson Atelier is at 60 Ward Avenue Extension, in Mercerville, New Jersey. (Telephone: 609-890-7777.) The Atelier is open Monday through Thursday from 8:00 A.M. to 5:00 P.M., but you should call before you arrive to make sure tours are available. You cannot wander through the foundry on your own.

DIRECTIONS: From New York: Take the New Jersey Turnpike south to exit 7A (1-95 Trenton). Take 195 West to 295 North to exit 63B (Route 33 West). Continue through three lights, and turn left at the fourth (Ward Avenue Extension). The Atelier is about $2/10$ of a mile farther, on your right.

Of similar interest . . .
You'll find another foundry described in chapter 25.

The Tim Prentice Studio: Contemporary Sculpture in the Woods

West Cornwall, Connecticut

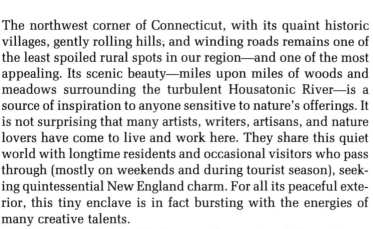

The northwest corner of Connecticut, with its quaint historic villages, gently rolling hills, and winding roads remains one of the least spoiled rural spots in our region—and one of the most appealing. Its scenic beauty—miles upon miles of woods and meadows surrounding the turbulent Housatonic River—is a source of inspiration to anyone sensitive to nature's offerings. It is not surprising that many artists, writers, artisans, and nature lovers have come to live and work here. They share this quiet world with longtime residents and occasional visitors who pass through (mostly on weekends and during tourist season), seeking quintessential New England charm. For all its peaceful exterior, this tiny enclave is in fact bursting with the energies of many creative talents.

On this walk you will discover the works of five of these artists, focusing on one particularly enjoyable outdoor studio/ gallery. The art is displayed on the grounds of these artists' studios, and can easily be seen from the road and in one case, at least, you may be able to visit the artist's studio.

We take you first to a wonderful outdoor art "gallery" belonging to Tim Prentice, just a few miles to the east of the village of West Cornwall.

As you're driving along a winding road from West Cornwall, you come to a point where there are broad views on your right and deep woods on your left and in front of you. On either side of the road your eye catches the light from shimmering objects reflecting the sun and swaying in the breeze. You've reached Tim Prentice's delightful place. The shimmering objects are in fact some of his many whimsical kinetic pieces on view for any passerby to enjoy. You will see a surprising array of works: some are tucked away off the road and into the woods, others are hanging from trees, draped in serpentine fashion, undulating in the air; still others are freestanding, next to the small barns and studios that adorn the property along with the main house. Two examples of his work that can be enjoyed from the road are *Plasmobile*, a 6′ × 8′ work and *Giant Spider*, a freestanding 8′ × 8′ piece showing just that (Figure 20). Most of the pieces are in fact visible from the road, but you can walk up to the house or studio and check to see if the artist is available to show you around. (The sculptor is an engaging individual who often enjoys explaining his work.)

Prentice's art reflects his fascination with space and motion. This architect-turned-sculptor is intrigued by objects moving naturally of their own accord, and his kinetic pieces—all made of very light materials—create an overall effect of an airy, floating world. Many are made of wafer-thin aluminum pieces connected with wire. But we were especially intrigued by his use of unlikely, odd materials: anything from bird feathers, straws, bits of discarded plastic and aluminum, to old milk cartons, small bottles, badminton birdies, or children's toys. His use of these materials is definitely witty. A particularly humorous work on display consists of a series of small yellow plastic toy Volkswagens in rows, hanging from wires.

Prentice's art is accessible, and will put a smile on anyone's face. As he has said, "I love the idea of art that's just on the edge of being art and that's not intimidating." His indoor studio and barn offer yet more pleasures to view at various stages of completion. As the many odd bits of bric-a-brac scattered about will attest, Prentice is an inveterate collector of discarded objects. He is able to transform many mundane items into one delightful, or even elegant, piece. The upbeat works of this prolific artist are well represented around the country and

20. Tim Prentice. *Plasmobile and Giant Spider.* 1985

abroad, in corporate headquarters, airports, restaurants, and private homes.

Other artists in the environs also have open studios or grounds with visible art.

Near Warren (south of West Cornwall), on Melius Road, off Route 45, you'll find the home/studio of the well-known abstractionist Alexander Liberman, where from the road, you can see some of his works on display right in his garden. The bright red and orange constructions stand out very visibly and will remind you of his works at Storm King Art Center (see chapter 46), but on a much smaller scale.

At the end of Flat Rock Road (also off Route 45) are the outdoor sculptures of Werner Pfeiffer. These bold geometric constructions are in brilliant primary colors or white, and are set dramatically on the artist's garden grounds.

At #76 Route 45 near Cornwall you will see some of the environmental works of abstract artist Dave Colbert. These are discreetly set in his wooded yard and can best be seen during the winter months when not hidden by the foliage.

Near Cornwall Bridge (a village four or five miles south of West Cornwall on Route 7) you will find the pottery studio of Todd Piker, on the left as you are going south. Here you can see the potter at work and enjoy a sampling of his creations.

While in the area, you can also enjoy one or more of the surrounding picturesque villages and can walk or ride through the lovely countryside, from one spot of artistic interest to another.

One of the most charming villages is tiny West Cornwall, beautifully situated on the banks of the Housatonic. If you are coming from the south on Route 7, look for unusual froglike cairns—conically-shaped stone mounds used as landmarks—on your right just before reaching the village. The main entrance into West Cornwall is by an antique covered bridge, painted a brilliant red. Built in the 1860s, during the horse and buggy era, this one-lane wooden bridge is one of three remaining covered bridges in Connecticut—there were once more than sixty! (If you're interested in covered bridges, you'll also find one in nearby Kent, another charming New England village, and another much farther east, near Colchester, Connecticut.) As you might expect, the bridge at West Cornwall is a popular stop for visitors; fortunately, the town has not been spoiled by tourism. The Grandma Moses-like village scene is hardly commercial with its somewhat offbeat little buildings, some curiously perched on the cliffs; but you will find a few small boutiques and craft shops lining the main streets. You might want to visit a Shaker furniture studio near the bridge and a pretty pottery shop, or follow any number of enticing little country lanes that lead into the surrounding woods.

Do not miss a visit to a most unusual vintage bookstore right in the center of town. Barbara Farnsworth Bookseller occupies two floors in an old Masonic Hall building and contains rooms literally crammed with some 50,000 volumes of every kind of book—from horticulture and gardening (the owner's predilections) to food, the arts, antique architecture, and local history. Barbara Farnsworth's eclectic collection will delight anyone who has time to browse in a comfortable environment. The cheerful and knowledgeable Barbara Farnsworth herself is usually on hand to chat about her books; on a recent visit she discussed the art scene in the Cornwall area, informing us of local artists and shows. You will find her a wonderful source of information.

INFORMATION: Barbara Farnsworth Bookstore telephone: 203-567-0748; open Saturdays and Sundays and "by chance or appointment" during the week.

DIRECTIONS: To West Cornwall from New York City: Henry Hudson Parkway to Cross County Expressway, to Hutchinson River Parkway, to Interstate 684 East, to 84 East. At Danbury take Route 7 north to West Cornwall.

From West Cornwall to Tim Prentice's studio (130 Lake Road, West Cornwall): Route 128 to the junction with Route 125; bear left to the junction with Town Street; the first right at the top of the hill is Lake Road. Take Lake Road to #130.

Note: If you wish to walk part of the way, we suggest you park your car at the Cornwall Hollow Church, a wonderfully stark country church on your left that stands alone in the surrounding landscape. From there it is about a two-mile walk to Tim Prentice's outdoor art gallery.

22

The Arthur Ganson Studio: Whimsical Machinery and Kinetic Constructions

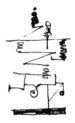

Somerville, Massachusetts

Arthur Ganson is a young artist who makes kinetic sculpture—machinery that is both art in motion and whimsical inventiveness. This "diverse machinery," as he calls his creations, ranges from tiny, delicate, linearly complex objects to monumental organic forms that engage repeatedly in an intricate series of movements. His work might be described as a form of performance art; it is a descendant of Dadaism and Constructivism, featuring a juxtaposition of chaos, chance, and humor, with organic machine elements.

Ganson recently had a one-man show at the De Cordova Gallery (see page 217), where a series of his sculptures were hooked up to electricity or could be hand operated. Small familiar motions like a hand grasping or a plant straining toward sunlight are among the gestures that the artist's machines articulate; the viewer is simultaneously transfixed by these tiny purposeful actions and by the abstract elegance of changing shapes and forms.

The complexity of Ganson's ideas and his mechanical ingenuity make a visit to his studio-workshop an especially interesting experience. The artist delights in showing visitors how he designs his diverse machinery—from mathematical plans to completion with gears and wires and found objects. You will be invited to see his creations throughout his house as well as in his modest workshop. The artist is an informative and enthusiastic host to visitors.

INFORMATION: Call for an appointment; telephone number is 617-776-4808 or 617-625-5541.

Of similar interest . . .
A large outdoor construction by the artist is on the grounds of the Discovery Museum in Acton, Massachusetts (508-264-4201). Made of drainage pipes and other innovative materials, Ganson calls it a form of musical instrument.

23

Stitches and Patterns: Quilters at Work

Putney, Vermont

We all know that the earliest American quilts were master-pieces of invention, using leftover scraps to keep freezing colonial settlers warm. But while the origins of patchwork quilting may have been necessity and thrift, the art long ago developed into an avenue for creativity and social pleasures. By the nineteenth century patterns were carried across the country in covered wagons (the tracing of various designs from settlement to settlement is one way of following westward migrations), handed down from generation to generation—and designed anew by imaginative women.

For this was, in fact, a woman's art form, in an era when few opportunities for creativity existed for rural women. The social enjoyment of a quilting bee was enhanced by the creative delights of pattern, color, and new designs. To some women, a quilt was more than self-expression; it was a representation of life itself. Here is what one woman had to say about making quilts:

> How much piecin' a quilt is like livin' a life! Many a time I've set and listened to Parson Page preachin' about predestination and free will, and I've said to myself, "If I could jest git up there in the pulpit with one of my quilts, I could make life a heap plainer than parson's makin' it with his big words."
>
> You see, to make a quilt you start out with jest so much caliker; you don't go to the store and pick it out and buy it, but the

neighbors give you a piece here and there and you'll find you have a piece left over every time you've cut out a dress, and you jest take whatever happens to come. That's the predestination.

But when it comes to cuttin' out the quilt, why, you're free to choose your own pattern. . . . The Lord sends us the pieces; we can cut 'em out and put 'em together pretty much to suit ourselves. There's a heap more in the cuttin' out and the sewin' than there is in the caliker.

Eliza Calvert Hall, the author of this comment, might have been describing many a creative person's thoughts. And certainly today, with a renaissance of quilt-making taking place all over the country (and fast spreading to Europe and even China), the art of quilting has a "heap more" to it than just the "caliker."

In fact, quilting, as well as fabric-based collage and cloth design, have become increasingly popular forms of art, blurring long-held distinctions between art and craft. While the superior craftsmanship necessary to the making of a first-rate quilt continues to distinguish the best of modern quilts, it is the variety and sophistication of contemporary design that makes today's quilting so special.

We decided to visit a small area in southeastern Vermont that is known for its artists and artisans. Putney and its environs have long been a center for creative people of various kinds, including quilters. Today a number of them live and work there year-round, but we recommend that you make your visit in late spring, summer, or "foliage" season. You will find that these are committed and exhibiting artists whose work areas—though in their homes—reflect the highly professional quality of their work.

Among these fabric artisans is a small group of quilters who have been working together one day a week since 1980, and three individual artists who each work alone. By phoning them in advance you can arrange to visit them in their home studios to see them at work.

The quilting group, which produces the most traditional work, meets every Tuesday at the home of Louise Ripley in Dummerston. Five or six women of various ages gather informally in a cheerful, warm, and unhurried atmosphere reminiscent of another era. Their numbers and hours vary, but Mrs.

Ripley's home is "open all day" and they can come and go as they please. Sewing together on a large antique quilt frame, they work on traditional patterns from a variety of sources, including colonial and Amish designs. It takes the group about two years to complete a quilt, which is then kept by one of the members (who has chosen design and colors), rather than sold. The works in process that you will see here are traditional in style and of heirloom quality, with minuscule stitches outlining delicately patterned images.

Eliza Greenhoe-Bergh, who is part of Mrs. Ripley's group, also works at home on her own designs. While in some quilts she uses traditional patterns, she also creates original designs, which often seem inspired by the Vermont landscape. Her own subtly colored, hand-dyed fabrics, are quilted totally by hand in the finest traditional technique. (Most quilting is now done by machine, and then hand-tied from back to front.) Ms. Greenhoe-Bergh exhibits her quilts widely and is a frequent prize-winner.

Our next visit takes us to the studio of Carlene Raper, who describes her quilts as "in between traditional and modern." She creates her own patterns, but they are not "wild" or asymmetrical. She begins with white goods which she dyes in delicate, predominantly cool shades; you might find hundreds of different tones in a bed quilt or wall hanging. Her studio is filled with color, and you will enjoy seeing the way she works, placing small squares into a larger context.

In a decidedly more contemporary mode are the quilts of Kathleen O'Connor. Her designs are bold and unconventional abstractions with unusual shapes and textures. Many are reminiscent of Japanese art. Her designs are created on a large wall in her studio. Free form, with swirling patterns, her fabric wall hangings incorporate a combination of appliqué, transparent materials (like window screening), painted fabrics, and unusual prints.

INFORMATION: To telephone the quilters:

Louise Ripley: 802-254-5414 (remember that her group meets on Tuesdays).

Eliza Greenhoe-Bergh: 802-387-5912

Carlene Raper: 802-387-5746

Kathleen O'Connor: 802-387-4172

DIRECTIONS: From New York City, take the Hutchinson River Parkway to the Merritt Parkway to Route 15 to Route 91 to Putney Exit (just north of Brattleboro, Vermont). From Boston take the Massachusetts Turnpike to Route 91. For specific directions to the homes of the quilters and other artisans, telephone the numbers listed above.

In addition . . .
While in the Putney area you might want to enjoy some of the other crafts offered here. An annual craft walking tour is held in the fall when you can visit the studios or workshops of weavers, woodworkers, potters, jewelry makers, or glass artisans. For information call 802-387-4032.

Of similar interest . . .
The Vermont Quilt Festival is an annual three-day event held in July on the campus of Norwich University in Northfield, Vermont. Here you will see 250 or more quilts of all styles, ranging from antique works to avant-garde designs. More than seven thousand visitors from all over the country and abroad come to look at the works on display and some even to participate in the many quilting classes offered during those three days. For information telephone Richard Cleveland at 802-485-7092.

24

The Richard Rulli Studio: Woodcarver in the Catskills

Neversink, New York

After driving for miles on the western edge of the Catskills, on winding country roads that take you past woods and fields, up and down hills, along a reservoir, and finally down a narrow steep driveway in a hemlock forest, you will reach the secluded world of sculptor Richard Rulli. To visit his remarkable home and studio is to enter a place where nature and art are in complete harmony.

When you first arrive you're immediately aware that you're in a special environment. Everything in and around the house has been made by the artist, from the two wooden totem poles in front (used as birdfeeders), to the large wooden bald eagle around which the house was built, to the house itself and its many works of art and furnishings. Rulli moved to this seventeen-acre property near the town of Neversink in the mid-1980s. Since then he has focused on his art, which reflects profoundly the natural world surrounding him.

Essentially self-taught—as many artists have been in the history of American art—Rulli learned his art through nature and not the academy: As a young boy, he spent hours in the woods observing animals and plants and carving them in wood. His need to be in close contact with nature shaped his life. At one time he traveled around the country living in a tepee—he still has a special affinity for Native American life-styles.

Rulli built his rustic house—which may be short on modern amenities but is rich in imagination, creativity, and charm— around the sculpture of the eagle. It was begun in 1986 and is still in progress. The house has the feel of a tree house: In the center is the eagle, whose broad wings invade the second floor. Throughout the living/working quarters (they are basically one and the same) are examples of the artist's work, many pieces finished, others still in progress. Each piece has its own story, which Rulli is happy to tell in detail. You will be intrigued not only by the various sculptures but also by the wooden objects, Indian artifacts, animal skulls and skins (tanned by the artist himself), and deer antlers scattered about. The rustic-looking furniture pieces are finely crafted works of art in their own right.

Rulli obviously enjoys talking about his work, its evolution, and his views on art. He mills his own wood, and before beginning to carve spends time—sometimes months—observing the wood closely. He says he waits for the wood to "speak" to him; he believes that each piece of wood has qualities that dictate what it should become and that the artist should not make something without considering these traits first. For Rulli there is a natural harmony between the tree and the work of art inherent in it.

In speaking about a large blue heron sculpture in his house he says:

> Some artists create by building, by putting things together step by step, starting from point zero. For me it's the opposite. That great blue heron was always in the tree. I just cut away enough of the wood so you could see him, too . . . [the sculpture is] my interpretation of him, of his spirit.

Rulli is mindful of the grain in the wood he works with, and of the knots he might find; he uses these elements to shape his work. In a wall piece depicting bears hunting for salmon, the knots in the wood have become the eyes of the fish and the pronounced grain, the rippling river and waterfall. Long wooden staffs have been carved, into animal shapes reminiscent of Eskimo art, following the natural configuration of the wood.

127

But the pièce de résistance is the eagle. Rulli talks about this sculpture with the same emotion that one might use in speaking of a close friend. He says he has dedicated some seventeen thousand hours to it so far. Approximately eleven feet high, it has a thirteen-foot wingspan, which can be viewed especially well from the second floor. You'll note the delicacy and expressiveness of the wings—surprising in so bold a work. You can touch them from above to feel their silky softness. Rulli has a photo album that chronicles the evolution of this extraordinary work. Its story begins in 1986, when he heard of a large black walnut tree that was to be cut down to make room for a flower garden. The tree was at least eighty years old and weighed more than four tons: handling it and transporting it in sections from downstate New York proved to be a daunting task, as can be seen in the photographs. It was during the process of building his house around the wood that its branches grew another four feet! The tree finally stopped growing when Rulli finished the roof, as if it were content to stay. This experience left a lasting impression on him and helped shape his view of the sculpture as an organic entity.

After your visit to Rulli's studio you might wish to take a walk in the thick surrounding woods, which extend far and beyond.

INFORMATION: To arrange for this studio visit, you must call Richard Rulli first at 914-985-2397.

DIRECTIONS: From New York City take the New York Thruway to exit 16, then Route 17 north to exit 100 (Liberty). Richard Rulli will give you directions to his home from here.

25

Tallix-Morris Singer Foundry: Today's Masterpieces in the Casting Process

Beacon, New York

The excitement of visiting a foundry is to see works in progress. The foundry plays a key role in the creative process of three-dimensional art. For it is here that an artistic concept, a model, or a clay sculpture becomes a finished work in steel or bronze or other metals. The foundry sees the work through its final realization, as envisioned by the artist.

The Tallix-Morris Singer Foundry in Beacon, New York, is a particularly impressive foundry to visit. It is the product of a recent merger between the twenty-or-so-year-old Tallix Foundry of Beacon with the 150-year-old Morris Singer, a venerable British foundry. (Two other foundries also make up the group: one in Ontario, the other in Birmingham, England, specializing in lost-wax technique and small sculpture casting.) Tallix-Morris Singer's huge size—eight acres, or eighty thousand square feet of massive hangarlike structures with forty-six-foot ceilings—enables it to produce giant sculptures. And its vast technological and craft facilities include everything from casting (in bronze, brass, steel, aluminum, lost-wax, sand, etc.) to restoration, reductions, enlargements, coloring, and much more—all of which make it a fascinating place to see in full action.

When you first arrive at Tallix you see what appears to be a collection of huge warehouses or airplane hangars. Were it not for the large pieces of sculpture scattered about on the surrounding grounds, you might think you were simply in a factory complex. But once inside, you've entered a different and quite magical world. You might be surprised, as we were, by the great variety of processes going on simultaneously throughout these vast quarters. Visitors are required to take a tour (for good reason, given the inherent dangers of wandering around unaccompanied) in which these fascinating processes are explained thoroughly and in some technical detail. You are shepherded from section to section, and from process to process, observing the staff (many of whom are artists in their own right) busily at work. The noise level can be deafening—when the machines are being operated at full blast—the air can be hard on the lungs, and you might have to walk through very dusty places, but you will find the experience engrossing and well worth any temporary discomfort.

A particularly intriguing process to watch is enlarging, which is long and laborious. It's incredible to see a small, unprepossessing clay sculpture become a massive piece that still retains all of its exact proportions. The artisan who does this has to work very carefully and mathematically to make sure that every line and every curve is respected in the exact way intended. And workers must be an unjudgmental crew, who work with similar attention to detail and apparent interest on the most realistic portrait heads as on massive abstract constructions.

We enjoyed wandering through the cavernous spaces seeing partial works—maybe a torso or a head being worked on, or a fantastically-shaped abstraction in its early stages—and realizing how privileged we were to be seeing these works before completion. We saw a giant black canoe with Native Americans rowing vigorously, being transported out of the foundry for an embassy swimming pool in Washington, D.C.

On your visit you might chance upon works in progress by such well-known artists as Roy Lichtenstein or Frank Stella—who have their works cast and fabricated here—or Nancy Graves, Julian Schnabel, Isamu Noguchi, Claes Oldenburg, and Jeff Koons, to name a few. It's interesting to learn that sculptors submit their works at different stages. While some might give the foundry only a conceptual drawing or small model to work from (which will then be transformed into the final work), others submit a full-scale work. Artist involvement with the sculpture at the foundry also varies: Whereas some are constantly available for input (and, indeed, want to be there to witness the final creation), others are happy to leave the major responsibility to the foundry.

INFORMATION: Tallix-Morris Singer Inc. is located at 175 Fishkill Avenue in Beacon. Hours: 8:00 A.M.-5:00 P.M., Monday-Friday; Telephone: 914-838-1111. Tallix has recently cut back on the number of visitors they can accommodate. In order to make a tour appointment, you should identify yourself as an artist, art-lover, or otherwise connected with the art world.

DIRECTIONS: From New York City take the Taconic Parkway to Route 84 (West); take exit 12 and make a left onto Route 52. Go for two miles to Beacon. Tallix will be on your left.

Of similar interest . . .
After you've visited the foundry you might like to see the finished works in situ. Cross the river and visit Storm King Art Center, the famous sculpture park (see chapter 46).

For another foundry visit see the Johnson Atelier in Mercerville, New Jersey (see chapter 20).

26

The John McQueen Studio: Unique Visions of Nature's Fibers

Trumansburg, New York

The continuing discussion as to what constitutes art as opposed to craft seems irrelevant when you view the extraordinary works of John McQueen. We might see them as organic sculptures; he emphatically refers to them as "baskets." They are, in fact, unique creations that defy categorization.

We were recently introduced to McQueen's work at an exhibition sponsored by the American Craft Museum in New York City, an experience which radically transformed our perception of what a basket is. His baskets come in extraordinary shapes and forms; and they inevitably stimulate philosophic discussion about the nature of space, the complexity of the natural world, and the individual's relation to nature. They are also a visual treat that everyone can enjoy.

McQueen's baskets are abstract forms, although they are sometimes reminiscent of whimsical imaginary animals, birds' nests, human body parts, or anything and everything. They can be round, like a reconstruction of an ancient vase; spiraled, like a reptile; gawky, squat, or oblong with strangely protruding "arms" and "legs"; twisted, like a porcupine or bonsai; or utterly delicate, like a gossamer web. But they are, first and foremost, meant to be baskets.

To McQueen a basket is a singular, three-dimensional object, a container with a bottom and a hole at the top—although he occasionally varies from this model. His baskets are made of woven or otherwise attached strips of natural materials that he gathers on his rural property in upstate New York: twigs, vines, patches of leaves, orange peel, moss, goldenrod, or the barks of an assortment of trees, in various combinations. Like traditional baskets, McQueen's are neither too large nor too heavy to be carried. Their function is to enclose and contain, like shells that divide inner from outer space.

"A basket is egocentric and imprisoning," he wrote in his 1983 journal.

> It holds tenaciously to its limits. It has its own organization and regulates its definition closely. By insisting on being a basket, it keeps itself confined. Let other objects try to be art. A basket is isolated, unique, separated from all but itself. Such defenses are tightly held. Uncertainty, movement, fear of being spread out is guarded against. The open object, the object of art leads to a larger reality. The basket must reject this even when inside, it secretly entertains it. These secrets lead to hero worship and flights of fancy. A basket must be careful. In such a state it could become unraveled.

McQueen sees the basket as a metaphor for the individual, whose self is separated from other beings or objects.

McQueen began as a sculptor, but his need to explore the nature of containment and his love for nature and its materials led him to basketmaking. He feels this form of expression has given him greater freedom as an artist. "Baskets have enormous variety, history, and distance," he says.

> I think sculpture, because of its place in the hierarchy of the fine arts, has more rules, requirements, and preconceptions. The advantage of having baskets ignored by modern western cultures is that baskets are allowed to be whatever I want—the rules haven't been determined. Baskets connect with the definition of a container—a very broad concept. This room is a container. I am a container. The earth is being contained by its atmosphere. This is so open, I don't need to worry about reaching the end of it.

He became interested in basketmaking while in New Mexico. With his natural ability for working with his hands (he had been an auto mechanic at one time) he learned to weave "three-dimensional structural things." Refining his craft, he began working with forms and molds, in order to control precisely the shapes of his works. As time went on, however, he began using parts of trees as his molds, particularly oddly shaped logs and branches that he found in the woods behind his house. In so doing, he was allowing nature to determine the shapes of his pieces and was achieving a more organic look in his works.

In his *Untitled #189* (Figure 21) he created a curious animal-like shape from what had probably been a protruding limb. The spruce bark is sewn together and fastened with plastic rivets, adding to the appearance of a blocky, armored body. In a work we saw entitled *Tree and its skin #112*, the artist obviously chose logs that looked like human torsos, and in *Untitled #187* he fashioned a basket in which the openings appear where limbs once emerged from the main trunk of the tree.

Some of McQueen's works include words. These are not only decorative but also structural elements. Occasionally they are hidden inside or underneath his baskets, or are shown as abstract and translucent calligraphy. The word "Understand" forms the base of one work and "Once" circles around another. In one of his most delicate works, the open-ended *Untitled #88*, the word "Always" creates two webs, as light as clouds disappearing into the sky. McQueen feels that words are powerful symbols from our culture, much like the ancient symbols of crosses or lightning bolts, and they can engage the viewer in a meaningful exchange.

John McQueen's works are exhibited frequently, but you can also see them right where they are made. The artist welcomes visitors to his studio, located on eight acres outside of Trumansburg, New York. The property includes his English-style cottage, a barnlike studio, pond, and deep woods. Here, in splendid isolation, McQueen is completely involved with the natural surroundings that provide him with the inspiration and physical materials he needs to create his works.

INFORMATION: To visit John McQueen in his studio, telephone him at 607-387-6098. He will give you precise directions to his studio.

21. John McQueen. Untitled #189. 1989

DIRECTIONS: From New York City take Route 80 to 380 North to Route 81 North, to Binghamton; then take Route 17 west to 14 north; at Watkins Glen take 414 north to Trumansburg. Then follow the directions given by the artist.

27

Folk Art and Modern Craft Workshops at Peters Valley

Layton, New Jersey

To witness the making of an art or craft object is a compelling experience for anyone interested in the creative process. At Peters Valley Craft Center in rural New Jersey you can watch a piece of metal, wood, or fabric take on a new identity such as a one-of-a-kind weather vane, a musical instrument, or a wall hanging.

Situated in a remote wooded site within the Delaware Water Gap National Park Recreation Area, Peters Valley is obviously far removed from the bustling urban scene. Still, this tiny community bursts with the creative energy of the artists and artisans who live and work here. Fortunately, they are willing to share their world not only with the students who come to learn about their art, but also with the more casual visitor who is interested in observing these works in progress.

Peters Valley is a genuine crafts community and not a contrived setup for tourists. Established in 1970 as a nonprofit craft education center, its role has been to promote traditional and contemporary crafts through a wide variety of programs. Professional artisans (one for each discipline) in blacksmithing, ceramics, fine metals, photography, textiles, and woodworking, are selected to live here for one year and manage their own studios with the help of an assistant. In the summer, a large and diverse number of artisans comes from all over the country to teach inexperienced as well as advanced students. A crafts store displays the work produced on the premises, and an art gallery hosts annual shows. And, of special interest to us, is the so-called "studio interpretive program" which enables the visitor (during the summer months) to see artisans at work in their studios.

A walk through Peters Valley will not only be of interest to those who like crafts, but also a treat for nature lovers, for this is a spot of great beauty. As you wend your way from one studio to the next, you will discover many an inviting path through the woods and might be tempted to wander farther afield into the vast surrounding national park after your visit.

Although Peters Valley is by no means an extensive community, it does include a good number of small buildings scattered about and tastefully integrated into the woods, some almost hidden from view. Not only are there the six main working studios (one dedicated to each craft), but also the Doremus Art Gallery, the Peters Valley Contemporary Craft Store, the Bevans Church (an old frame building sitting prettily behind a quaint graveyard and used for social gatherings), and several dormitory and other service facilities.

To get your bearings, pick up a self-guided walking tour map available at the Peters Valley Craft Store. This is the first house you see when you reach this tiny community after your fairly circuitous route over winding roads: a charming frame house with an old-fashioned porch, directly in front of a most unusual, tall house in the Greek Revival style (which turns out to be the photography studio). The craft store is filled with the works of the on-site craftspersons and is a great place to browse. Across the street you'll find the Peters Valley office, from which you can get all the information you'll need. You can either walk from one studio to the next on your own or take a guided tour. In the same building as the office, on the second floor, is the Doremus Gallery, which features three annual shows: the Summer Faculty Show, the Studio Assistants' Show, and a show dedicated to works from the anagama kiln behind the ceramics studio.

Before you start out on your studio tour remember that what you will see at each studio will depend, of course, on the workshops in progress and on the particular area of expertise of the artist on the premises at the time. But we can assure you that you will be treated to a wide variety of techniques and materials of interest to any crafts buff.

Begin your walk at the craft store. A small path from there will lead you to the photo studio, unmistakable with its Greek-columned facade. Here, in addition to the basic developing and printing of black and white and color prints, you might chance upon workshops dealing with nineteenth century platinum/palladium printing techniques, or alternative photographic techniques such as infrared film, toning, hand-applied colors, or discussions on photographic thought and vision.

At the nearby fine metals studio, next on your self-guided walk, you might see anything from silversmithing and metal casting to forging and soldering, to jewelry making or designing of metal furniture.

On your next stop, at the wood studio, you might find an artist at work in the fascinating process of traditional gilding—from the preparation of gesso to the laying and burnishing of gold; or you might see the making of a shoji screen, an acoustic guitar, or even a wooden canoe. Here, the unusual seems usual!

At the textile studio objects are made from a wide variety of materials using different techniques. You might see individuals at work on vine basketry, tapestry making, paper marbleizing, or silk screening, to name only a few of the possibilities.

The ceramics studio is fun to visit, especially if the fifty-foot long anagama kiln is being fired. The six-day firing of it starts with a slow but constant fire and builds up to one in which the temperature reaches an amazing 2,400 degrees, with smoke and flames surging on all sides. Clay tiles, pottery, ceramic jewelry, and functional pots are among the items made here.

At the blacksmith studio you might see the making of a weather vane, forged furniture, or decorative metal objects.

The best time to visit Peters Valley is from June 1 to August 31, when everything is open. You might also enjoy the annual craft fair which takes place during the last weekend of July. Here, again, you can watch a variety of craft demonstrations and browse through the many works on display by some hundred or more artisans. Nature lovers might prefer to come to Peters Valley during the off-season: true, some of the studios and other facilities may be closed to the public, but the woods are quiet and you will have the place almost all to yourself.

INFORMATION: Peters Valley Craft Center is located on Route 615, Layton, New Jersey. It is open seven days a week, year-round, from 10:00 A.M.-5:00 P.M., although the studios are open to the public daily from 2:00-4:00 P.M. only from June 1-August 31. Guided tours are offered on Saturdays and Sundays at 2:00 P.M. and leave from the craft store. The Doremus Gallery is open seven days a week during the summer, from 9:00 A.M.-5:00 P.M., and only on weekdays during the rest of the year. For general information telephone 201-948-5200.

DIRECTIONS: From New York City: Cross George Washington Bridge and take Route 80W to exit 34B to Route 15N to Route 206N, left onto Route 560W through the blinking light in the center of Layton. Take Route 640 for about a mile and turn right onto Route 615. Go approximately one mile and follow signs to Peters Valley.

In the vicinity . . .
The Delaware Water Gap is one of the East's most picturesque spots. Now a national recreational area, it is accessible at many different points for walking and viewing the spectacular vistas. A number of nineteenth century landscape artists chose the site for painting; among them was George Inness whose panoramic painting of it can be seen at the Montclair (N.J.) Art Museum.

Artistic Gardens: Formalizing Nature

28

Old Westbury Gardens: Elegance on Long Island

Old Westbury, New York

The magnificent black iron gates and the grand allée beyond introduce you immediately to the glamorous ambience of Old Westbury Gardens. Here is the splendor of the magnificent European-style formal gardens of the past, their harmonious elegance graced with outdoor sculpture. This is a great estate on the grand scale, bringing to mind hazy romantic scenes involving Edwardian images and moonlit nights. In fact, the gardens are used frequently for movie sets and picture-book weddings, as well as by historians of landscape architecture of the past.

Just a stone's throw from the ultimate contemporary highway landscape, this site is all the more intriguing in its contrast with Long Island sprawl. The estate, built in 1906 by John S. Phipps, a financier and sportsman, is not the only grand house in Old Westbury, where many of the rich and fashionable built their homes at the turn of the century. (Nearby are the William C. Whitney Racing Stables, for example.)

Mr. Phipps hired the London architect George Crawley to construct a Stuart-style "country" mansion, to please his English wife. Westbury House was built atop a hill; its symmetrical elegance is set off by a master plan of landscape design. In fact, the estate is a rare example of landscape and architectural planning that went hand in hand; the complementary designs of the house and its surroundings are worth noting and are of great interest to modern designers.

The interior of the house is elegant and formal. It is open to the public and will appeal to those who enjoy seeing how such country retreats were designed and furnished—from fluted Corinthian columns and French windows, to polished antique tables and Ormolu clocks. You will also find paintings by John Singer Sargent, George Morland, Joshua Reynolds, and Sir Henry Raeburn.

But of particular interest and delight to us were the gardens, which—even without the many sculptures—are a work of art in themselves. Designed by both Crawley and a French landscape architect named Jacques Greber, the master plan called for a formal geometric arrangement of grand allées, softened by English "romantic" or picturesque gardens. The combination, based clearly on the layouts of the grounds of English stately homes, is an unqualified success.

Among its charms are a lake walk—yes, of course, there is a lake—leading to a "Temple of Love," a boxwood garden, a garden with flowers of all the colors of the rainbow, a "ghost walk" of dark hemlock trees, and a walled garden where you can easily imagine—or enjoy—the most romantic of trysts. There are numerous rare and magnificent trees and plantings, including many from the Orient. Almost three hundred species of trees are flourishing at Old Westbury Gardens. Depending on the timing of your visit, you may see profusions of rhododendrons, lilacs, roses, and too many other of nature's most beautiful flowers to list here.

Sprinkled liberally throughout these enchanting areas are neoclassical sculptures and columns and various other art works that add to the ambience of European elegance. Ceres is sheltered in a pergola of wisteria, while a terra-cotta Diana the huntress graces a curving colonnade within the boxwood garden. There are ornamental cherub fountains in pools of lotus and lilies; a pair of bronze peacock statues with topiary tails; an elaborate shell mosaic in the style of Italian grotto decoration of the seventeenth century; a sundial topped with rampant lions; groups of nymphs and satyrs on the roofline of the house; a pair of lead eagles and stone vases on pediments, surrounded by lilacs; and a sculpture of the quasi-mythical athlete, Milo of Cortona, wresting a tree stump from the earth. (You will surely discover additional sculptures tucked away in niches and along walkways.)

Old Westbury Gardens are not unknown in the New York area, so we suggest visiting on a weekday if you can. There is a moderate admission charge. (Holiday festivities are occasionally held at the estate.) You can pick up pamphlets and guides to the garden at the mansion.

INFORMATION: Old Westbury Gardens are located at 710 Old Westbury Road. Their hours are 10:00 A.M. to 5:00 P.M. every day except Tuesday, May through December. Telephone: 516-333-0048

DIRECTIONS: From New York City, take the Midtown Tunnel to the Long Island Expressway to Exit 39S (Glen Cove Road). Continue east on the service road of the expressway $1^2/_{10}$ miles to Old Westbury Road, the first road on the right. Continue ¼ mile to the garden entrance on your left. (Also reachable by Long Island Railroad to Westbury from Pennsylvania Station in New York, and by taxi from the Westbury station.)

29

Ladew Topiary Gardens: Plant Sculpture in Eccentric Forms

Monkton, Maryland

A fox hunt within the grounds of a formal garden? As unlikely as it may sound, you will indeed find one at Ladew Topiary Gardens in Monkton, Maryland. But, instead of a lively scene of red-coated riders and yelping hounds, you'll find a quiet, green sanctuary. Fortunately for the potential victim, no real fox hunt takes place here—only a giant topiary version of one.

Topiary art, in which yew and other growing plants are trimmed into artistic shapes and forms, is rare in this country. Though many public gardens clip hedges into pyramids or other geometric forms, a garden of representational topiary shapes is unusual and certainly great fun, particularly for children.

Ladew Gardens were the creation of Harvey Smith Ladew, a prominent and somewhat eccentric New York socialite; he moved to the Maryland countryside to pursue his equally great passions for fox hunting and building gardens. The fifteen gardens that comprise this twenty-two-acre site were recently restored to their former splendor, some years after his death. Filled with surprises at every turn, they reflect Ladew's wit, whimsy and peculiar interests.

One of the most delightful spots is, unquestionably, the plant sculpture fox hunt tableau, which includes two horses and riders jumping over a fence following six yew-covered hounds in hot pursuit of a fox. Grassy walks throughout these green acres take you to other topiary delights, interspersed among hedges, behind fountains, around walkways: a flock of twelve graceful swans "floating" atop a hedge; seahorses, a lyrebird, a Scottie running toward his bowl and ball; and the somewhat incongruous forms of Winston Churchill's victory sign, a Chinese junk, and a large Buddha.

More conventional gardens representing a variety of styles also grace the elegant premises: a carefully tended wild garden (not such a contradiction of terms within this context); an old-fashioned Victorian flower garden, a rose garden enclosed in a circular brick wall; a yellow garden, white garden, water lily garden, iris garden, and even a Garden of Eden—with a statue of Adam and Eve surrounded by azaleas and . . . apple trees. A terrace garden features steps flanked by austere-looking topiary obelisks in formal rows. A Temple of Venus (Ladew's "folly," perhaps) overlooks the entire scene from a lofty perch.

The Ladew Gardens are both formal and romantic in tone. Their combination of charm, surprise, and beauty will appeal to young and old alike. (Children will delight in finding and identifying the topiary forms.) The estate also includes an elegant home filled with travel memorabilia, artifacts, and photographs reflecting Mr. Ladew's active social life and travels.

INFORMATION: Tours are required to visit the house and garden, although you can wander around on your own in the garden. There is a moderate entrance fee. Telephone: 410-557-9570.

DIRECTIONS: The Ladew Gardens are located at 3535 Jarrettsville Pike, Monkton, Maryland. From Baltimore take Route 83 to 695; exit 27B (Route 146); cross over the bridge and bear left onto Route 146, the Jarrettsville Pike. Travel fourteen miles to Ladew Gardens.

Of similar interest . . .
For another visit to a topiary garden, see Green Acres in Portsmouth, R.I. (chapter 33).

30

Wethersfield: The Delights of Trompe L'Oeil

Amenia, New York

There are many ways in which gardens can be artistic—or appear to be art themselves. Topiary gardens (see chapters 29 and 33) are like parks of living sculpture, while sculpture parks are themselves gardens of art. In this collection we include gardens designed as Chinese paintings (see chapter 32) and gardens that have been the inspirations for paintings (see chapter 7).

At Wethersfield, a country estate near Amenia, New York, you'll find gardens that are at once repositories for sculpture and themselves a kind of spatial work of art. As you walk through the landscaped grounds of Wethersfield you'll have a sense of trompe l'oeil—that French description of art that plays spatial tricks on the unsuspecting (but delighted) viewer.

Wethersfield's gardens are so artful that the eye can be deceived by the long allées and decorative gates, and the geometric shapes of pruned bushes and trees that form the setting for its marble statuary. The gardens within gardens, the sense of perspective, the carefully placed statuary, reminded us of the surreal gardens of René Magritte's paintings, where a hat may appear over a hedge in a dreamlike green garden of distant proportions and uncertain boundaries.

The gardens are the high point of the visit to this gentleman's country estate (and working farm). There are also tours of a spanking carriage barn with elegant vehicles of the past, all shined up and ready to go (the owner participated in carriage driving competitions), and a house tour through the large interior, which, despite some real art treasures, is not terribly interesting.

If you want to see everything, you must call for an appointment. On your (prearranged) arrival you can decide which parts of the estate are of most interest, but you will surely want to explore the gardens (which can be visited separately), even if you skip the carriage barn or the house tour.

Wethersfield has just opened formally to the public. It was the home of Chauncey Stillman, an investor and philanthropist, who purchased it in 1937. The estate now consists of one thousand four hundred acres. The setting of the house and gardens is magnificent, overlooking a vast panorama of fields and mountains—the Catskills to the west and the Berkshires to the north. The gardens cover more than ten acres of the estate and provide a marvelous place to walk. There are also woodland paths that you can enjoy at your leisure.

The Georgian-type mansion, built in 1940, is in a traditional colonial style. It houses Stillman's collection of antiques, paintings, furniture, and decorative objects. Elaborate and somewhat overwhelming frescoes by the present-day Italian artist Pietro Annigoni cover a number of walls in a sort of neo-Baroque fashion. There are several paintings of serious interest, including a wonderful *Boy with a Dog* by Toulouse-Lautrec, two Mary Cassatts, an Ingres, a Sargent, and a Degas, as well as many lesser works.

There is a great mix of styles and attitudes in these interiors, ranging from the owner's rather chummy den with its duck-embroidered pillows, to a room that functioned as a Catholic shrine to the Pope, with a Murillo painting over the mantel. The most startling room is the south wing which Stillman called the "Gloriette," an addition to the house in 1973, which can only be described as eccentric in style and taste. The guide will describe it all.

And now to the gardens. Leave yourself plenty of time to see them, and even to walk through the woods to the Palladian arches at the edge of the field. Pick up a map at the upper parking lot, where you leave your car. You'll find the brochures in a basket between two stone lions.

The gardens, which you will enter here, are generally neo-classical and French in style. They are simultaneously grand and intimate. You might even see occasional peacocks strolling through them. Each garden is separated from the next with hedges or wrought iron gates. Though there are formal flower beds, it is the geometric design of borders and flagstone paths, reflecting pools, and green walls of hedges that create the special ambience of this place. There are cones, balls, columns, and boulder-shaped topiary designs, as well as gargoyles and cherubs, temples, animal sculptures and classical figures everywhere, nestling into the greenery and demarcating each individual area.

You'll find a lily pond with sculptured turtles, deer sculptures by John Flannagan, two Pans by an Englishman named Peter Watts, two nymphs and a Hercules of limestone, some charming recumbent sheep, a naiad by the Swedish sculptor Carl Milles gracing a fountain, and a stone stairway leading to a "Belvedere" with a stunning view of the landscape.

A Polish artist named Joseph Stachura made many of Wethersfield's sculptures, including the Madonna and other religious works around the grounds. They are representational marble carvings that are graciously placed here and there in shrinelike settings.

All of the sculpture is traditional—this is not a venue for the latest in abstract works. Instead, it is a period setting with a strikingly "modern" sense of space. Like an outdoor gallery, the gardens are a form of three-dimensional art, ornamented with sculpture; the emphasis of the landscape design has surely been on form.

But this is not to say that there are not charming flower beds and wonderful trees. There are, in fact, a rose garden, perennial gardens, a cutting garden, and many other distinctive sections. (An army of gardeners works year-round.)

INFORMATION: Wethersfield House, Gardens and Carriage House are open Wednesday, Friday and Saturday, June 1 through September 30. To visit the house or carriage house or garden you must make an advance reservation. The gardens are open noon to 5:00 P.M. There is a moderate entrance fee. Telephone: 914-373-8037.

DIRECTIONS: Wethersfield is located in northern Dutchess County, New York. From the Taconic Parkway, take Route 44 north of Millbrook, then take Country Road 86 (Bangall–Amenia Road) and turn right onto Pugsley Hill Road. Follow signs about 1⅓ miles to the entrance on the left.

In the vicinity . . .
The beautiful gardens of Innisfree are not far away. (See chapter 32.)

Untermyer Park:
The Neoclassical Tradition

Yonkers, New York

If you are looking for a way to introduce young children to the pleasures of art and architectural discovery outside of the confining walls of a museum, try taking them to Untermyer Park in Yonkers. Here, in a short and delightful walk, they can discover a variety of interesting sculpture, architectural details and classical era art without knowing they are being educated at all! If you do this walk in the form of a treasure hunt, they will enjoy it all the more.

Untermyer Park was once the estate of Samuel Untermyer, a well-to-do lawyer who made his home, Greystone, there at the turn of the century. (Greystone was an imposing place where a governor of New York State, Samuel J. Tilden, lived from 1874 to 1876. The house was demolished some time ago.) But the 113-acre garden, designed by William Welles Bosworth for Untermyer (an amateur horticulturalist himself) was saved. In 1946 it was donated to the city of Yonkers, and through the efforts of preservationists and city and state with federal funds is still being restored.

And there is a lot worth saving. In addition to the beautifully landscaped gardens, there is literally a treasure trove of small art details in the neoclassical revival style favored by Bosworth and Untermyer. Perched on a hill with a great Hudson River view to the west, the park is a large rectangle surrounded on the other three sides by a high brick wall, which increases the lovely sense of isolation from the modern noise and confusion of a busy roadway just outside the gates.

The park is a formal arrangement with a central reflecting pool bordered by shrubbery. There are wonderful-looking columns and white walkways that make you think you are strolling among ancient ruins. At the north end of the park is an amphitheater with Ionic columns; at the western side is a circular temple in classical style overlooking a pool decorated with Roman-looking mosaics (perhaps best seen when the park is not in season with pools filled). There are several flower gardens that are also decorated with different ancient ornamentation, as well as an artificially constructed rocky area that is reminiscent of a grotto. In addition to seasonal plantings of flowers (particularly nice, of course, in spring and summer), there are wonderful old trees here, including beech, Japanese maple, firs, and spectacular massive oaks.

You might begin your walk, if you want to do it as a treasure hunt, by telling your children (or enthusiastic adults) to search for the following sculptural, architectural, or pictorial treasures at Untermyer Park:

Two Sphinxes: These strange creatures look like crouching lions but have wings.

Head of Hermes or Mercury: The Greek god Hermes (or Roman god Mercury), the messenger, wears a winged cap to show his speed.

A Round Classical-Style Temple: A small, round temple, complete with classical columns and ornamental fountains.

Two Kinds of Vine Patterns: The use of leafy patterns for decoration can be found in at least two places.

Greek-Style Amphitheater: An outdoor theater ornamented with columns and two sphinx sculptures (by sculptor Paul Manship).

Roman-Style Pool: This beautiful pool is decorated with multicolored mosaic designs.

A Lobster

A Crab

A Skate Fish

A Sea Lion

A Star Fish
An Octopus
A Snail
A Red Fish
Ionic Columns: Ionic Greek columns are long and slender with an ornamental curling design at the top.
Doric Columns: Doric columns are shorter and more massive and solid.
Columned Walkway: This walkway leads to the rock garden.
Ancient Gateway: This Assyrian-style entranceway contrasts with the delicate Greek columns opposite.
Wave Pattern
Snowflake Pattern
Whirlwind Pattern

INFORMATION: Untermyer Park is located on U.S. 9 in Yonkers. It is open from dawn to dusk daily, year-round.

DIRECTIONS: From New York City take the Hutchinson River Parkway north to exit at 250th Street. Go north on Riverdale Avenue, which becomes Warburton Avenue. Take Warburton into Yonkers, where you come to a small cross street called Odell; turn left. It will bring you to Route 9. Turn left on 9; Untermyer Park is on your right.

In the vicinity . . .
The Hudson River Museum is about one mile away. See page 262.
   Philipse Manor Hall, Warburton Avenue and Dock Street in Yonkers (telephone: 914-965-4027) is a historic Dutch colonial house filled with paintings (including important American masterworks) and many things to interest children, including special events.

Innisfree Garden: Bringing Chinese Landscape Painting to Life

Millbrook, New York

The artistic gardens of Innisfree, near Millbrook, New York, are well worth a foray into the countryside. Created in the 1920s to reflect the philosophy and aesthetic of Chinese gardens, they bring you to a very different world from that of most gardens in our region. Experiencing Innisfree means taking an inspiring journey and exploring nature through ancient Chinese artistic tradition. In fact, a walk here is akin to finding a series of Chinese landscape paintings that are real and three-dimensional, and then strolling right into them.

Walter Beck, a painter, and his wife, Marion, spent twenty-five years creating these vast gardens. Their inspiration came primarily from the eighth century Chinese scrolls of the poet/painter Wang Wei, where scenes in nature are unfolded gradually. The basic design idea of Innisfree is the "cup garden"—a Chinese tradition dating back hundreds of years. The Chinese would set apart an object by "framing" it in such a way that it would be distinct and apart from its surroundings. According to Lester Collins, the landscape architect who has been in charge of Innisfree for many years, "You build a picture out of nature; you control the floor and the walls, and you bring the sky down." Walking through Innisfree is analogous to walking through an art gallery from one picture to the next—from a meadow to a rock covered with moss, to a lotus pool—in each case concentrating on the element before you. As in the case of a work of art, each destination has been created carefully to affect the viewer's senses in a certain way. Nature has been tamed completely and, even though the terrain at Innisfree may look wild and free, nothing has been left to chance. The land has been cleared, and waterfalls, streams, and pools have been created. "In their gardens," says Collins, "the Chinese express life and death and everything together—the pain and the wonder." The two main elements of Chinese gardens—mountains and rocks (yang) and water (yin) are very important in this garden and provide the necessary counterpoint of life. Yin is passive, dark, and moist; and yang is active, bright, and aggressive. According to the Chinese, a harmonious arrangement of mountains and water can give the viewer a spiritual experience of universal harmony. Water and rocks of all sizes and shapes are everywhere set amid soft foliage, shrubs, and trees. Flowers are not an important element in Chinese gardens, but here you will find delicate clematis growing on an arbor, primroses, forget-me-nots, water irises, and hydrangeas.

Innisfree is a garden for all seasons, since it emphasizes the architecture of its basic elements in harmony with one another. (Note, however, that it is open only from May 1 through October.) You can enjoy it under any weather conditions, as a great garden "is good aesthetically and has nothing to do with climate," according to Collins. In fact, on one of our visits we experienced torrential rains. But the downpours only echoed the usual sounds of the nearby streams and waterfalls, and the soft colors of the foliage were rendered the more vivid by the rain.

Before setting out on your walk you can pick up a map near the parking lot. A network of paths will take you around the lake (from where you'll see a tantalizing little island of pines that can be explored) and up and down gently sloping hills. Chinese gardens are supposed to be miniatures of nature's way; here, too, you will walk past small evocations of mountains, streams, and forests, experiencing each sensation as a traveler might in the open countryside, or as a viewer who encounters an unfolding Chinese handscroll landscape painting. You'll come across a mist fountain, a rock garden waterfall, a curious

"Fu Dog" stone statue, a hillside cave, a brick terrace (where you can rest and take in the view), fantastic rocks in the shapes of turtles and dragons, bird and bat houses, water sculptures, and hemlock woods. Don't fail to look about you at distant views as well.

INFORMATION: Innisfree is open May-October: Saturday and Sunday, 11:00 A.M.-5:00 P.M. (small admission fee), Wednesday-Friday, 10:00 A.M.-4:00 P.M. (no admission); telephone: 914-677-8000.

DIRECTIONS: From New York City take the Henry Hudson Parkway to the Saw Mill River Parkway, to the Taconic State Parkway; exit at Poughkeepsie/Millbrook (Route 44) and go east on 44. Look for Tyrrel Road on your right. Entrance to Innisfree is from Tyrrel Road.

In the vicinity . . .
Nearby Millbrook also has an unusually pleasant town park, if you haven't had your fill of nature walking.

Of similar interest . . .
Another exquisite garden, also in Dutchess County, is Wethersfield (see chapter 30) in nearby Amenia.

33

Green Acres:
An Animal Kingdom
Made of Yew

Portsmouth, Rhode Island

If you like animal sculptures prettily set along garden paths—and wish to see some whimsical examples that are neither stone nor steel—make a visit to this topiary garden where growing trees and bushes are trimmed into myriad shapes, both abstract and realistic. Green Acres is a small estate whose gardens are filled with members of the animal kingdom, including a giraffe, a giant camel, a bear (see Figure 22), a swan, an elephant, a rooster, and even a unicorn, all made of greenery. Set into a formal garden of flowers and hedges and geometric pathways, these cavorting animals are a particular delight to children.

Green Acres, not far from Newport, overlooks Narragansett Bay. It is the oldest topiary garden in the country. The seven-acre estate includes a summer house with original furnishings from its nineteenth century past and a toy collection, but it is particularly the topiary garden that draws visitors.

Green Acres garden was the idea of a family named Brayton who were enchanted by topiary gardens they had seen in the Azores. They and their gardeners, Joseph Carreiro (a native of the Azores) and his son-in-law, George Medonca, designed the gardens, beginning their work around 1893.

22. Topiary bear at Green Acres, Portsmouth, Rhode Island

Green Acres' sculptures, made from nature, are both realistic and fanciful. The garden includes about one hundred pieces of topiary art, including geometric shapes, arches and ornamental designs, and some twenty-one animals and birds. The topiary works are made from yew and privet. Other specialties of the garden are thirty-five seasonally planted flower beds in the most perfect condition. There are peach trees and fig trees and grape arbors and various other horticultural pleasures.

In pleasant weather children can sit on tiny animal-shaped rocking chairs out among the topiary fantasies. Green Acres is included in a combination ticket with several of the mansions of Newport, or can be visited separately (at what we thought was an unfortunately rather steep price). If you would enjoy visiting Newport's great houses with their elegant period furnishings and art, however, the combination ticket is well worth the cost.

INFORMATION: Green Acres is on Cory's Lane in Portsmouth. It is open daily from 10:00 A.M. to 5:00 P.M. from May to November. There is a moderate admission charge. Telephone: 401-847-6543.

DIRECTIONS: From Providence take I-95 at the Wyoming exit and Route 138 east to Newport. At junction of R.I. 138 and Route 114, take 114 and continue for about seven miles north to Cory's Lane. Entrance is on the left.

In the vicinity . . .

Newport. The great mansions of Newport are not far away; these glamorous, art-filled reminders of the gilded era are filled with art and artifacts. Many are open to the public. For information on the combined ticket with Green Acres call the Preservation Society of Newport County at 401-847-1000.

North Kingston. Gilbert Stuart's birthplace in North Kingston, Rhode Island (815 Gilbert Stuart Road, telephone: 401-294-3001), is a charming eighteenth century snuff mill with a water wheel. Though there are no original Stuart portraits here, you'll find a nice atmosphere and interesting colonial displays, including material on Stuart's career.

Of similar interest . . .

Another major topiary garden is described in chapter 29.

Master Painters and Sculptors of the Past: Artists' Homes and Ateliers

34

An Impressionists' Boardinghouse

Old Lyme, Connecticut

> [Old] Lyme . . . was found by many of our masters in landscape to possess remarkable advantages in its great variety, which ranges from the low land of estuaries and salt meadows to the rugged, romantic beauty of rolling glacial hills . . . the village is one of the oldest in New England and is one of the few remaining places which still possess the characteristics expressive of the quiet dignity of other days.

So rhapsodized the painter Frank Vincent DuMond in 1903, in describing the charms of Old Lyme, Connecticut, and its environs—an area to which he and many of his contemporaries first went to live and paint around the turn of the century. Soon Old Lyme became one of the most famous art colonies in the country. Today, anyone who walks along the village's un-spoiled tree-lined streets, leafy lanes and romantic riverbanks can still appreciate what so captivated these artists.

Old Lyme's enchanting natural setting—its network of water-ways surrounding the Connecticut River and Long Island Sound—its soft, impressionistic countryside of salt meadows, lowland estuaries, and open fields, and its brilliant summer light made it a paradise for painters. As Henry Ward Ranger, the most prominent of the colony's early artists, said, "It looks like Barbizon, the land of Millet . . . it is only waiting to be painted." Here, as in the Barbizon School in France, landscapists were to paint out of doors, "en plein air," to catch firsthand the impression or essence of their natural surroundings.

The painter Clark Voorhees (who first explored the area by bicycle, a much recommended way even today) encouraged Ranger to come in 1899. He took his room and board at the then somewhat dilapidated—but still gracious—Georgian mansion of Miss Florence Griswold, an enterprising, energetic, and committed art lover whose personal fortunes had come upon hard times. Her boardinghouse, the Florence Griswold House (today an elegant museum housing many important works and memorabilia of the Lyme artists), became the home of the art colony, and Miss Florence (as she was affectionately called), its muse.

This cheerful and accommodating lady did everything she could to make the artists feel at home. She encouraged their creativity by providing an environment of intellectual stimulation, camaraderie, and good spirits. Her property included some eleven acres of meadows and orchards abutting the Lieutenant River, where artists could wander around and paint at will. Scattered about were a number of outbuildings that could function as studios, making the entire setup ideal for an art colony. And so it flourished, mainly as a summer place for artists dedicated to living in tune with nature's cycles and capturing on canvas the lovely landscape.

At first the "American Barbizon" included such "tonalists" as Ranger, Lewis Cohen, Alphonse Jongers, and Henry Rankin Poore, among others. In 1903 its artistic clientele changed upon the arrival of the already well regarded and peripatetic Childe Hassam and his fellow impressionists.

Hassam had come to Old Lyme after having traveled abroad and up and down the New England coastline, painting as he went, always searching for new, unspoiled seaside locales to capture on canvas. He found this area quite similar to that around the farm of his friend and like-minded painter, J. Alden Weir, in Ridgefield, Connecticut (see chapter 39), and was immediately drawn to it. And with him came such artists as Willard Metcalf, Walter Griffin, Edward Simmons, Edward Rook, William Chadwick, and Bessie Vonnoh—all friends of Hassam's and followers of the impressionist style. Unlike the "tonalists," who painted nature in its darker, more brooding brown hues, these artists played upon the bright summer light and used intense color schemes in their work. Many of them had studied in France and had been inspired by Monet, Sisley, and others who were many years ahead of them; but their work had a distinctive American stamp and a greater fascination with the factual.

Impressionism had already been launched in the late nineteenth century in this country by such influential painters as Weir, John Twachtman, and William Merritt Chase, all of whom taught at the Art Students League in New York City. But it was at Old Lyme that the movement coalesced and became so influential, largely due to the energy and work of Hassam. Clearly the leader among his peers at the art colony, he became a great favorite of Miss Florence's and was given the most desirable studio on the grounds—facing the Lieutenant River. Here he painted many of his most famous works, among them *Late Afternoon (Sunset)*, which portrays the river in softly dimming crepuscular light. This theme particularly inspired Hassam, who was intrigued by the poetic effects of light over water. (You can see this painting at the Griswold Museum, where it is part of the permanent collection.)

The Griswold Mansion itself became a popular subject to paint. Will Howe Foote's *Summer Night* (1906) shows a dreamy moonlit view of the facade of the house. He had clearly been inspired by his colleague Willard Metcalf, who just a few months before had painted *May Night*, which won a grand prize at Washington's Corcoran Gallery of Art and became the most celebrated of the Old Lyme paintings. William Chadwick's *On the Porch* (1908) (Figure 23) depicts the outdoor dining room on the mansion's veranda, where the artists enjoyed eating and conversing alfresco. A seated female figure (probably Chadwick's wife, Pauline) is shown savoring the last remnants of a meal, after her luncheon companions have adjourned, probably to rest or paint. In a typical impressionistic mode the essence of the scene is captured through color, texture, and play of light within a natural setting.

After the great artist Claude Monet began painting at his idyllic country estate at Giverny in northern France, it became a center for the impressionist movement. Americans, eager to

23. William Chadwick. *On the Porch.* c.1908

follow the new directions in French painting, sought a "Giverny of America" where they too could paint outdoors and explore the impressionist style in views of local subjects. Old Lyme became their "Giverny." They created colorful canvases, such as Matilda Browne's *Clark Voorhees House* (1905) and Edmund W. Greacen's *The Old Garden* (1912), which are part of the collection at the Griswold Museum. They painted local trees—especially the stately elms, oaks, and chestnuts that enhanced the countryside—(as in Clark G. Voorhees's *Winter Landscape*) and the meandering rivers and streams. Popular sites along the river included the Bow Bridge over the Lieutenant River, quite near the Griswold Mansion. This picturesque bridge—alas, long since gone—can be seen in Hassam's painting *Bridge at Old Lyme* (Georgia Museum of Art, The University of Georgia). It evokes a bygone era of quiet pleasures in a peaceful setting.

A favorite theme of Hassam's was the First Congregational Church, a stately landmark colonial church, which he depicted several times, much as Monet had painted several versions of the Bourges Cathedral under different conditions of light. The church, with its tall spire towering above the village's clapboard houses and winding lanes, was to Hassam quintessentially New England in its spirit. The pediment is supported by four Ionic columns topped by a square clock tower; above that, a spire is ornamented by a finial. (You can see Hassam's works picturing this church at the Corcoran Gallery of Art in Washington and the Smith College Museum of Art in Northampton, Massachusetts.) The church burned down in 1907, but was immediately rebuilt to replicate the original; it can be visited on this outing.

The paintings that were produced at Old Lyme were usually exhibited in the town library at the end of the summer season, until the artists finally formed the Lyme Art Association in 1914 to raise money and build their own gallery right next to the Griswold House. (It became the first self-financed art gallery built by a summer art colony.) The colony continued to thrive well into the 1920s. It was among the most highly acclaimed art colonies in America during the teens and attracted to its exhibits many collectors, dealers, and art enthusiasts. But by the 1930s, with the strong currents of modern art, Old Lyme became more of a historic site than an active art colony.

The Florence Griswold Museum was officially opened in 1947 and joined in 1955 with the Lyme Historical Society to form an organization dedicated to furthering the public's awareness and appreciation of the Lyme artists.

To gain a fuller understanding of the artists, their life-styles and times, we recommend that you visit the museum and then explore the village and countryside that so inspired them. A walk around Old Lyme is pleasant in all seasons, although you might prefer visiting during the spring and summer months, when the artists mostly worked here, and the landscape is green and inviting.

Begin at the Florence Griswold Museum on Lyme Street, where you can easily park your car. The gracious, immaculately kept Georgian mansion was designed by Samuel Belcher (the architect of the First Congregational Church of Old Lyme) and is considered an important landmark. Here you will find over nine hundred paintings, drawings, watercolors, and prints by some 130 American artists, most of whom were members of the colony. (Obviously the collection is not on display in its entirety.) For history buffs there are thousands of documents relating to the colony, as well as amusing photographs showing the artists' life here. You'll see them enjoying a jolly summer lunch on the porch (there seemed to have been quite a number of bon vivants among this group!) or engrossed in a painting class out of doors, or on a horse-drawn wagon en route to a beach picnic.

The centerpiece of the museum is Miss Florence's famous dining room, the site of many bountiful feasts, still kept much as it was during the heyday of the colony. On the walls and doors is a unique collection of panels painted by the artists as a special gift to her. (Apparently she had adopted a somewhat laissez-faire attitude when it came to financial arrangements with her artists, for which they were most grateful.)

The museum organizes temporary exhibitions each year to illuminate certain features in the permanent collection. Recent exhibits have included "Notable Women of Lyme," "A Summer Day" (focusing on Old Lyme as a summer resort with related paintings, photos, and memorabilia), and "Old Lyme: The American Barbizon."

You might enjoy walking around the grounds surrounding the museum, although they are much reduced from the eleven acres of Miss Florence's time.

On your walk, bike ride, or walk/car ride (depending on your inclination) through the village you will pass several spots that recall the halcyon days of the colony—from some of the artists' homes (now private) to sites they painted. (Some artists bought their own homes after discovering Miss Florence's Inn.) Just two doors to the right of the museum (as you face the entrance) is the former home of Edward Rook, now a private house; and to the left of the museum is the Lyme Art Association, which has continued to have group shows and is open to the public.

If you continue your walk past the Art Association on Lyme Street, you'll come to the main street in the historic district. You will walk past antique, well-preserved clapboard houses with charming old-fashioned flower gardens and fine old trees. After about ½ mile you will come to a little side street on your right, Beckwith Lane. Go down the lane to the end and turn right onto Lieutenant River Lane (it may not be identified, but you can't miss it). You will see a small parking area for cars and behind it a grassy path leading to a small dock right on the Lieutenant River, one of the few public accesses to this often painted site. The narrow meandering river surrounded by tall reeds and marshes is a rare and peaceful spot and as unspoiled as it must have been when Miss Florence's artists worked at this site. (You would find it hard to equal this idyllic spot for a picnic.)

Retrace your steps back to Lieutenant River Lane and go a few feet in the other direction for your second view of the river at another small public access. Return to the lane and continue to Ferry Road. This small intersection is the former site of the Old Lyme Inn, where some of the artists, their friends, and patrons occasionally stayed. (Today's Old Lyme Inn is across the street from the museum, on Lyme Street.) Turn left on Ferry Road to the Congregational Church. This fine reconstruction of the famous 1817 structure is totally convincing. It is a key spot in the village. Walk back to the museum along Lyme Street, just under a mile's trek. (If you don't wish to make this long loop on foot starting and ending at the museum, you can drive to the Town Hall on Lyme Street, park in the lot behind, and walk from there.)

INFORMATION: The Florence Griswold Museum, at 96 Lyme Street, is open Tuesday-Saturday, 10:00 A.M.-5:00 P.M., and Sunday, 1:00-5:00 P.M. There is an inexpensive admission fee. For further information telephone 203-434-5542.

DIRECTIONS: From New Haven take I-95 north to exit 70; go left at the end of the ramp, then right at the light; take a left at the intersection with Route 1. The museum is the second building on the left.

Of similar interest . . .
A visit to two other Connecticut sites for American impressionists will take you to Weir Farm (see chapter 39) and the Bush–Holley House in Cos Cob.

The Bush–Holley House and the waterfront in this village were at the center of Cos Cob's days as an art colony around the turn of the century. As many as two hundred artists worked in Cos Cob, beginning with the impressionist John Henry Twachtman, who, with his close friend J. Alden Weir, began painting there in about 1890. Two generations of painters, ranging from the first American impressionists to the early abstractionists who helped organize the Armory Show in 1913, made Cos Cob a mecca for artists.

Twachtman and other artists and writers gathered at the Holley family boardinghouse, where room and board ran to about $8 per week. You can visit the house, now a museum (39 Strickland Road, Cos Cob). Telephone: 203-622-9686.

Like Old Lyme, Cos Cob was the setting for dozens of landscape paintings. A walking tour is given on Sundays that will take you to some of the painters' favorite sites including the many clapboard houses that led Childe Hassam to describe the colony as "the Cos Cob Clapboard School of Art." Telephone the Greenwich Library Information Center at 203-622-7910.

35

Winslow Homer's Studio

Prouts Neck, Maine

The coast of Maine with its rushing sea crashing against rocky shores has been the subject for many American painters. But Winslow Homer is the artist who immediately comes to mind when we think of the ocean's magnificent and terrifying power. Homer, perhaps this country's greatest nineteenth century painter, made the theme of the individual against nature's stronger forces his own.

Homer pictured fishermen struggling against the waves in a small boat, women almost blown off their feet by the wind, clusters of people huddled against the crashing of the waves on the rocks and dramatic rescues from the terrors of the sea, as in *The Lifeline*, 1884 (Figure 24).

His great artistry and the force of these images make his works masterpieces that are quintessentially American. Though their subjects often suggest a particular moment and place—late nineteenth century coastal Maine—there is a timeless dramatic element that makes them equally powerful today. In fact, Homer lived by the sea for more than twenty years, and it was there—on the coast of Maine—that many of his greatest works were created.

In 1882 he decided to move permanently to a small fishing village on Maine's southern coast, called Prouts Neck. His family had visited there in the 1870s, and two brothers had already settled there. It was a secluded, rocky spit of land projecting out into the ocean. Its deep green firs and weathered houses

24. Winslow Homer. The Lifeline. 1884

faced the wind and waves and coastal storms. Homer found its isolation and beauty an ideal place to work and to study his own sense of the meaning of nature.

Today you can visit the home and studio of the artist in a most appealing way. Homer's place (on Winslow Homer Road) is not a tourist site, nor are there brochures, tour buses, entrance fees, or the other trappings of public sites. To visit, you simply telephone the Homer family, still in residence in Prouts Neck, and ask to come. You will be left to wander about the studio—kept in its historic state of musty charm—and to take in the spectacular ocean view. No studio visit could be more evocative of the past than this one.

INFORMATION: Winslow Homer's house is located on Winslow Homer Road in Prouts Neck. It is open from 9:00 A.M. to 5:00 P.M., June through October. Telephone: 207-883-2249.

DIRECTIONS: From Portland, Prouts Neck is seven miles south of Portland; take Route 77 to Winslow Homer Road.

In the vicinity . . .
The Portland Museum of Art (7 Congress Square; telephone: 207-775-6148), an unusually fine small museum with up-to-date shows and a very good collection of its own.

Victoria Mansion (109 Danforth Street, Portland; telephone: 207-772-4841), a landmark American–Victorian palace in the Italian villa style built just after the Civil War. In addition to its noteworthy architecture, the interior is filled with trompe l'oeil paintings and carvings that will delight your "deceived eyes."

36

Chesterwood: The Home and Studio of Daniel Chester French

Stockbridge, Massachusetts

The lovely region of western Massachusetts known as "The Berkshires" is endowed with charming vistas, mountains, rivers, lakes, and little New England villages. The area has long attracted seekers of unspoiled natural beauty, including many artists and writers.

Daniel Chester French, the famed neoclassical sculptor of monumental works, came to establish a summer home and studio in the shadow of Monument Mountain near Stockbridge, Massachusetts. When you visit Chesterwood, his remarkable country estate, you will come away feeling that he could not have chosen a more idyllic spot. He was an artist who really knew how to live.

French became the nation's leading classical sculptor in the early decades of this century. After studying the Beaux-Arts style in Paris in the late 1880s, he returned to America to establish his own studio. He began his illustrious career making allegorical figures that represented the lofty civic and patriotic aims of the nation.

Along with Augustus Saint-Gaudens, he produced many of the most important neoclassical statues at major sites all over the country. Among his colossal allegorical female figures were sculptures titled *The Republic* (a commission of the World's

Columbia Exposition in Chicago in 1893), and the *Four Continents* (at the New York Custom House, now the home of the National Museum of American Indians).

Later works combined portraiture with personification. Giant figures that were both lifelike and monumental brought him increasing fame and public commissions, among them his most notable work, *The Lincoln Memorial* in Washington, D.C. (You will see the various working versions of this statue at Chesterwood.) French's ability to create heroic, allegorical figures in a naturalistic style was well-suited to the taste of the nation, and even after the advent of modernism, he continued to receive honors and awards.

At the height of his career, internationally known and able to live in grand style, French decided to create a perfect working and living environment for himself and his family in the country (although he continued to maintain a winter studio in New York). He and his wife first saw the rustic farm that was to become Chesterwood while on a horse-drawn carriage trip through the Housatonic River Valley in 1896.

Beautifully situated on a rural road, the 150-acre property—now a museum operated by the National Trust for Historic Preservation—would become the Frenches' summer home for the next thirty-three years. It was at Chesterwood—amid the enchantment of romantic gardens, lawns, and woodlands—that French was inspired to create many of his most important works, including the *Lincoln Memorial*, the *Minute Man* for Concord, Massachusetts, and the *Alma Mater* for Columbia University.

Chesterwood itself became a lifelong project for the sculptor. Carefully he fashioned the estate to provide an ideal ambience for his creative needs, as well as for the many brilliant social gatherings he was fond of hosting for his prominent neighbors and friends. (Edith Wharton came regularly from her nearby estate.) The main house and studio, overlooking majestic Monument Mountain, were designed by his architect friend Henry Bacon; but it was French himself who laid out the garden and woodland walks.

To him gardens were like sculptures: a basic design had to be drawn up in order for them to work as art. He planned a central courtyard, an Italianate garden with a graceful fountain, and English flower gardens. Beyond the formal areas he arranged a network of paths leading into and through the hemlock forest, where the walker could enjoy peaceful views. He enjoyed creating aesthetic effects that influenced the quality of daily life. For example, he built a berm (an artificial little hill) abutting the road leading to the house; in that way one would not see the wheels of approaching carriages, which would appear to be "floating" by.

French spent a great deal of time in his garden, from which he derived much of his inspiration. He regularly studied the effects of light and shadow on sculptures that were destined to be out of doors. He found an ingenious solution to moving these massive works from his studio to the outside. He would put these pieces onto a revolving modeling table set on a short railroad track and roll them out into the sunlight, where he could test them in the natural light. You can still see this unusual contraption when you visit the studio.

French and his wife lived and thrived at Chesterwood with their daughter, Margaret Cresson French, also a sculptor. In 1969 the property was donated to the National Trust and converted into the museum you see today.

When you arrive at Chesterwood you are struck by the beauty of the site: with spectacular mountain views on all sides it is little wonder that French and his family wanted to be here. The house and landscaping are tasteful and harmonious in every sense; there is nothing pretentious or ostentatious about this estate. As the artist once remarked, "I live here six months of the year—in heaven. The other six months I live, well, in New York." A possibly discordant note (and a recent one) is an ongoing modern sculpture exhibit, which is on view on a rotating basis throughout the grounds (including the woods). The pieces we saw had nothing to do with French, his style, or his era and were in striking contrast to the gracious nineteenth century setting.

In order to visit the house and studio you must take an organized tour—about forty-five minutes of fairly detailed information (more than you might want to hear), including a great deal about the social life of the French family and mores of the time. However, you are free to roam the grounds and woods at will, and can do so at no cost. After you have purchased your tickets for the house and studio you will probably be directed to the barn to begin the tour. This rustic building, originally part of the working farm that French purchased, has been remodeled into an exhibition gallery. You can wander about and look at the vintage photographs and works by Margaret French Cresson, Augustus Saint-Gaudens, and others.

Aside from the gardens, the studio visit is by far the most satisfying part of the tour. The beautifully designed twenty-two-foot high structure provided the perfect airy and spacious working environment. It is kept much as it was during French's time, with materials, notebooks, tools, and sketches on view. You'll see plaster cast models and preliminary sculptures of some of his most important works, notably his seated Lincoln (of which there are several versions) and his graceful Andromeda. You'll also see the massive thirty-foot double doors that were constructed to accommodate French's many large works; they were built when French first made his impressive equestrian statue of George Washington, now located in the Place d'Iena in Paris. Off to the side of the studio is a cozy room with couch, piano, and corner fireplace where French entertained. Apparently he enjoyed having friends around even when he worked. In back of the studio is a wide veranda (which he called a "piazza") with wisteria vines and fine views and the rail tracks on which his massive sculptures rolled away.

The thirty-room colonial revival house (built in 1900) is nearby. Its gracious rooms, wide hallways, and appealing surroundings are what you would expect from a man of French's refined tastes. Surrounding the house are the charming gardens that French carefully planned and so enjoyed. Take a stroll in them and beyond, on the pine-laden woodsy paths in the forest.

INFORMATION: Chesterwood is open May-October 31, from 10:00 A.M.-5:00 P.M. It is recommended you phone first to check on the next schedule; telephone: 413-298-3579. There is an inexpensive entrance fee.

DIRECTIONS: Chesterwood is about two miles west of Stockbridge. From Boston take Route 90 (the Massachusetts Turnpike), to exit B3 to Route 22; go about one mile to 102 to Stockbridge. Take Route 102 west to junction with Route 183. Turn left onto 183 for one mile to a fork in the road. Turn right onto a blacktop road, travel a few yards, and turn left. Continue ½ mile to Chesterwood.

In the vicinity . . .

Hancock Shaker Village (at the junction of Routes 20 and 41 in Pittsfield; telephone: 413-443-0188). Once a Shaker community at its peak in the 1830s, this collection of simple houses and community buildings—including a round stone barn—is an architectural pleasure. You can also watch crafts being made in traditional Shaker style.

The Morris School (West Street, Lenox, on the way toward Tanglewood). George L. K. Morris and his wife, Suzy Frelinghuysen, were leading American abstractionists in the '30s and '40s who built the first modern house in the entire area. Their home became a meeting place for artists (both American and French). The Morris School, which adjoins the original property, boasts a three-paneled outdoor mosaic by Morris, which you may drive into the school grounds to see.

The Mount (at the junction of Routes 7 and 7A—Plunkett Street, Lenox; telephone: 413-637-1899). The Mount was Edith Wharton's Gilded Age mansion and summer "retreat." Now a certified landmark with tours, resident theater company, etc., it is quite a tourist attraction. But if you enjoy gardens and interior decoration of the period, or are familiar with her influential books *The Decoration of Houses* and *Italian Villas and Their Gardens*, it's a "must see" spot, for she based the design of the imposing house and extensive gardens on her own precepts.

Butler Sculpture Park (Shunpike Road, Sheffield; telephone: 413-229-8924). A sculptor named Robert Butler has turned his hilltop grounds with a panoramic view of the Berkshires into an outdoor sculpture park. His works are contemporary and abstract and visitors are welcome.

Of similar interest . . .

For a visit to the home and studio of a contemporary of Daniel Chester French, visit Aspet, the Augustus Saint-Gaudens estate. (See chapter 38.)

In Peace Dale, Rhode Island, you can see an unusually fine example of a Daniel Chester French monument. (See page 264.)

37

The Thomas Cole House and Frederick Church's Olana

Catskill and Hudson, New York

The Hudson River painters—the American Romantics who glorified nature on canvas in the mid-nineteenth century—drew much of their inspiration from the Hudson Valley, where many of them lived and worked. Thomas Cole, known as the "Father" of this school of painting, and Frederick Edwin Church, his illustrious pupil, both lived here. This outing takes you to their homes, which are located on opposite sides of the river (see directions at the end of the chapter), just minutes—but light-years —apart.

The Cole House, an unpretentious, white clapboard structure, was the residence of Thomas Cole. Olana, the grand Persian-style villa dramatically perched atop a hill overlooking the Hudson, was the home of Frederick Church. The Cole House is as modestly understated as Olana is wildly extravagant: While the former is an ordinary early nineteenth century American farmhouse, the latter is the result of an imagination fueled by the aesthetic fantasies of exotic lands. The contrast between them could not be greater—in architectural style and ambience—yet each provided an inspiring setting for the creation of important works of art.

Thomas Cole moved to his farmhouse in the village of Catskill, located 115 miles north of New York City on the west bank of the river, in 1836. His desire was to live and paint in this glorious spot with its views of the river and the Catskills. (Today these views have been partially obscured by overgrown trees on the property.) As he grandly stated, "The Hudson for nature magnificence is unsurpassed ... The lofty Catskills stand afar—the green hills gently rising from the flood, recede like steps by which we may ascend to a great temple, whose pillars are those everlasting hills, and whose dome is the boundless vault of heaven." While living here he painted some of his great Catskill landscapes (see chapter 5). His pictures are odes to nature, with their unusual sensitivity to its nuances and intensity, its lights and shadows. He was able to nurture his mystical need to commune with nature in these environs, without having to go far afield. "To walk with nature as a poet is the necessary condition of a perfect artist," he wrote. As his concerns were for spiritual and aesthetic—rather than material—values, it is not surprising that he was not a commercially successful artist. His home reflects his simple life-style and tastes.

The Cole House remains much like it was, except for the overgrown vegetation on its three-and-a-half-acre property. The small foundation that now operates it has tried to keep the place as Cole knew it, without giving it the new gloss of a facelift. (You might think that it could use a coat of paint here and there!) Because most of Cole's furniture and personal belongings were sold some years ago, the interior of the house is now quite bare and you will find few personal mementos. But a visit to this quiet and refreshingly uncommercial spot will give you a sense of who Cole was as an artist and person. You will most likely be able to enjoy the place by yourself, as there are few visitors and no guided tours.

To reach Olana you travel only three miles but enter another world. A spacious 250-acre park surrounds the sixteen-room villa, which is often crowded with tourists. The approach to the house is itself on a grand scale, with a network of roads winding up the hill. The house is at the top, with commanding views that Frederick Church captured so beautifully in several of his paintings.

Church was first introduced to the Catskills—"Nature's great Academy of landscape art"—in 1844, when he came to study with Thomas Cole, but it was not until fourteen years later that he decided to live here. By then he had become an international celebrity. He had traveled throughout the Americas, from Ecuador to Labrador, as well as in Europe and Asia, to experience firsthand natural wilderness at its most elemental. He had created showpiece landscapes that literally galvanized the public, who flocked to see them. His *Niagara* was hung by itself; it was so popular it could only be viewed by ticketholders. His *Heart of the Andes*, a massive $5\frac{1}{2}' \times 10'$ canvas that became one of the most celebrated American paintings of the century, was actually preached about in pulpits, where ministers extolled Nature's glories. It would have been unlikely for Church, with his flamboyant style, to have gone off to paint in a quiet spot, as Cole did.

After marrying in 1860 he bought a 126-acre farm south of the town of Hudson, intending, in fact, to live a quiet, rural family life. But with time he inevitably thought in grander terms and acquired more land. Seeing himself as landscape designer in addition to painter, he began to convert the property into a Romantic landscape garden; he created reflecting ponds, planted thousands of trees and many flower gardens, and constructed carriage roads that were carefully placed to enhance a sequence of views. He also decided to build a larger house. What began as plans for a French château changed dramatically, when Church returned from a trip to the Middle East, enthralled with Moorish architecture. The architect Calvin Vaux (the co-designer of Central Park with Frederick Law Olmsted) was engaged to design something exotic, but it was Church himself who ultimately created Olana ("our place on high," in Arabic).

Church made sketch after sketch, followed by elaborate drawings, much as if he were conceiving a large painting; and he became involved in every detail of the house—from the colors, shapes, and sizes of the rooms to the placement of windows to frame river views, from the interior decor to the colorful stencils inside and out. He further enhanced the surrounding gardens to complement the house, adding lookout points where views could be captured. Olana became much more than a place to live; it became a work of art to Church.

25. Frederick E. Church. *The Catskills from Olana.* 1870-72

You can appreciate Olana as Church's personal creation when you visit the house and surrounding grounds. A forty-five-minute conducted tour leads you through the house, now a museum, where you enter the private world of the artist. In contrast to the Cole House, Olana is filled with artifacts, objects from years of travel, vintage furniture, works of art, and memorabilia that vividly recall Church's rich and fulfilling cultural and family life. But perhaps the best way to understand Church's art is to wander through the vast property, which you can do on your own, and enjoy the naturalistic gardens and breathtaking views that so inspired him. Before you begin your walk pick up a guide to the landscape, available at the ticket office. A map indicates points of interest, including the site of the studio where Church first painted. (He later designed and built a new studio wing onto the main house.) It was probably from this spot that he captured the views immortalized in such landscapes as *The Catskills from Olana* (Figure 25).

INFORMATION: The grounds of Olana are open daily all year, from 8:30 A.M. to sunset. You will find joggers, walkers, and picnickers enjoying the surroundings. The museum is open by guided tour only, from April 15-October 31, Wednesday-Saturday, 10:00 A.M.-5:00 P.M. and Sunday from noon to 5:00 P.M. (Note: The last tour begins at 4:00 P.M.) Tours are limited to twelve people, so reservations are recommended, particularly in view of the fact that Olana is a popular place with some 25,000 visitors to the house annually. There is a moderate entrance fee. Telephone: 518-828-0135.

The Cole House is open Wednesday-Saturday, 11:00 A.M.-4:00 P.M. and Sunday 1:00-5:00 P.M. during the summer season. There is no admission fee. Telephone: 518-943-6533.

DIRECTIONS: To get to the Cole House: From New York City take the New York Thruway to Exit 21 in Catskill, then Route 23 east to the traffic light at Route 385. Turn right and go about fifty feet to the entrance of the Cole House on the left.

To get to Olana from the Cole House: Take Route 385 to Route 23, turn right and cross the Rip Van Winkle Bridge (where you should note the extraordinary views). Turn right on Route 9G for one mile, following the signs, and wind your way up the hill to Olana.

Of similar interest . . .

Other outings relating to the Hudson River painters are described in chapter 1 (West Point) and chapter 5 (Kaaterskill Falls).

38

Aspet: Home and Studio
of Augustus Saint-Gaudens

Cornish, New Hampshire

If your idea of the nineteenth century artist living in the depth of a city in a dreadful Bohemian garret needs changing, visit the home and studio of Augustus Saint-Gaudens. Now a National Historic site complete with Park Rangers and one of the most beautiful landscapes imaginable, Aspet, the artist's summer place and eventual year-round home, is a rarely visited treasure. You may come away thinking that life as one of America's most famous sculptors must have been heavenly.

The National Park Service has made this memorial to Saint-Gaudens an elegant, tasteful, and fascinating place to visit. Though Saint-Gaudens' own experiences there were not so universally glamorous and moneyed as they now appear (the docent told us that several disastrous studio fires and a $30,000 loan to keep the place going were among the less glorious facts of Aspet's past), this estate shows off his art and architecture in a noble fashion. From the distant vistas of fields and mountains, to the charmingly columned and arbored studios, to the delicately set sculptures along garden paths, this is how we would like to imagine an illustrious artist's estate.

The site of Aspet is in rural Cornish, New Hampshire, just beyond the longest covered bridge in the nation. It crosses the Connecticut River from Vermont at Windsor. Nearby, a perfectly kept roadway into the deep woods takes you to Aspet.

Despite its original use as a posting house along a traveled route, the house and its surroundings seemed to us wonderfully remote, like some Shangri-la amid the picturesque New England countryside. The large property includes a number of studios in addition to the sculptor's home, formal gardens, a deep wooded ravine, and enough fields and lawns to satisfy even a walker without a taste for sculpture. A striking view of nearby Mount Ascutney adds to the vista. But the art is, of course, the featured attraction, magnificently displayed with architecture and nature as its allies.

Augustus Saint-Gaudens was one of America's premier artists and probably its most beloved nineteenth century sculptor. Born in 1848 in Dublin to a French shoemaker's family from the small village of Aspet in the Pyrenees, Augustus was brought to the United States as a baby. At thirteen he was apprenticed to a cameo cutter. (And, in fact, his large bronze cameos later became a staple of his work; many are displayed at the estate.) At nineteen he left for Europe to study art, working as a cameo cutter in Paris and Rome to support himself. In Paris he experimented with naturalistic representation and the modeling of surfaces; in Rome he studied the works of Donatello and delicate low relief.

At twenty-seven he returned home and began his American career. He worked briefly with John LaFarge (as a mural painter), and began his lifelong friendships with the architects Stanford White and Charles McKim. They eventually collaborated in many projects, some of which can be seen at Aspet.

It was the commission in 1876 to create a statue commemorating Admiral David Farragut that brought Saint-Gaudens lasting recognition and success. The statue was exhibited in Paris, cast in bronze and placed in Madison Square in New York. Set upon Stanford White's unusual pedestal, Saint-Gaudens' unconventional, powerful figure of the admiral made him a celebrity. (A cast of this work is prominently displayed at Aspet.)

Saint-Gaudens' naturalistic approach contrasted with the smooth, controlled surfaces and contours of neoclassical sculpture that had been in vogue. By 1880 he had become an acknowledged leader of American sculptors in an era in which the memorial statue was a necessity in every city square. Other artists joined him in rejecting academicism; in 1878 he was a founder of the Society of American Artists, which sought to free both painting and sculpture from academic and banal styles of portraiture.

His commemorative statues of famous people (including Abraham Lincoln) were in great demand and are familiar images to us today. But perhaps his best known and most beloved work—beautifully displayed at Aspet—was his venture into a more emotional style: his *Adams Memorial*. This grieving, hooded figure was arguably the most original and haunting sculpture yet achieved by an American.

Saint-Gaudens became a widely respected teacher and leader of other artists. In 1885 after he bought the old staging inn that was to become Aspet, Cornish became the center of an artists' colony that grew up about him. (Legend has it that a friend persuaded him to go to New England in the summertime; he was then at work on an important Lincoln portrait and was told that he would find among the natives of New Hampshire many "Lincoln-shaped" men to use for models.)

Aspet became a center both for sculptors and other creative people; Saint-Gaudens' salon attracted poets, novelists, journalists, and actors. You'll find a flyer describing the Cornish Colony's illustrious members at Aspet. The artists included sculptors Frederick MacMonnies, Philip Martiny, and James Earle Fraser; among the painters were George deForest Brush, Thomas Deming and Maxfield Parrish.

For some twenty-two years Saint-Gaudens worked at Aspet, adding continually to the estate by building new studios and gardens and redesigning the old. During these full years he created some of his most famous works, advised presidents and museums, and won numerous international prizes and awards. (Agreeably, the displays at Aspet are devoted to his art rather than to his illustrious life as important artist.)

Aspet became a National Historic site in 1965, the first home of an artist to be so designated. (The second is Weir Farm, see chapter 39.) Like other National Park sites, this one provides guided tours of the house and grounds, but you can also wander on your own throughout the estate (but you cannot enter the house unaccompanied).

Begin your visit at the sculptor's home. Here, in a perfect white New England house with a grand columned veranda shaded by grape leaves, you can sit and contemplate the vista (or wait for a house tour).

The house, which dates to about 1800, is small roomed and Victorian within, hardly reflecting the grandeur of Saint-Gaudens' sculptural conceptions. Deep peach and rose-colored drapes and shades, a large faded tapestry, and dark Victorian furniture set the tone. A few small, curious paintings enliven the interior—one by his friend and colleague architect Stanford White, another by the sculptor's wife.

The spectacular veranda was added to the house, and is its most inviting feature. Its classical columns and magnificent view conjure visions of the Cornish Colony seated in the prevailing westerly breeze and discussing art and literature one hundred years ago.

But to begin your tour, leave the veranda from the far steps and make your way to the gardens below. Saint-Gaudens had a taste for landscape design, white marble paths, and formal gardens. Of particular note are the rare clumps of mature white birches which are carefully maintained, and the individually designed rectangular flower gardens. Each part of the estate has its own plan with borders and hedges of pine or hemlock. Small sculptured heads appear above the boxwood here and there. There are pools, fountains that shoot jets of water through the mouths of fish and turtles (designed by the sculptor), and marble benches for the proper contemplation of it all. (The white bench decorated with figures of Pan playing his pipes is, however, the work of Augustus' brother Louis, also a sculptor of note.)

Your next stop is the Little Studio, an enchanting building that was once a hay barn. Transformed for Saint-Gaudens into a romantic workplace, the Little Studio reminds us of the sculptor's fascination with the images of antiquity. George Babb, an associate of Stanford White, redesigned the old barn into an Italianate classical structure. It has brilliant white columns now ornamented with clinging vines, contrasting with a rose-red wall (described as "Pompeiian red") and a frieze that copies the figures of the Parthenon.

187

Inside the Little Studio, which was the sculptor's personal workplace, is a charming room filled with natural light. It contains small Saint-Gaudens works, including low-relief portraits, many books, and a small corner where a twenty-eight minute video of the sculptor's life is shown. (This seems to be the only modern-tech touch except for lawn mowers droning on the vast grounds.) Another room houses a discreet shop of memorabilia and books on the sculptor. The Little Studio is as pretty a place to picture an artist creating as you can imagine, but today there is little sign that he actually worked there. (How to present a "working" studio to the public is an ongoing debate in preservationist circles.) The Little Studio also presents a series of chamber music concerts.

On leaving this building, follow the path toward the *Adams Memorial* in its own garden, grandly surrounded by a square hedge and plantings. Arguably Saint-Gaudens' most stunning work, this is a cast of the original in Washington (Figure 26). The shrouded, seated figure was commissioned by Henry Adams on the death of his wife in 1885. It is not a portrait but a symbol of mourning which brought American sculpture to a new depth of emotion, anticipating expressionism by many years.

When the British novelist John Galsworthy saw it, he remarked that it gave him more pleasure than anything else he had seen in America, commenting, "That great greenish bronze figure of [a] seated woman within the hooding folds of her ample cloak seemed to carry [one] down to the bottom of [one's] soul."

Through the hedgerow and along the birch-lined pathway you'll see the bowling green, where the family and friends played lawn bowls. Next you'll come to a well-known portrait head of Abraham Lincoln and then to the *Shaw Memorial*. This large bronze bas-relief commemorates the Fifty-fourth black regiment from Massachusetts in the Civil War. (This is also a cast of the original, which stands in the Boston Commons.) Saint-Gaudens worked for fourteen years on this major sculpture. It is surrounded by a white grape arbor in a sun-dappled garden.

Nearby is a carriage barn filled with highly polished carriages and sleighs. (Saint-Gaudens enjoyed tobogganing and other sports at Aspet.)

6. Augustus Saint-Gaudens. *The Adams Memorial.* 1891

Returning to the path, bear left across the open lawn to the Gallery. This comparatively modern building houses both Saint-Gaudens' sculpture and pretty gardens, as well as a changing exhibit of contemporary painting, sculpture and photography. In the atrium of the gallery there is a reflecting pool. The sculptor originally had built a studio for his plaster molder and areas for his assistants on the site; it burned in 1904 with the loss of many works in progress, sketchbooks, and correspondence. Its replacement was also destroyed by fire in 1944.

Among the high points of Saint-Gaudens' works in the gallery are his famous massive statue called *The Puritan*, and a particularly appealing wall-size bas-relief of the ailing Robert Louis Stevenson, bedridden, but nonetheless a romantic figure. The gallery for today's artists is a nice bright space that was showing the work of Louis Iselin at our last visit. (Needless to say, his sculptures looked shockingly modern in this nineteenth century environment.)

Outside the gallery is the *Farragut Base*, the original stone pedestal for the monumental and influential statue that brought Saint-Gaudens such celebrity. Designed in collaboration with Stanford White, it is indeed impressive with its rough texture and free form.

From here, follow signs to the Ravine Studio, which Saint-Gaudens used occasionally. This is still a real and well-used studio where a contemporary sculptor is generally at work and will welcome you as part of the interpretative program of the Historic Site; the artist is in residence in season Fridays to Mondays from 9:00 A.M. to 4:30 P.M. It is a nice touch to see sculpture in process after so much finished work.

The estate also includes a dramatic and rather steep descent into a forested ravine. (A nature trail guide is available where you park.) If you choose to take this walk you will find it exceptionally beautiful, but be sure you are wearing proper shoes for a climb!

The path eventually will bring you to the bottom of the great field in front of the house where the Cornish Colony had a Greek-style, columned temple erected in 1905 to celebrate twenty years of Saint-Gaudens' residence at Aspet. It became the family burial place.

190

This is but a thumbnail sketch of the many pleasures to be found at Aspet. A true student of sculpture might spend a long day noting the many works of art—some almost hidden among the shrubbery—while a nature buff could hike the paths of Aspet for an equally long time. You will choose your own pace here, perhaps resting on a marble bench in front of a well-known statue, or examining the many small bas-reliefs on Saint-Gaudens' studio walls. Whatever style is yours, this is an artwalk to savor.

INFORMATION: The Saint-Gaudens National Historic Site is open daily from the last weekend in May through October 31. The buildings are open from 8:30 A.M. to 4:30 P.M. daily and the grounds from 8:00 A.M. until dark. There is an inexpensive admission fee for persons over sixteen. The mailing address is RR 3, Box 73, Cornish, NH 03745; telephone: 603-675-2175.

DIRECTIONS: From Boston take the Massachusetts Turnpike to Route 91 north to exit 8; take Route 131 East and go left onto Route 12A north. Aspet is located just off Route 12A in Cornish, New Hampshire; it is twelve miles north of Claremont, New Hampshire and two and a half miles north of the Covered Bridge at Windsor, Vermont.

In the vicinity . . .
For another New Hampshire art site in the vicinity, visit the campus of Dartmouth college to see the great Mexican painter José Clemente Orozco's murals (see chapter 47).

Windsor, Vermont (almost directly across the Connecticut River from Cornish), is known as the birthplace of Vermont; in addition to its wonderful covered bridge, it has several attractions worth noting. Windsor's historic district is comprised of forty-five buildings including several houses and a church designed by Asher Benjamin, a Colonial portrait painter. The Vermont State Craft Center is in the center of town. The American Precision Museum in an old water-powered factory is intriguing; its fascinating glimpse of tools and machinery may remind you of some contemporary kinetic constructions now regarded as art. Open May 20-November 1, Monday-Friday 9:00 A.M. to 5:00 P.M. and weekends and holidays 10:00 A.M. to 4:00 P.M.

At Bellows Falls, Vermont, you'll find another artistic curiosity: About fifty feet down river from the Vilas Bridge, on the west side of the Connecticut River (but best viewed from the opposite side) are some interesting Indian petroglyphs. These are stone pictures incised and/or painted in yellow onto boulders at the edge of the river. (You can find them just beyond the white fence.) There are six heads including a horned shaman's head thought to be the work of the Pennacook Indians.

Of similar interest . . .

To visit the summer home and studio of Saint-Gaudens' colleague Daniel Chester French, see chapter 36.

39

Weir Farm: Home and Studio of J. Alden Weir

Ridgefield, Connecticut

Western Connecticut is an area of gentle hills, stone walls, fine old oak trees, and red barns. Its rolling landscape is tranquil and picturesque, rather than dramatic. It is the kind of place that is inviting for walkers, particularly at its greenest, in late spring or summer, when the light and the colors seem wonderfully fresh.

Some time after dozens of painters had begun flocking to Giverny in France to learn about impressionism from the master, Claude Monet, a small but significant group of Americans started painting outdoors in Connecticut, taking the first steps toward American impressionism. In fact, Weir bought the farm six months after Monet moved to Giverny.

These outdoor artists were brought to the area by the artist J. Alden Weir, who purchased an old farm in Branchville (now part of Ridgefield) for $10 and a still-life painting in 1882. With his colleague John Twachtman, and many friends including John Singer Sargent, Childe Hassam, and Albert Pinkham Ryder, Weir explored the Connecticut landscape. Weir and Twachtman began painting outdoors and examining the light's effect on color—taking the first gentle steps toward the European style of impressionism. Weir Farm, just recently dedicated as a National Historic Site, the first National Park in Connecticut, was the scene of great artistic activity from the 1880s until

Weir's death in 1919. Its studios and the surrounding landscape (a delightful stroll covering sixty-two acres) were saved from development at the last minute. Though the farm has shrunk from its original 238 acres, it is still large enough to include many a picturesque landscape, and even a lily pond that Weir built, perhaps with Giverny in mind.

In order to appreciate the setting fully, however, a little bit of art history might be welcome, for Weir Farm was—in its simple, picturesque way—an important location in the development of American painting.

Weir, the son of drawing professor at West Point Robert Weir (who taught both Generals Grant and Lee, by the way), and younger brother of landscapist John Ferguson Weir, was for many years a conservative, academic painter. When he went off as a young man to study art in Paris he wrote back in 1877:

> I went across the river the other day to see an exhibition of the work of a new school which call themselves "Impressionists." I never in my life saw more horrible things. They do not observe drawing nor form but give you an impression of what they call nature.

For Weir had come from an American academic artistic background, painting realistic topographical scenes, and giving drawing and form major importance in his compositions. The hazy impressionistic painting that he saw abroad opposed the principles with which he had come to Europe. He shared America's anti-European feeling about "foreign" styles of art, though he—like all young artists—went there for traditional art study.

On his return to the United States, Weir settled in New York where he was a successful painter of delicate, naturalistic still life, flower pieces, portraits, and domestic scenes. But Weir was a great nature lover, having been raised on Emerson and "back to nature" themes.

In 1882 he moved his family to the farm in Connecticut to escape urban life; soon the beauty of his surroundings beckoned him to begin outdoor painting. Before long, Weir—a gregarious and magnetic figure in the art world—had brought other painters to his home in Branchville. He was to paint there every summer for thirty-seven years. By 1890 he and Twachtman were experimenting with impressionistic canvases of scenes on the farm, using pure colors from the prism to create the sense of flickering light and impressionistic changes in the atmosphere. They became so excited by outdoor painting that they even devised a portable winter studio. (You will see the sites of these forays on the farm when you visit.)

Weir went on to guide and organize the Ten, a loosely knit but nonetheless influential group of American impressionists. Their collective withdrawal from the established exhibitions in New York to show their works together was a revolutionary moment in American painting. But Weir and his colleagues did not consider themselves rebels. They never abandoned entirely their American artistic roots; American impressionism retained subject matter and interest in the factual (though Weir never minded adding or transposing a tree or flower—he called it "hollyhocking").

Their paintings and explorations of light were an outgrowth of a tradition of luminism in American art, and they saw their experiments in painting light through the use of prismatic color as a natural step forward. They never issued a manifesto of impressionism, nor sought to make dramatic political statements. Both Weir and Twachtman, as well as their colleagues in the Ten, were somewhat surprised by their designation as American impressionists.

Weir Farm became a center for artists, and Weir himself held open-air classes. Nearby Cos Cob soon became an art colony, where Weir's friends took summer homes (see page 169). Weir was a busy man, painting, teaching, encouraging and supporting his colleagues, serving on the board of the Metropolitan Museum of Art, and as president of the National Academy of Design. His personal charm and dynamism (he was known as "the diplomat") enabled him to move the static world of academic art forward, without dramatic means or revolutionary art.

Weir lived at the farm until his death. His daughter married the sculptor Mahonri Young, who built the beautiful second studio and continued to work there. Your tour of the farm will include studios used by both artists, and a variety of memorabilia from both of their careers.

Since Weir Farm's dedication as a Federal Historic Site has just happened, its full program is not completely in place. (The house is still occupied by an artist, who will show it on designated days.) The grounds are always open for walking, however. We particularly liked the studios, with their clutter and confusion, including friezes, potbellied stoves, plaster casts, old photos, souvenirs, shelves of still life, and quite a bit of nice carved wainscoting. An addition houses etching machinery and armatures and bookbinding materials. We recommend visiting on a day when the studios are open so that you can see them all. (Hours and days are listed below.)

Plans for the future of Weir Farm include rotating exhibitions, artists working on the site, and lectures and classes. We hope that the powers-that-be will leave the studios as they are, rather than clean them up to resemble some fictitious studios where an artist might never have dropped a spot of paint on the floor. In fact, the tranquillity of Weir Farm can only be retained with the most careful management. This is not yet a tourist attraction, and—for the sake of both art lovers and walkers—we hope it stays the way it is.

In order to visit Weir Farm's buildings, you must telephone for an appointment. When you arrive, you will receive a map and walking guide that identifies the sites of some of the Branchville paintings by Weir. The view shown here (Figure 27) is *Upland Pasture* (1905), which is still part of the property and looks remarkably the same. You will receive a map at the central office and can wander off to find various sites and views on your own. But the studios and house can only be seen by appointment with a guide. (At our visit, the guide was the artist in residence.) Other views of Weir Farm painted by Weir and his colleagues include the barns, the pond, laundry on a line, and trees in the snow.

You will also find a nature preserve adjacent to Weir Farm. The Weir Preserve consists of 110 additional acres of unspoiled Connecticut landscape given by the artist's daughter and several other residents of the area. A map with listings of wildflowers and trees is available at Weir Farm.

INFORMATION: The grounds at Weir Farm are open Monday-Friday, 8:30 A.M.-5:00 P.M. all year. The studios are open one day a month (usually on a Thursday) during spring, summer, and fall. For information call 203-834-1896. There is an inexpensive

27. J. Alden Weir. *Upland Pasture.* 1905

entrance fee. The Weir Preserve's telephone number is 203-762-0237.

DIRECTIONS: Weir Farm is located in southwestern Connecticut in the towns of Ridgefield and Wilton. From New York City take the Merritt Parkway to Route 7 North, through Wilton and Branchville. Go left on Route 102; take the second road on your left, Old Branchville Road; turn left on Nod Hill Road to Weir Farm. The Weir Preserve is entered at either Pelham Lane or Nod Hill Road; signs are posted.

In the vicinity . . .
For a complete change of pace, visit the nearby Aldrich Museum of Contemporary Art at 258 Main Street in Ridgefield. This attractive museum is particularly noted for its modern sculpture garden and for its very trendy changing exhibitions. Without visiting the Soho galleries in New York you can get a taste of the latest in avant-garde paintings, sculpture, constructions, and conceptual art.

Of special interest is its outdoor sculpture collection. Using a map given out at the desk, you can spot large works by Tony Rosenthal, Arnaldo Pomodoro, Robert Morris, Lila Katzen, David Von Schlegel, Sol Lewitt, Alexander Liberman, and other contemporary sculptors and construction artists.

There is an inexpensive entrance fee for the museum, but the sculpture garden can be seen separately without going indoors. Telephone 203-438-4519 for hours and information on new exhibitions.

Of similar interest . . .
For more American impressionist art sites in Connecticut see Old Lyme and Cos Cob (chapter 34).

Indoor and Outdoor Collections:
Art in Public Settings

40

Outdoor Art in the Philadelphia Region

Montgomery County, Pennsylvania

The outskirts of Philadelphia are a particularly lovely area for walking and for enjoying art. The rolling terrain, luxuriant foliage, and great old fieldstone estates make an incomparable setting for sculpture. A number of these old mansions and their surrounding grounds have become colleges, museums, private schools and arboretums. This country artwalk will take you into the grounds of several former estates that now provide wonderful combinations of artistic and natural beauty.

Our first stop is at the Abingdon Art Center in Jenkintown, northwest of Philadelphia. The township of Abingdon has recently made Alverthorpe Manor—an old and gloriously landscaped estate—available to serve as an art center for the surrounding communities. Its first exhibition opened in 1990 with large outdoor sculptures and a small indoor gallery. The center plans to change exhibitions yearly, to hold three month site-specific exhibitions, multifaceted art programs (some 250 courses in art are offered), and a variety of gallery events.

Of major interest to us were the magnificent space for open air sculpture and an ongoing environmental art project in a woodsy area. The sculpture garden lies behind the charming stone central building. A veranda behind the house looks out on a vast greensward, set with modern sculptures. This is a good walk if you wish to view each artwork close up. The ancient trees and beautiful lawns make this a particularly nice outing for springtime. Be sure to pick up a brochure describing each piece of sculpture at the central desk before you set out.

When we were there the year-long exhibition included works by Alice Aycock, Melvin Edwards, Roy Wilson, George Greenamyer, Mary Ann Unger, and Jude Tallichet. All of these artists are well-known in the world of contemporary sculpture, with site-specific pieces in many other public locations, and numerous solo and museum exhibitions.

But Abingdon also offers juried sculpture shows for what are known as "emerging" sculptors from the Delaware Valley area. A recent juried show (judged by Alice Aycock) featured stipends to artists and teams of artists to construct new works on the sculpture garden grounds. Another exhibition, called "Ancient Sources: Contemporary Forms," explored ancient and archetypal imagery in modern sculpture. No matter what show is on exhibit when you visit, you will find a wide variety of contemporary styles and ideas awaiting you in the luxuriously landscaped gardens.

In addition, you will want to veer to the side of the major sculpture garden to visit the environmental site of one of the more unusual art setups we have encountered. There we found a sculptor and landscape artist named Winifred Lutz working away on a wooded area of the estate. Deep among the fallen trees, roots, overgrown bushes and piles of leaves, she is attempting to "reevoke a sense of woodland history by reclaiming the land." The artist intends to restore one or two acres, making "a register of wood that has fallen" and several large installations involving the fallen tree trunk and paths that follow the footsteps of deer. While this description may make her objectives sound somewhat obscure, you will find the site work itself intriguing, for she has stacked up wood by sizes in giant piles, filled in the vee of a fallen tree with wood, and laid out a series of pathways leading to a stone folly she has found, that is perhaps a hundred years old. If you are lucky she will be there working with axe and saw and will tell you how her plan is materializing and how she visualizes the finished result. This may be a rare opportunity to watch an environmental artist at work. (If you visit when she is not there—or in the unlikely possibility that this massive undertaking is permanently finished—the curator at the center will no doubt explain it to you.)

While you are in this immediate area, you might want to detour to the nearby Tyler School of Art, the fine arts division of Temple University. The campus is open to visitors, who will enjoy the exuberant young talent displayed all across the grounds and in a nice gallery within the main building. We saw some avant-garde works, including large outdoor sculptures—one called *Metabolism and Mortality* involved a kiln and six burners sending flames through the portholes of a vast globe stuck with sticks—and an indoor exhibition relating to shoes and costume constructions. If the latest student art is to your taste, stop by this campus—you'll enjoy a walk here.

Also not far away is the campus of Beaver College, whose central building is a sight to behold. One of those grandiose concoctions of the late nineteenth century, Grey Towers was the home of William Welsh Harrison, a sugar refining magnate. The well-known Philadelphia architect Horace Trumbauer (see outing to West Laurel Hill Cemetery, chapter 16) designed this medieval style castle, with crenellated turrets, forty rooms, a grand staircase and—of particular interest to us—a large number of hand-carved medieval-style gargoyles. You don't have to go to Europe to see gargoyles! The carved stone heads of gods and demons with grimacing faces ornament Grey Towers in many easily seen spots. You'll find them all around the porticoed entranceway. These will be "finds" that children will particularly enjoy.

You can also walk into the main hall to see the grandeur of the building, including fine decorated ceilings (nymphs, garlands, and clouds) in a mirrored ballroom, commissioned tapestries, and gold and cream carved, decorated walls that rival those in the finest palaces abroad. (The decorator's bill in 1898 came to $50,000 for painting and tapestries alone.) Other artistic oddities include Pompeiian-style murals in what was Mr. Harrison's smoking room, and a flat-vaulted ceiling in the Great Hall that is modeled after one at the château of Chambord in France.

In contrast with the grand and ancient style of Grey Towers there used to be a number of contemporary outdoor sculptures

visible on the campus. But at our last visit they had been removed for a major construction project. You can inquire in
Grey Towers as to their whereabouts.

Finally, make your way to Morris Arboretum of the University of Pennsylvania. Located well outside the city in a green-
belt, this is a lovely, hilly, Victorian-style park, filled with both
flowers and sculpture. Though the plantings and pathways are
quintessentially Victorian and some of the loveliest we have
seen, the sculpture is anything but old-fashioned. In fact, you
might consider most of it totally unrelated to its surroundings.

The Morris Arboretum is at the site of a great house called
Compton, which once belonged to a prominent Quaker couple
named John and Lydia Morris. Though the house is now gone,
the 166 acres of landscaped grounds remain, and are kept in
the most beautiful condition. This is a rather long and hilly
walk if you want to see everything—and you should.

Originally designed by Charles Miller (an American of Anglo-
phile tastes), the park is a marvel of charming paths, flowering
shrubs, fountains and clustered garden areas. There is a Temple
of Love on a Swan Pond. There are numerous great trees—including twelve redwoods bordering a stream—a grove of cedars, the most magnificent flowering cherry tree we have ever
seen, and many rare trees from the Orient. (You can pick up
material on the arboretum—including a map and information
on what's blooming—when you enter.)

There are also many flower beds in the English style, as well
as an indoor grotto with more than five hundred types of tropi-
cal ferns. The rock garden, azalea meadow, and holly slope are
all worth seeing. In June don't miss the rose garden bordered
by a wisteria allée. We could go on and on about the flowers and
trees—but you will discover for yourself the natural beauties of
Morris Arboretum. Be sure to plan your visit according to the
season you most enjoy.

Now to the sculpture: The art works are somewhat dwarfed
by the beauties of the landscape. The Butcher Sculpture Garden
contains predominantly contemporary art of which there are
about a dozen permanently installed sculptures.

Several Cotswold sheep made of two-dimensional Cor-Ten
steel by Charles Layland are "grazing" at the base of Magnolia
Slope. A kinetic steel sculpture by George Rickey called *Two*

Lines moves in the wind. You'll see several constructivist pieces on the grounds including Israel Hadany's *Three Tubes*, Buki Schwartz' *Four Cut Stones*, and a painted metal sculpture, *Untitled*, by George Sugarman. Linda Cunningham is represented by a giant bronze and steel sculpture that evokes the garden idea; its name is *Germination*.

At the center of the sculpture garden is a group of modern works by Scott Sherk based upon classical Greek mythology (but without classical visual connotations). Robert Engman is represented with a rotating geometric sculpture called *After B.K.S. Iyengar* (a yoga master). Thomas Sternal has made two wood sculptures from felled trees from the Arboretum's own grounds; one is called *Table*, the other, *Altarpiece*.

The Morris collection also features several more traditional pieces, including a *Mercury at Rest* (a copy of an antique sculpture excavated at Herculaneum) and some portrait sculptures of the Morrises themselves. Children will enjoy the Lorraine Vail whimsical animal characters, including a five foot frog and a bull.

The sculpture is widely separated by glorious patches of nature, which may give some viewers a sense of the art as a secondary source of decoration (as in Edwardian times). In fact, this type of massive contemporary art does not readily lend itself to such cultivated surroundings—except for young Mercury seated on a stone. Nonetheless, you shouldn't miss the experience of kinetic sculpture amidst the blossoms.

INFORMATION: Abingdon Art Center is at 515 Meetinghouse Road in Jenkintown. Telephone: 215-887-4882. There is no admission fee for the sculpture garden.

Tyler School of Art is at Beech and Penrose Aves. Elkins Park. Telephone: 215-782-2700 The campus can be visited during daylight hours, year-round.

Beaver College's Grey Towers Castle is at Easton and Church Roads in Glenside. Telephone: 215-572-2969.

The Morris Arboretum is at 100 Northwestern Avenue, Philadelphia; telephone: 215-247-5777. It is open 10:00 A.M. to 4:00 P.M.

daily; guided tours are available on Saturdays and Sundays at 2:00 P.M. There is an admission fee.

DIRECTIONS: All of the sites listed are north of Philadelphia. From Philadelphia take Route 611; from the Pennsylvania Turnpike, take exit 27 to Route 611. To reach the Abingdon Art Center in Jenkintown take Meeting House Road from 611. Tyler School of Art is in nearby Elkins Park; go south on Route 611, right at Cheltenham Avenue, take third right on Penrose Avenue. Beaver College is on Church Road which also intersects Route 611. To reach the Morris Arboretum take Stenton Avenue (which also intersects Route 611 a bit farther south) and head northwest (right). The Arboretum is between Stenton Avenue and Joshua Road on Northwestern Avenue.

41

Masterworks on Campus at Princeton University

Princeton, New Jersey

American college campuses are well-known for charming shaded walks and Gothic buildings. Few, however, can compare with Princeton University's beautiful campus, nor—of particular interest for us—with its outdoor sculpture collection. Princeton has acquired over the last decades an unusually fine selection of contemporary sculpture. These works are scattered across the campus, making an expedition to see them a most attractive, and artistically satisfying, artwalk.

As you will discover if you set off from the center of the campus, these works have been placed with great care among the walkways and lawns of the campus. You'll see the jagged forms of a Lipchitz against a background of buildings, a huge Picasso in front of Princeton's fine art museum, the gently moving kinetic forms by George Rickey on an open lawn, and works by David Smith, Louise Nevelson, and Isamu Noguchi, among many others. In all, some twenty-one sculptures are to be found on campus, aside from the major collection in the art museum (also open to the public).

If you enjoy strolling on a campus and looking at sculpture as you walk (along with the endlessly fascinating scenes of college life that go on around you), this tour will definitely be a favorite, to which you will return many times. (We recommend a thorough visit to the art museum in conjunction with your walk, for this museum has an outstanding collection of antiquities, European and American paintings, African sculpture, and many other treasures. It is used by scholars from the University and around the world.) Following, however, is specifically a sculpture walk.

Enter the University campus from Nassau Street at the gate opposite Palmer Square. You must go on foot. Park at a meter in town, or leave your car at the University parking lot and take the shuttle bus to campus. The guard at the gate will direct you to the lot or to town parking. Pick up a campus map at the information desk near the gate before you start. (Numbers in this walk refer to this map.)

A fitting beginning to this tour of twentieth century sculpture is a Henry Moore called *Oval with Points*. This commissioned work was installed in 1971 between Stanhope Hall and West College, at F2 on the map. It is made of bronze, its inside surface now burnished from contact with the thousands of students who have lounged on it (to the sculptor's delight). The sculpture bears some resemblance to an elephant skull which was given by Sir Julian Huxley to Moore and placed in the sculptor's garden. "Henry," wrote Huxley, "not only took it to his heart but proceeded to explore its massive outline, its tunnels and cavities, its recesses and blind eye-sockets . . ." You will find the Moore easily recognizable, with or without the knowledge of its relationship to the elephant skull, and you'll enjoy its graceful placement on the green.

An entirely different sculptural experience awaits you at your next stop. Walk on away from the gate to the pathway behind West College. Turn left on the path. At F3 on the map you'll see the slightly undulating forms of George Rickey's *Two Planes, Vertical Horizon II*. Don't miss the Rickey work; it is just off the pathway, and somewhat above your head, where its kinetic parts catch the breeze and move almost imperceptibly. Back away to look at it. Rickey is perhaps the leading exponent of this type of sculpture today, though it was Alexander Calder, whose work you will shortly see, who led the way in inventing kinetic sculpture.

Continue on the path and then turn left at its end. Between the University Chapel and Firestone Library (at G2) you'll see the Jacques Lipchitz sculpture called *Song of the Vowels*, one of a series in which the artist worked with a harp motif. This soaring bronze is a cubist structure suggesting a harpist in Lipchitz's familiar curvilinear style. The artist said that the title had to do with a legendary prayer of ancient Egypt in which the forces of nature were called upon. It was installed on the campus in 1969.

In the lobby of Firestone Library itself is another work by a master of contemporary sculpture, Isamu Noguchi. *White Sun* is one in a series of works in various media portraying the sun that the sculptor created in the 1960s. Made of white marble, it is a large, irregular circle with an open center, like many Noguchi sculptures that explore circular and disc-shaped forms.

When you leave the lobby to go back outdoors you'll see another modern "classic" between the Library building and Nassau Street bordering the campus (also G2). This is *Atmosphere and Environment X* by Louise Nevelson (Figure 28), whose work will probably be recognizable to you from many of the other sculpture walks in this book.

Nevelson, a major figure in contemporary sculpture for decades, described her works in her own way:

> Say an architect builds a house. Well, now let's say that he builds the whole thing inside, all the rooms and everything, but he doesn't have an outside wall. Well, it's not a house, it's a veranda. I want the total house, I don't want my sculpture to be a veranda.

Like other Nevelsons, this one is made of Cor-Ten steel and is quite large—twenty-one feet high and sixteen feet long. It is made up of interlocking black, white and gold geometric shapes set in a shallow relieflike form. You will enjoy watching the play of light and shadow on it if you happen to have a sunny day for your walk, but at any time it is an impressive and monumental work. It was Nevelson's first major work in Cor-Ten steel, a medium that was to become a hallmark of Nevelson sculpture.

Between Firestone and Dickinson Hall (still G2), you'll discover George Segal's memorial to the Kent State massacre: *Abraham and Isaac, in Memory of May 4, 1970, Kent State University*. Segal's very realistic style is a clear contrast with

28. Louise Nevelson. *Atmosphere and Environment X.* 1969

the abstract sculptures we have just seen; his human figures look strikingly real, and though they represent Biblical figures, their contemporary message is very clear.

Walk along Washington Road toward the School of Architecture (G3). If you wish to go inside the building, you'll find in the stairwell Eduardo Paolozzi's imaginative *Marok, Marok, Miosa*, a contemporary work. Paolozzi was the principal exponent of England's junk sculpture movement, making works from found objects.

Here you might gauge your energy and decide whether to cross Washington Road and head several blocks across the campus to the Engineering Quadrangle where three more sculptures are situated. If you want to make this detour, you will walk along Prospect Avenue to Olden Street, where you will turn left and continue until you reach the Engineering School (J2).

At the entrance to the quadrangle you'll see Clement Meadmore's *Upstart 2*, a work made in 1970. This minimalist form, also made of Cor-Ten steel, could be said to resemble a letter of the alphabet or a hard-edge snake; it rises from a slab base, giving an impression of surprising lightness. Meadmore is said to see his sculpture "as being like a person who inhabits a place."

While in the Engineering Quad you can see two more works: Masayuki Nagare's *Stone Riddle* (K2), a contemporary example by the well-known Japanese artist, and *Spheric Theme* by Naum Gabo (K2), a leading figure in Russia's early modern style of constructivism. Gabo's work, a kind of spatial puzzle, involved replacing several of the planes of a cube with interlocking diagonals. The completed stainless steel work, which is eight feet high, is an attempt by Gabo to show that "the visual character of space is not angular . . . I enclose the space in one curved continuous surface."

Turn toward the center of the campus now, walking back along Washington Road toward the gym complex. You will cross Prospect Avenue and Ivy Lane (whether you are coming from the Architecture School or Engineering Quad).

Just beyond Ivy Lane you'll find your next piece of sculpture within the Fine Hall Library, the well-known portrait head of Albert Einstein by the renowned American/British sculptor Jacob Epstein (H5). As you no doubt know, Einstein was a beloved figure in Princeton for many years, and this tribute to him is appropriately placed in the physics library. Epstein's portrait heads were modeled in clay for casting in bronze and are characterized (as this one is) by many small jagged planes that break up the surface of the work.

In the plaza between Fine Hall and Jadwin Hall (H5) is another major work of the Princeton collection: Alexander Calder's *Five Disks: One Empty*. Though this giant work is a stabile rather than one of Calder's more familiar mobiles, it nonetheless has the unmistakable Calder style, with its cut-outs and circular and pointed forms of black steel and its mood of playfulness. Though originally painted orange (to honor Princeton's traditional colors) the artist blackened the forms after the work was set on the campus in 1971.

Just behind Fine Hall is Jadwin Hall. Here in the courtyard of the hall (H5) is Antoine Pevsner's *Construction in the Third and Fourth Dimension*. Pevsner was the elder brother of Naum Gabo; together they were active in the constructivist movement in Russia in the 1920s. Pevsner's work is also involved with spatial ambiguity. This sculpture, which rises to more than ten feet, is a bronze abstraction set on a black granite pedestal. It explores the contortion of flat metal planes into shapes that suggest the possibility of infinite continuity.

Cross Washington Road once again and head toward the Computer Science Building, if you are still feeling energetic. (We don't deny that this is a long walk.) Here (F6) you will see Michael David Hall's work *Mastodon VI*, another contemporary sculpture.

Slightly closer is *Sphere VI* by Arnaldo Pomodoro, an Italian sculptor. You'll find this work in Butler College Courtyard (F5). Pomodoro specialized in negative/positive casting, in which parts of the surface were gouged out, giving his forms an imagery of motion from within. *Sphere VI* is a giant polished bronze with a type of interrupted surface that the artist described as "an expression of interior movement."

If you cross the tennis court area to your left, you'll find yourself at some newer dormitory buildings near the train station. Here (E5) is one of the campus' favorite pieces: David Smith's *Cubi XIII*. Situated on the lawn of Spelman Hall, Smith's stainless steel, nine foot high sculpture is one of a series of twenty-eight works that he called *Cubi*. An exploration of Cubist principles in welded steel, these works were designed for outdoor positioning with particular reference to the architecture around them.

Turning back to the heart of the campus, you will pass Dillon Gym and come to a street called Elm Drive. Turn left until you reach a dorm quad called Cuyler. Cross in front of Cuyler to see Prospect Gardens, the lovely formal gardens of the college (and a good place for a quick rest). Prospect House, which overlooks the gardens, has a sculpture on its lawn. It is by the American artist Tony Smith and is called *Moses* (G3).

A strong cubistic work, *Moses* is a painted steel abstraction of angular planes. The artist felt that the parallel uprights suggested the horns of Michelangelo's *Moses* (Moses wears horns because of a misunderstanding by Latinists of the Hebrew for "shining," also the root of the word for horns) and Smith continued the symbolism. But whether or not you see this geometric work as Moses, you will find it interesting to compare with the other studies in contemporary, angular, hard-edged abstractions on this walk.

You arrive next at the Art Museum itself. (We expect you will want to return to it after your last few stops.) You can easily identify it by the imposing Picasso in front of it. *Head of a Woman* (F3) is one of those works that is so identified in our minds with Picasso that it hardly needs introduction. It is constructed of cast concrete, was executed by Carl Nesjar (who did many of Picasso's sculptures) from a maquette made originally in 1962, and was made specifically for this Princeton site. As it was constructed on campus, students watched the process—a unique experience!

Your final stop on the central campus is in the courtyard of Hamilton Hall (E2), back near the gate you originally entered. Here is *The Bride* by British sculptor Reg Butler. This tall slender figure (it stands seven feet high) is a bronze semiabstract female, whose forms suggest something of the shapes of trees and leaves. The work is in the tradition of British postwar figurative style.

As you leave the campus (don't forget your parking meter!), you may wish to drive to the last two destinations on our sculpture walk. They are both at the Graduate College, which is beyond the golf course to the left of the gate. (See map.) You are headed to A6 where you will want to see Gaston Lachaise's *Floating Figure*, made in 1927. (You may recognize this work from the Museum of Modern Art's Sculpture Garden, where another copy of it is a favorite of sculpture lovers.) A typical example of Lachaise's bronzes, the seated figure balances its rounded forms gently and weightlessly.

Our final destination is to see Kenneth Snelson's *Northwood II* (B6), also in the Graduate College. This is a fitting conclusion to our sculpture walk, for Snelson has become a leading member of the current sculpture stylists. His towering aluminum and steel constructions are supported by cables within the framework. "My concern," he says, "is with nature in its fundamental aspect; the patterns of physical forces in space."

INFORMATION: The University campus is open year-round. For tours and information telephone 609-258-3603.

DIRECTIONS: Take the New Jersey Turnpike to exit 9. Take Route 1 south, then Route 571 west to Princeton. Follow signs for the University.

In the vicinity . . .
The Johnson Atelier, a foundry in nearby Mercerville, is described in chapter 20.

42

Spiritual Sculpture Retreat at Pacem in Terris

Warwick, New York

A walk through Pacem in Terris is a very unusual experience, for it combines contemporary art and a highly spiritual environment. In fact, when we first called there, it was made clear to us by the owners that they weren't sure they wanted to be in a book. In light of the rampant commercialism pervading so much of today's art scene, that in itself was refreshing, but the best was definitely yet to come.

Pacem in Terris is the creation of a Dutch-born artist, Frederick Franck, and his wife. Franck had been a doctor who worked for two years with Dr. Albert Schweitzer in Africa. When he came to the United States he devoted himself to painting and sculpture and philosophy, but his dedication to humanitarianism and religious spirituality led him to seek a common ground between art and the spiritual. His art—sculpture, paintings, drawings, banners, mobiles, and stained glass—and his many books testify to this pursuit.

In 1963 he left New York for rural Warwick, to establish a "transreligious sanctuary" which he dedicated to Pope John XXIII and to "Reverence for Life." The location was an eighteenth century watermill beside a rushing little river. The site was to provide a beautiful haven for numerous outdoor sculptures, as well as an extraordinary indoor environment for art, music, and contemplation.

This is a beautiful place, for nature has been left quite untouched. A walk along the riverbank with its waterfall and rather wild look would be a pleasure, even without the surprising sculpture that dots the landscape between wildflowers and forest and even hangs suspended above the river. There are some garden areas, a few remnants of long-ago wood or stone farm sheds, a dovecote, and an ancient and imposing cherry tree.

And then there is the sculpture. Franck's work is modern in style, often made of welded and cut-out steel or found objects in the contemporary mode. What distinguishes it particularly is its emphasis on the reverential and mystical. There are eyes everywhere: They are carved into doorjambs, on otherwise abstract works, and on a giant sculptured fish turning in the wind above the river. The sculptures all have subjects, ranging from a striking series of receding abstract figures that diminish in size (a memorial to the Iroquois), to a large black and white mask called *The Face of Everyman*, to a huge circular serpent eating its own tail called *Ouradouros*, the most ancient symbol of eternal life.

We were soon made aware that even the fenceposts and flagstones underfoot bore either statements of peace and religious experience or decorative symbols ranging from Egyptian to Chinese. Franck's beliefs are truly cosmic and multicultural. A walk through the gardens is indeed a walk through a sanctuary, but the spiritual aura is neither intrusive nor didactic.

After seeing the outdoor environment, you will visit the pointed-roof building that lies across the little river. Here, more mystical quotations and symbols appear, decorating an extraordinary old building with a modern raised roof. The interior is of dark and ancient stone. Though used primarily as a studio, it also houses concerts and various meetings of humanitarian groups; but it is in itself a fascinating work of art. Its rising stone levels are inlaid with bits of glass; iron and steel mobiles twist in the air. An interior waterway rushes under the floor. More eyes and hands and masks and totems intermingle with the ladders and equipment of contemporary use. You will not visit a studio quite like this one anywhere else.

Pacem in Terris has added another tract of land to accommodate its growing collection of art. Just across the road (and the railroad tracks) is an area called the "Meadow of Signs." Here you'll find sculptures dedicated to fighting persecution, and a memorial to the victims of Hiroshima (replicas of this work are at St. John the Divine in New York and in Japan). A wooden shrinelike construction called *The Mother of the Earth* is made of many small carved wooden figures that fuse eastern and western religious belief in the mother-goddess. Other works include a *Death and Transfiguration* and a *Buddha's Eye*, made with mirrors.

The site also includes a gallery and the Francks' home, which are both filled with the artist's work. A visit here is an experience unlike any of the others we have described. If you like to see art "pure"—without the trappings of titles and extra-aesthetic meanings—this may not be the outing for you. But if you are open to a spiritual-cum-artistic experience, you will surely be glad you came to Pacem in Terris. We found that it was the overall ambience—perhaps more than the individual works of art—that captured our imaginations.

INFORMATION: Pacem in Terris is open without charge (though contributions are accepted) Saturdays and Sundays from May to October. The hours are 11:00 A.M. to 6:00 P.M. (Telephone: 914-986-4329.)

DIRECTIONS: From New York City, take the George Washington Bridge to Route 4 to Route 17 North to Route 17A. At junction in Warwick take 94 West. Make a left on 94 and go three miles to Fancher Road, on your right. Pacem in Terris is at the end of Fancher Road.

43

De Cordova Sculpture Garden: Modern Forms Upon a Hill

Lincoln, Massachusetts

The combination of fine modern and contemporary art in an unusually beautiful setting makes the De Cordova Museum and Sculpture Park a remarkable site not to be missed. Situated on the shores of a quiet pond in Lincoln, outside of Boston, its bucolic ambience would be reason enough for a visit: The thirty-five acres of rolling hills, woods, and sweeping lawns with views of the New Hampshire hills, create an inviting environment for a walk. De Cordova also happens to be New England's most important outdoor exhibition space with more than thirty large-scale sculptures on view.

Once the country estate of Julian De Cordova (1851–1945), an eccentric, art-collecting Boston entrepreneur, the property with its odd castlelike structure was bequeathed in 1930 to the town of Lincoln. It was first simply a recreational area; it gradually evolved into a museum, when its potential as an exhibition site was realized. The De Cordova began acquiring and displaying large sculptures by prominent American artists. Since the mid-1980s the museum has included a permanent sculpture park—the only one of its kind in New England—an indoor museum (housed in what once was De Cordova's mansion), and several additional buildings used for classes, studios, and workshops.

Scattered about the spacious grounds—like silent abstract sheep in a pastoral tableau—are modern and contemporary works by a wide variety of American artists. (A map of the grounds and art works is available at the museum desk.) These range from sculptures of such major artists as Alexander Liberman, George Rickey, and Mark DiSuvero, to the latest, most innovative environmental pieces. While some works remain at De Cordova as part of their permanent collection (see below), others come and go with the continuous flow of changing exhibits. The sculptures have been carefully placed so they interact harmoniously with the beautifully arranged park, creating a landscape that is in itself a sculpted environment.

Although sculptors of national and international stature are well represented here, a large number of artists shown are from New England. De Cordova is considered to be the premier showcase of the region's most promising artists and is committed to generating public appreciation of its local artistic community. Some of the art has a particular New England focus.

Recently a site-specific work by Gail Rothschild called *Women of the 19th Century: A Conversation* was installed in a quiet hemlock grove. Drawn from the writing of a nineteenth century New England feminist, Margaret Fuller, a transcendentalist colleague of Thoreau and Emerson, it features five giant rocking chairs, each with inscriptions from Fuller and her contemporaries. Placed in each rocking chair is a larger-than-life female figure made of hay held together by chicken wire. The women are kneeling in a way suggestive of the stocks that were used in this region during colonial times. You might draw your own conclusions from this unusual grouping, but the New England context is unmistakable.

Every year De Cordova commissions site-specific works that often speak of environmental issues. A recent show of such work included a sculpture called *Bat House* by Christopher Sproat. It was built as a real haven for these much maligned creatures. Placed in an open field, the sculpture heralds our need to protect these flying mammals. The appropriately Gothic-looking spear-shaped work has a pointed roof and soars fourteen feet into the air. It is without question the only artist-designed bat house you will ever see.

Another unusual installation is Allan Wexler's *Floor Becoming Table on a Hill*, which he located at a leafy site overlooking Flint's Pond. The artist is known for his original—and somewhat eccentric—constructions and arrangements of furniture that reflect the relationships among individuals, architecture, and landscape. This conceptual picnic site includes two sixty-foot-long wooden paths that intersect at a junction where people, landscape, art, architecture, and furniture meet and connect. Philosophy and art aside, you can imagine its being a fine place to dine alfresco.

Another artist, Patrick Dougherty, decided to create something that would respond to the castlelike appearance of the museum's building. The result is *Spin-Offs*, an installation in which natural materials have been woven into conical windswept forms that actually appear to move from the top of the turreted structure to the ground.

These sentiments and concerns for the environment find expression throughout the sculpture park. You may not find all of the specific works mentioned here, since many are not permanently installed. However, the De Cordova has a number of sculptures on its grounds that were gifts to the collection, and that should be on view at all times. Look for:

George Rickey's *Three Lines*, a stainless steel work that focuses on linear movement.

Richard Fishman's *Colleoni*, a contemporary bronze homage to Andrea del Verrochio's equestrian monuments.

Hugh Townley's intriguing concrete work called *Group of Three*, which spells the word ART in abstract manner.

Alexander Liberman's *Cardinal Points*, one of the well-known sculptor's abstract welded steel constructions.

Ed Shay's *Acadian Gyro*, an intriguing bronze construction that he describes as "a skeletal structure of a fish-boat with winged oars" that functions as a symbolic spiritual gyro.

George Greenamyer's *Mass Art Vehicle*, a welded steel construction of a pyramid-shaped vehicle on tracks.

Mags Harries' topiary garden constructions that can be seen as "intimate rooms" when viewed from above.

Lila Katzen's weathered steel *X Notion Like an H*, which explores the "identity" of the letter X.

Paul Matisse's *The Musical Fence*, made of aluminum sounding bars and concrete, a kind of sculptural vibraphone that stretches to more than twenty feet across the lawn.

The museum's gallery shows sometimes relate to the works in the park. A recent museum show featured thirty plastic models created by Allan Wexler in his investigation of ideas for his picnic area.

The De Cordova is an active, vibrant museum complex with many facilities and activities, including classes and workshops. Visits to artists' studios are also arranged. Docent tours of the museum and sculpture park are available for those who enjoy discussing art with others as they view the pieces. However, you are welcome to walk around on your own.

INFORMATION: Museum hours: Tuesday-Friday, 10:00 A.M.-5:00 P.M.; weekends, noon-5:00 P.M.
Sculpture park: open every day of the year from dawn to dusk. There is an inexpensive admission charge for galleries, but not for the sculpture park.
Telephone: 617-259-8355

DIRECTIONS: De Cordova Museum and Sculpture Park is located on Sandy Pond Road in Lincoln, MA. To get there from Boston: From Route 128: Take exit 28B, Trapelo Road/Lincoln. Take Trapelo Road about 2½ miles to intersection with Sandy Pond Road and follow the signs to De Cordova.
From Mass Pike: Take 128 North and follow directions above.
From Route 93: Take 128 South and follow directions above.

44

An Inviting Sculpture Park on Corporate Grounds: The Donald M. Kendall Sculpture Gardens at PepsiCo

Purchase, New York

We have no hesitation in inviting you to take this artwalk; it is truly one of our favorites both with and without children in tow. You may wonder how PepsiCo—so well known for its mainstream popular culture advertising—would find itself in a book about public art and gardens. But you are in for a wonderful surprise. While there are many corporate art collections in America, few are available to the public to enjoy with the scale, variety, and quality of the Donald M. Kendall Sculpture Gardens at PepsiCo.

A walking tour of these 112 acres (more an estate than a garden in the traditional sense) will introduce you to some forty-two major works of sculpture, as well as to a shining example of how a corporation can enhance its surroundings and bring art to people outside of a museum. The former CEO of the company, Donald M. Kendall, conceived the idea and was active in collecting the sculpture to provide "an environment that encourages creativity and reflects essential qualities of corporate success." (While you may find that few of these works of art seem to relate in any way to corporate success, the sense of creativity is indeed all around you.)

In 1970 Edward Durell Stone's massive building was opened on this exquisite site—formerly a polo field. The building (which is not open to the public) is made up of seven square blocks that form three courtyard gardens around a central fountain. The architect's son laid out the surrounding acreage of rolling green terrain; there are fields, pathways, a lake, distinctive trees, flower gardens, fountains—and everywhere you look—sculpture.

The gardens themselves were planned by the internationally known landscape designer Russell Page. Each piece of art is carefully placed in relation to its surroundings, so that each knoll or valley provides a gentle setting for its work of art. There are both formal gardens—where smaller pieces of sculpture are surrounded with clipped hedges and precisely groomed plantings—and vast fields—where monumental examples of contemporary sculpture stand starkly against the horizon. There is a lake and well-tended woodland. This park is so carefully designed and maintained that even the parking lots are concealed by plantings, and an army of gardeners seems to be always at work. (A list of some of the most interesting trees and plantings appears at the end of this chapter.)

To begin your artwalk, leave your car in one of the hidden parking lots (to which discreet signs direct you). No appointment is necessary, but check the hours listed below. You will seldom find this vast place crowded. After you park, you'll go to the Visitor Center, pick up a numbered map, and enter the "Golden Path"—a nice, winding walkway through the entire acreage. (You may wander on your own if you prefer, or stay on the path and follow the map, which identifies all works of art.)

1. As you come to the fork in the path, go to your right. The first sculpture, just to the left of the path, is Alexander Calder's *Hats Off*, a giant work in orange-red metal, unmistakably Calder's. It is set against a backdrop of white fir and Colorado blue spruce, bringing its brilliant color vividly to life.

2. Also to the left of the path is Jean Dubuffet's painted black and white abstract work *Kiosque Evide* (Figure 29). This 1985 sculpture by the renowned French artist does look like some

29. Jean Dubuffet. *Kiosque L'Evide*. 1985

fantastic kind of kiosk with its whimsical shapes and painted designs. Dubuffet described his works in this style not as sculptures but as "unleashed graphisms, drawings which extend and expand in space."

3. A little farther, also to your left, is a work by Arnaldo Pomodoro called *Grande Disco*, a variation on the form of the globe—eaten away by some mysterious forces. (Another Pomodoro work—and one of the major sculptures of the entire collection—is described below.)

4. Leave the path and walk left toward the building entrance to see a work by the well-known David Smith. This piece, called *Cube Totem Seven and Six*, is set just in front of the trellis to the giant headquarters building. You will no doubt recognize Smith's style in this delightful shiny metal work. (In fact, one of the characteristics of this sculpture collection is that each work is highly typical of its artist's style; you may enjoy identifying the works, if you are familiar with contemporary sculpture, without benefit of this guide.)

5. and 6. On the terrace in front of you, you'll find works by two twentieth century Italian masters. First, you'll see Marino Marini's charming *Horse and Rider*. Now somewhat of a "classic," Marini's signature horse and rider images are familiar, but always a pleasure to see anew. Also on the terrace are two Alberto Giacometti statues: *Standing Woman I and II*, their tall, thin figures sharply defined against the building's wall.

7. Auguste Rodin's *Eve* is perhaps the most traditional work on this artwalk, but it is interesting to see the origins of contemporary sculpture in this lovely 1881 work. It is charmingly set among holly trees and shrubbery.

8. One of the most interesting works is Max Ernst's *Capricorn*, to the right of the path. Don't miss this surrealistic group of figures with animal parts suggesting fish, a cow, and birds.

(Here is an opportunity to visit the courtyard gardens that contain ten additional works of art. You can either enter the gateway at this juncture, or leave them for the end. They are described as numbers 33 to 42.)

9. One of today's leading sculptors is represented next; in a kind of garden area to your left you'll find Kenneth Snelson's *Mozart II*. This is a giant aluminum construction of geometric shapes and wires, a most contemporary tribute to Mozart.

10. Go back to the path and go left at the fork, near the building's walls. Here you'll see George Segal's *Three People on Four Benches*, a characteristically superrealistic work that may remind you of PepsiCo's workers relaxing during their lunch hour break.

11. Claes Oldenburg's *Giant Trowel II* (Figure 30) is one of the most memorable sights at PepsiCo. In fact, it is so startling against its background of pine and dogwood trees that you blink to see if the giant spade is really there, digging into the green earth.

12. Moving farther along the path you'll next see George Rickey's *Double L Eccentric Gyratory II*, a typical Rickey work made up of stainless steel windmill-like blades that shift gently in the breeze.

13. and 14. Here, on the edge of the cultivated lawn area, and in front of a wooded section you'll come to Tony Smith's abstract *Duck* and Richard Erdman's *Passage*.

15. and 16. David Wynne's *The Dancers* is close to the entrance to the park, near an area called the stream garden, as is Art Price's *Birds of Welcome*, a rather folksy, but contemporary work that reminded us of Pennsylvania Dutch design.

17., 18. and 19. Also nearby are *The Search* by Victor Salmones; another David Wynne figure piece, *Dancer with Bird*; and William Crovello's *Katana*. These works are all surrounded by shrubbery and little woodsy walkways, in contrast to those on the terraces or open fields.

20. Some way past these works, to the left of the path, you'll come upon a fascinating work in the collection: Judith Brown's 1982 sculpture *Caryatids*. This is an interesting postmodern work which is reminiscent of ancient art—using old car parts in a highly contemporary manner. Don't miss this impression of crumbling ruins made of steel bits.

21., 22. and 23. Gidon Graetz is represented by *Composition in Stainless Steel No. 1*, which you'll find near the building on your left, while *Personnage*, a 1970 work by the "old" master, Joan Miró, is up on the terrace near the lily pond. (Don't miss this delightful garden spot with its perennial flower border and water lily pool. Here also is a charming pavilion inspired by eighteenth century English lanscape design—and it is a perfect

30. Claes Oldenburg. *The Giant Trowel II.* 1982

place for a quick rest.) Nearby is Robert Davidson's *Frog*; you'll see a more imposing work by this sculptor later on.

24. Next you'll come to one of the most memorable and defining works in the sculpture park: Arnaldo Pomodoro's *Triad*, a dramatic group of three modern, but ancient-looking, columns set starkly against the landscape.

25. and 26. The well-known British sculptor Barbara Hepworth is also represented with a typical work in this collection. Her *Meridien*, a 1959 piece, is to the left of the path near Bret Price's *Big Scoop*.

27. and 28. Next you'll find the works of two of the most often mentioned sculptors in our book: Isamu Noguchi and Louise Nevelson. Both have defined contemporary sculpture in our time, in very different ways. Noguchi's work, *Energy Void*, is a characteristically formalistic work; Nevelson's *Celebration II* is a dark collection of geometric metal forms set in soft ground cover amid a stand of copper beech trees that reflect the color of the sculpture.

29. You have now reached the lake. In your walk around it you'll see several of the major works in the collection. First is Robert Davidson's three giant totems that will remind you of northwest coast native American carvings. This work, appropriately called *Totems*, stands out by its audacity, bright colors, and dramatic design.

30. and 31. Another contemporary work, Asmundur Sveinsson's *Through the Sound Barrier* is also next to the circular path around the lake. And at the intersection of the lake path and your original entrance to the grounds is one of the most beloved sculptures (particularly by children), David Wynne's realistic *Grizzly Bear*.

32. The last work on the grounds is Henry Moore's *Double Oval*, which sits on the edge of the lake as a splendid monument to contemporary art.

33.-42. If you haven't already detoured to the courtyards, you will now wish to see the works in the courtyard gardens, charmingly landscaped collections of plants and art. These are in the center of the building complex. The majority are representative of the earlier schools of contemporary sculpture, including two Henry Moore works, two Henri Laurens and an Aristide Maillol. There is also a Seymour Lipton work and a

David Wynne *Girl with a Dolphin* in the center of a fountain. Of particular note are the wonderful heavy figures of Laurens, *Le Matin* and *Les Ondines*, which you reach by walking on stones through a watery environment that heightens your appreciation for the art so beautifully placed.

For those of you who enjoy nature as well as sculpture, notice rare plantings, including some from Japan and China. A list of these trees is available at the Visitor Center; but we will also mention a stand of birch trees, an oak grove, a stand of witch hazels, lacebark pine from China, European hornbeam, black locusts, sweet gum, walnut, hemlock, cypress and dawn redwood. Among the wonderful flowering plantings are azaleas, rhododendrons and crabapples, so you might want to take this walk in April or May—at the height of the flowering shrub season. In any case, we think you'll find this combination of natural and artistic pleasures a rare treat.

INFORMATION: The Donald M. Kendall Sculpture Gardens at PepsiCo's headquarters are on Anderson Hill Road in Purchase, New York. Telephone: 914-253-3000. The Sculpture Gardens are open free from 10:00 A.M. to dusk, seven days a week, year-round.

DIRECTIONS: From New York, take the Hutchinson River Parkway north to exit 28 (Lincoln Avenue). Note sign indicating SUNY/ Purchase. After exit go left on Lincoln Avenue to its end. Turn right onto Anderson Hill Road; entrance is on the right.

In the vicinity . . .
Also in Purchase is the Neuberger Museum at the State University of New York. See page 261.
Reader's Digest headquarters (by appointment only) has a large collection of master paintings. See page 261.
The Katonah Art Museum is also nearby. See page 260.

45

Griffis Sculpture Park: Contemporary Works in A Natural Setting

Ashford Hollow, New York

A giant crab, an Amazon, a giraffe, a twenty-eight-foot cobra, a reclining nude, a monumental toadstool, and a variety of other astonishing creatures, towers, and constructions dot the grassy landscape of Griffis Sculpture Park. These four hundred rolling acres in upstate New York (about forty-three miles south of Buffalo) are an appealing art site for the walker and sculpture lover.

You'll find sculptures all over this varied terrain of grassy hills, open meadows, woods, and deep ravines. Some two hundred works have been placed at the park for the enjoyment of the art-loving public by the Ashford Hollow Foundation for the Visual and Performing Arts. There are 120 sculptures by artist Larry Griffis, the CEO of the Foundation, and about eighty works by other artists.

As you make your way over ten miles of hiking trails through this lovely landscape, you'll see art in a wide variety of styles. There are mixed media, huge steel and iron constructions, traditional marble statues, wood carvings, and sculptures made of a great mix of junk

Among the most interesting works are a collection of oversize human and insect forms, and a number of imaginative abstractions that tower over the viewer. A series of twenty-five-foot-tall iron figures with dangling earrings are posted like guards along one road. Called *Ladies in Waiting*, they are designed to "alert and greet visitors," according to Griffis. But you will hardly need alerting at this art site; a visit here will certainly keep you awake!

The sculptors, in addition to Larry Griffis, include Wes Olmstead, Richard Gustin, James Suris, Joe Panone, John Bjorge, Frank Toole, Dennis Baraclough, and—surprisingly—the Neighborhood Youth Corps. (The latter created a fountain with an airy design of flying birds.)

Larry Griffis had the inspiration for his own sculpture park while picnicking with his family amid the classical ruins of Rome. He envisaged a large parklike setting with trails and meadows for contemporary sculpture instead of ancient ruins. On his return to New York State, he set about making his Roman vision a reality. In 1967 his family purchased the vast acreage of rolling hillside, a foundation was set up, the first of his own works were placed on the grounds, and his sculpture park came into being. Since then it has grown to include works by dozens of other artists in a wide variety of styles.

This is a particularly enticing outing for children, a kind of artistic adventure that is surefire. They can allow free rein to their imaginations, touch the works of art, scamper through the vast fields at will, get lost in a brightly colored wrought iron maze, and perhaps capture the magic of the collaboration between art and nature that the best sculpture parks create.

"Visitors can touch the sculptures, climb on them," Griffis said recently. "The sculptures become an environment, and the whole park becomes a work too. People are part of the flow here." Periodically, he creates new trails and paths to accommodate the wanderings of both art and nature explorers at the park.

The foundation that sponsors the park also runs the Essex Arts Center in Buffalo, which houses artists' living and studio spaces, a foundry, and a gallery. There are musical events at the sculpture park in warm weather. The foundation has provided these acres of art for the pleasure of the public without charge. (Contributions, however, are gratefully received.)

INFORMATION: Griffis Sculpture Park is open daily until 9: 00 P.M. from April 1 to November 1. If you prefer a tour, call for an appointment. Telephone: 716-257-9344.

DIRECTIONS: Griffis Sculpture Park is at 6902 Mill Valley Road, in East Otto, New York. From Buffalo, take route 219 south. East Otto is between Ellicottville and Springville.

46

Spectacular Sculpture and Scenery at Storm King Art Center

Mountainville, New York

If you have never been to Storm King Art Center in Mountainville, New York, you can look forward to an extraordinary experience; if you have already been there, it is surely time to go back. For this great museum can be enjoyed again and again, with new discoveries to be made on each visit.

Storm King is one of the most important and impressive outdoor sculpture parks in the country. You are struck by the sheer drama and scope of the site the minute you enter through the stone gates. Large, compelling sculptures—many in brilliant primary colors—suddenly appear before you like enormous creatures, in striking contrast to the gently rolling hills and vast grassy fields of the surrounding Hudson Valley. It would be hard to find another place where outdoor sculpture it so dramatically exhibited.

The four-hundred-acre park includes more than two hundred modern sculptures—some of truly massive proportions and fantastic shapes—imaginatively set throughout the spacious grounds. Mostly made of metal or stone, these abstract forms range from the smaller, more delicate works on display around the manor house and indoor museum to the boldest of sculptures beyond. You can walk on grassy slopes, wooded paths, and fields, from one work to another to view each piece up close, or stand on top of one of the hills and admire them from afar. The combination of first-rate art with extraordinary spaciousness makes Storm King unique.

This great property once belonged to a lawyer named Vermont Hatch, who built the elegant Normandy-style stone mansion that is now used to show temporary exhibits and smaller works from the permanent collection. But it was his neighbor and friend, Ted Ogden, an energetic and visionary entrepreneur and art collector, who had the imagination to convert the estate into a sculpture museum. He had seen photographs of Henry Moore sculpture set on a sheep ranch in Scotland and thought Storm King would lend itself to display contemporary art in an even more inspiring way. In a bold move, Ogden acquired fourteen David Smith sculptures all at once. They became the core of the collection. (These sculptures can now be seen on the grounds near the house, as well as inside.)

He gradually added pieces by other well-known artists such as Alexander Calder, Mark DiSuvero, Louise Nevelson, Robert Grosvenor, Barbara Hepworth, Henry Moore, Charles Ginnever, and many others. Since his death in 1974 many more have been added to what was an already impressive collection, including works by lesser-known contemporary artists, or what are now known as "emerging artists." To accommodate this large body of works—some of which are monumental in size—it has been necessary to clear more land and to create hills and paths. Today's Storm King is still in the process of evolution and expansion; it is an ever-changing landscape.

You will find Storm King a wonderfully inspiring place to walk and contemplate art and nature at your own pace and leisure. There are daily one-hour guided tours that are informative and interesting. However, we preferred seeing the museum on our own, roaming freely from one spot to the next. The walk can be a very long one, indeed, if you are determined to examine each piece of sculpture; you can cover miles, climbing up and down hills and treading through broad fields. Or you can choose to see a selection of works that particularly interest you, reserving the others for a future visit, or perhaps view some of the works from a distance.

The quality of Storm King's art in combination with its unique environment makes it special to a wide variety of visitors, including foreign tourists who relish this taste of the vast

American panorama. It is also a perfect place to introduce children to contemporary sculpture. Here they can experience fine art without the usual museum restrictions, and can enjoy running about in the grass, from one piece to the next. Although visitors are in principle not allowed to touch the sculptures, there are two notable exceptions: Siah Armajani's *Gazebo For Two Anarchists: Gabriella Antolini and Alberto Antolini*, a recent acquisition, and Isamu Noguchi's *Momo Taro*. The latter is an impressive forty-ton granite sculpture that was created with the idea that people would sit in it. You will often see family groups crowded inside its inviting hollows, posing for a photo—a scene that would undoubtedly please the artist. Considered to be one of Noguchi's major works, *Momo Taro* sits on a small hill that was especially created to accommodate the work (Figure 31).

And now for the actual walk. After you've reached Storm King, paid your entrance fee and collected your visitor's map at the gate, you will drive along a beautiful allée graced by tall trees, catching your first glimpse of the enormous abstractions that punctuate the landscape on either side. Park your car near the museum center and walk inside, if you wish, to see exhibits within and to collect whatever literature you may find of interest. Note that each piece of sculpture at Storm King is clearly labeled on site, so you may not need an elaborate guidebook in addition to your map. Perhaps you will be impatient to set out at once to see the outdoor exhibits, reserving the interior ones for later.

The grounds closest to the house include semiformal gardens with relatively small sculptures tastefully set around shrubbery, planted areas, and walkways. An unmistakable Louise Nevelson black abstract construction called *City on the High Mountain* is located near the entrance; and a brilliant orange Calder stabile called *Sandy's Butterfly* is just beyond. (You will find an entire hillside of Calders on the other side of the house, as well as his bold fifty-six-foot-high work, *The Arch*, a dramatic black steel construction reminiscent of a prehistoric creature, close to the entrance of the park. This artist is certainly well represented at Storm King.

Near the manor house are fairly representational works by such artists as Emilio Greco and Henri Etienne-Martin, all set

31. Isamu Noguchi. Momo Taro. 1977

within view of a striking group of Ionic columns. These columns—brought here from nearby Danskammer, a Hudson River estate that was dismantled some time ago—add to the idyllic setting but are not considered part of the art exhibit. From here you look over a vast valley accented by a number of bold works. Among these are Mark DiSuvero's monumental *Mother Peace* and *Mon Père, Mon Père* and Alice Aycock's stunning *Three-Fold Manifestations II*, a recent acquisition. To walk to some of these sculptures will take some stamina. Near the columns is an area that is reserved for annual temporary exhibits. Especially interesting recent shows featured the works of Ursula Von Rydingsvard and Siah Armajani. Just beyond is a grouping of eight of the original series of David Smith sculptures overlooking the Calder stabiles mentioned above. These delicate and subtle works are in sharp contrast to much of the sculpture at Storm King.

As you move away from the house, the landscaping becomes more open and the sculptures larger and more daring. Don't miss a naturalistic grouping of stone *Spheres* by Grace Knowlton, tastefully set on a hillside near a clump of trees. A casual observer might think of them as part of the landscape, a tribute to the artist's ability to integrate them into the environment, in much the same spirit as the works of Noguchi. In sharp contrast is Kenneth Snelson's gracefully contrapuntal geometric work in brilliant metal called *Free Ride Home*.

To see Noguchi's *Momo Taro*—certainly one of the most popular works at Storm King—you must walk up a knoll to its commanding site. The breathtaking view from here takes in a stunning group of works. Directly in front of you is Menashe Kadishman's *Suspended*, a massive steel suspension that seems to defy all the laws of gravity. (You will be unable to resist going up to test it.) On your left, piercing the sky above the trees, is Tal Streeter's bright orange *Endless Column*, an original metal zigzag; Alexander Liberman's massive steel structures in bright primary colors as well as deep browns, *Ascent, Eve*, and *Adonai*; and many other works. If you walk down the hill, then up again and proceed left you'll find a wooded path that will take you to a newer area where smaller, more naturalistic stone pieces have recently been placed. Undoubtedly there will be new discoveries to be made on each visit to Storm King.

We recommend bringing a picnic lunch on your visit: There are few restaurants in the vicinity and a charming picnic spot with tables (in a grassy area near the lower parking lot) awaits you.

INFORMATION: Storm King is open daily, except Tuesday, from April 1-November 30, from 11:00 A.M. to 5:30 P.M. Because of its vastness, it never seems crowded, so you should not fear coming on weekends. Free walking tours are offered daily at 2:00 P.M.; no reservations are required. Admission fees are moderate. For information telephone: 914-534-3115 or 534-3190.

DIRECTIONS: From New York City take the George Washington Bridge to the Palisades Parkway north, to the New York State Thruway. Take exit 16 (Harriman) to Route 32 north. Go about 10 miles and follow the signs to Storm King Art Center.

47

José Clemente Orozco: A Master's Murals at Dartmouth College

Hanover, New Hampshire

Hanover, New Hampshire, may seem an unlikely place to find a series of brilliant wall paintings by a major Mexican painter. But here, amid the ivy-covered buildings, white frame houses, and quintessential New England campus setting of Dartmouth College, you can see the impressive three thousand square foot mural "An Epic of American Civilization" by the twentieth century Mexican master José Clemente Orozco.

Orozco was commissioned in 1932 to paint murals for Baker Library, one of the central buildings on the Dartmouth College campus. These vibrant frescoes are a riveting depiction of some five thousand years of Latin American life, beginning with the Mayan and Toltec civilizations. (It should be kept in mind that Dartmouth has had a particular interest in Native American peoples, since its charter stipulated that indigenous peoples should be among its students at its inception in the seventeenth century.)

José Clemente Orozco was one of the twentieth century's premier muralists. A native of Mexico, he established a monumental and expressive style, using subjects drawn from Mexican history and other political events. The plight of the native peoples of Mexico under the yoke of the conquistadores, and

Latin American revolution, were themes that reappeared in many of his murals.

Orozco was one of several Mexican artists in this century to turn to a contemporary style of fresco painting to express profound humanist and political beliefs. Combining their own pre-Columbian artistic heritages with a modern European sensibility, these painters revitalized an art form that had been in large part dormant for centuries.

Following the Mexican Revolution and the subsequent decades of political upheaval, these artists first became prominent in the 1920s and '30s. Using their own styles of expressionism and pre-Columbian forms and images, they found a way, through mural painting in public buildings, to bring their artistic and political messages to the people. Major murals by Diego Rivera, David Alfaro Siquieros and Orozco can be seen in public spaces in many parts of our hemisphere.

In 1932, after a trip to Europe where he saw some of the greatest European frescoes, including the ancient wall paintings of Pompeii, Orozco began the series of murals on the walls of Baker Library. For two years he worked on these dramatic paintings, bringing to the austere New England campus a brilliant taste of his political view and emotional style.

The murals at Baker Library, considered among the major murals in the United States, represent the history of Mexico as a parable for the destruction of humanity. The murals depict the ancient indigenous world of Mexico under Quetzacoatl, the conquest by Cortés, the rise of science and mechanism, and Christ the avenger, who destroys his own cross as civilizations fall. The panel shown here (Figure 32) is on the west wall, and is called *The Golden Age*.

You can visit the library (identifiable by its two hundred foot tower) at any time that the college is in session—including summer—and there is no admission fee. For more information about the murals, you can listen to a descriptive telephone recording available at the reserve book desk in the library.

Also on the Dartmouth campus are a number of other notable works of art.

Outdoors on the campus, just outside Sanborn Library, you'll find Mark DiSuvero's metal and wood abstraction called *Chi Delta*.

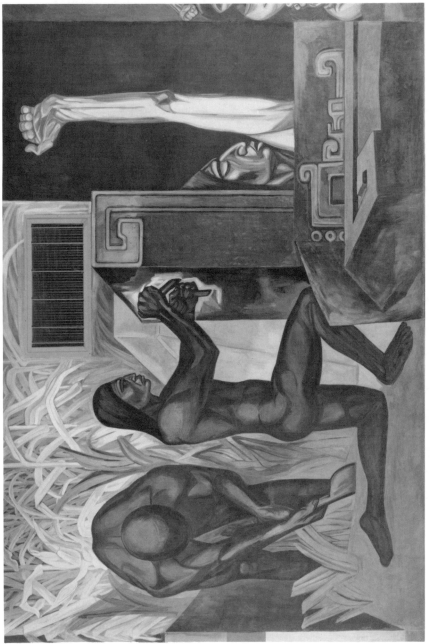

32. José Clemente Orozco. The Epic of American Civilization, panel #6: The Pre-Columbian Golden Age. 1932-34

Beverly Pepper's outdoor sculpture called *Thel* is a triangular steel work that can be seen on the lawn of the Fairchild Science Center. The artist intended its white panels to disappear under the snow in winter and to emerge anew in the spring.

Inside the Hopkins Center, there are three galleries that present a variety of exhibitions from the college collections and other sources.

In Wilson Hall you'll find an anthropological museum that features pre-Columbian North American arts and crafts—an interesting counterpoint to the Orozco murals.

The Dartmouth College Museum and Galleries in Carpenter Hall has an impressive collection of Greek and Russian icons and some monumental Assyrian reliefs from the sixth century B.C.

INFORMATION: A map and guide to many other sites of interest can be obtained at the College's information desk. This is a beautiful campus with many historic buildings; we recommend planning to spend some time here. Tours of the campus are available. The telephone number for College information is 603-646-1110.

DIRECTIONS: From Boston, take the Massachusetts Turnpike to Route 91 north. Dartmouth College is north of Lebanon, New Hampshire.

In the vicinity . . .

Dartmouth is a short distance north of the Saint-Gaudens house and studio (see chapter 38), with which you might wish to combine your visit.

Montshire Science Museum in nearby Norwich, Vermont, has a kinetic sculpture that can be operated by viewers. It was created by Fred Crusade. For hours and information, call 802-649-2200.

48

Johnson & Johnson: Art to Enhance Corporate Corridors

New Brunswick, New Jersey

Though many large corporations collect art and display it within their buildings, few allow the public at large to enjoy it too. This is particularly true of nonurban headquarters. Despite their reputations for fine collections, we were disappointed that security and other concerns had simply withdrawn large numbers of paintings and sculptures from public view. (There is an extensive book listing the art holdings of corporations, but almost all of them in our region refused even to comment about what art they owned. One public relations person thought we were industrial spies!) Fortunately, Johnson & Johnson Inc., the health-care conglomerate, has a much more public-spirited attitude.

The sleek and spare Johnson & Johnson International Headquarters, in the heart of New Brunswick, New Jersey, houses a large collection of contemporary American art. This elegant building complex, designed by I. M. Pei in the early 1980s, is a fairly extensive art "gallery," as well as the home of the conglomerate's headquarters.

The Johnson & Johnson art collection was started in the early twentieth century but not formally organized until 1983. Some twelve hundred works—prints, gouaches, paintings, photographs, and sculpture—form the collection from which pieces are selected to adorn offices, hallways, atria, and nooks and crannies. The art is moved around regularly—which means that you will likely see different pieces at different times. To view the art you must take a tour, which will lead you mostly through the common rooms (private offices are usually off-limits). You will see maybe 20 percent of the entire collection.

The parts of the collection which we saw included a wide variety of styles and media. Among them were a number of prints and smaller works by leading contemporary American artists. As you wind your way along circular passageways leading from one "maze" to the next, or through long expanses of corridors, you will find the collection is eclectic and somewhat unpredictable, but you might well be surprised by some unexpected artistic treat tucked away in an unlikely spot. All of the art is American, with the exception of a Henry Moore reclining *Mother and Child* (1983), also the only outdoor piece. You will find art by Louise Nevelson, George Segal, Jim Dine, Alexander Calder, Jasper Johns, Robert Rauschenberg, and Joseph Cornell, to name only a few, as well as many lesser known New Jersey artists.

Don't miss the lovely long gallery connecting two buildings, where you can admire an impressive group of exhibition posters by Chagall, Braque, Gris, Villon, and Dufy. The tour also includes the various views of the surrounding panorama and of the buildings' lower roofs, punctuated with unmistakably Pei pyramid-shaped skylights. Pei's concept for Johnson & Johnson was to create "a city in a park, a park in a city," which is, in fact, what he accomplished.

INFORMATION: To arrange for a tour, phone the curator, Michael J. Bzdak (908-524-3698). Tours last about thirty to forty minutes and can be taken during the week as well as on the weekend, when you might see works in areas usually off-limits.

DIRECTIONS: From New York City take the New Jersey Turnpike to exit 9 to New Brunswick. Mr. Bzdak will give you directions to the headquarters.

In the vicinity . . .
Quietude Garden Gallery in East Brunswick, an outdoor sculpture gallery, is described on page 255.

Of similar interest . . .
For another corporate art site, visit the extraordinary sculpture park of PepsiCo in Purchase, New York (see page 221).

. . . AND BEAR IN MIND

Additional Art Sites and Museum Collections of Interest*

CONNECTICUT

BRIDGEPORT
Housatonic Museum of Art (510 Barnum Avenue; telephone: 203-579-6727). Nineteenth and twentieth century European, American and Latin American art.

BROOKLYN
New England Center for Contemporary Art, Inc. (Route 169; telephone: 203-774-8899). Contemporary art from the People's Republic of China and temporary exhibitions of Asian and Oceanic art.

COS COB
Bush–Holley House (see page 169)

FARMINGTON
Hill–Stead Museum (35 Mountain Road; telephone: 203-677-9064). This elegant country mansion was designed by Theodate Pope, the first licensed woman architect in the country, in collaboration with Stanford White in 1901. Its art collection includes Monet, Manet, Degas and Cassatt, as well as prints by Whistler, tapestries, porcelains, and sculptures. The museum may only be visited by guided tour. Farmington is also noted for its many other elegant historic houses. Another of Theodate Pope's designs is the Avon Old Farms School (in nearby Avon), an unusual rambling complex of brick and stone buildings reminiscent of sixteenth century Cotswold architecture, with slate roofs, leaded glass windows, heavy timber frames, and iron hinges. No carpenters' level or plumb lines were used (under the architect's strict rules), giving the structures their handcrafted look and picturesque charm.

LITCHFIELD
The Historic District of Litchfield (for information call the Historical Society; telephone: 203-567-4501)

---

*(This list does not include sites in major urban centers)

One of the best preserved—and most beautiful—eighteenth century villages in the nation, Litchfield's architectural gems reflect its illustrious past, including the country's first law school. There is an elegant steepled church on the green. Walking tours are available.

MIDDLETOWN

Davison Art Center, Wesleyan University (301 High Street; telephone: 203-347-9411, ext. 2401). Prints from the fifteenth through twentieth centuries and photography. The Ezra and Cecile Zilkha Gallery (Wesleyan Center for the Arts, telephone: 203-344-8544)
Exhibitions of contemporary art.

NEW BRITAIN

New Britain Museum of American Art (56 Lexington Avenue; telephone: 203-229-0257). American art from colonial times to present, including paintings, sculpture, graphics and a collection of illustrations.

NEW CANAAN

Examples of houses designed by leading contemporary architects abound in the area of West Road. More than twenty homes including Philip Johnson's glass house (Ponus Ridge Road) and designs by Marcel Breuer (628 West Road), Eliot Noyes, and John Johansen (among others) can be seen in this wooded area. All are private residences.
New Canaan also has a number of historic houses from its early days. For information call the Historical Society (13 Oenoke Ridge; telephone: 203-966-1776).
Silvermine Guild Art Center (1037 Silvermine Road; telephone: 203-966-5617). Silvermine was one of the first art colonies in the nation. Sculptor Solon Borglum lived in Silvermine in the early 1900s. The Silvermine Guild Art Center now has exhibitions of contemporary art, juried shows, and a print collection.

NEW LONDON

Lyman Allyn Art Museum, Connecticut College (625 Williams Street; telephone: 203-443-2545). American, European and African arts.

NORWALK

The Lockwood–Mathews Mansion (295 West Avenue; telephone: 203-838-1434). This fifty-room mansion built by LeGrand Lockwood in 1868 has a central rotunda of such grand proportions that it is now used for changing art exhibitions. You will also see delightful ceiling frescoes in several rooms and the de rigueur "Moorish Room" of high-Victorian design.

NORWICH
The Slater Memorial Museum (108 Crescent Street; telephone: 203-887-2506). Casts of Greek, Roman, and Renaissance statues; Oriental, African, and South Sea Island art.

RIDGEFIELD
The Aldrich Museum of Contemporary Art (See page 198)

STAMFORD
Whitney Museum, a branch of the Whitney Museum of American Art in New York City, (One Champion Plaza; telephone: 203-358-7652) Contemporary American art.

First Presbyterian Church (1101 Bedford Street). This most unusual building, designed by Wallace K. Harrison (one of the architects of Rockefeller Center and the United Nations), is a rarity: a contemporary American church of grace and originality. Its sanctuary floor plan and elevations are in the shape of a fish, a well-known Christian symbol, and the striking windows are made up of some twenty thousand shards of stained glass. Despite its contemporary use of angled reinforced concrete panels and buttresses, the overall effect is that of a twentieth century Gothic cathedral. Don't miss the stained glass chapel window.

STORRS
The William Benton Museum of Art, Connecticut State Art Museum, University of Connecticut (245 Glenbrook Road; telephone: 203-486-4520). More than three thousand European and American works from the sixteenth century to the present, including prints by Käthe Kollwitz and Reginald Marsh.

UNCASVILLE
Tantaquidgeon Indian Museum (Route 32 Norwich–New London Road; telephone: 203-848-9145). Native American art and artifacts.

WILLIMANTIC
Windham Textile and History Museum (Union and Main Streets; telephone: 203-456-2178). This museum is housed in two buildings directly across from an old textile mill. Here you will find recreations of the textile mill era, including nineteenth century textile machines, looms, artistic weavings, and other items of interest.

DELAWARE

ODESSA
Historic Houses of Odessa, Delaware (Main Street; telephone: 302-378-4069). Group of historic houses open to the public.

WILMINGTON
Nemours Mansion and Gardens (Rockland Road between Routes 202 and 141; telephone: 302-651-6912). This 102-room Louis XVI-style château on three hundred acres was built by Alfred I. du Pont in 1910. The magnificent formal gardens extend a third of a mile from the house. Guided tours of the house will take you through room after room of European antiques, tapestries, and works of art.

WINTERTHUR
Winterthur Museum and Gardens (Route 52; telephone: 302-888-4600). In this sumptuous setting you'll find the largest (some 89,000 items) and most famous collection of American antiques and decorative arts from the seventeenth to the nineteenth century. The two hundred period rooms within the nine-story mansion are surrounded by one thousand acres of meadows and woodlands. The museum provides all sorts of tours, from regular guided tours to specialized tours, to do-it-yourself walks. There is something for every art or nature enthusiast to enjoy, if you don't mind crowds.

MAINE

BAR HARBOR
Abbe Museum (Sieur de Mont Spring, Acadia National Park; telephone: 207-288-3519). Archaic to modern Native American art.

BRUNSWICK
Bowdoin College Museum of Art (telephone: 207-725-3275). Wide-ranging collection of notable American art and world art.

CUSHING
Olson House Museum (Pleasant Point; telephone: 207-596-6497). Andrew Wyeth used this house as his studio from 1940 to 1968 and made some two hundred paintings here. It was the home of Christina Olson, subject of *Christina's World*. Approximately seventy of Wyeth's paintings are currently on display.

LEWISTON
Museum of Art, Bates College (Olin Arts Center; telephone: 207-786-6158). Marsden Hartley Memorial Collection and American and European arts.

OGUNQUIT
Museum of Art of Ogunquit (Shore Road; telephone: 207-646-4909). Twentieth century American art.

ORONO
University of Maine Museum of Art (Carnegie Hall; telephone: 207-581-3255). American, European, and contemporary arts.

PORTLAND
Portland Museum of Art (7 Congress Square; telephone: 207-775-6148). Large collection including works by Winslow Homer and other American masters.
Victoria Mansion (109 Danforth Street; telephone: 207-772-4841). Decorative arts.

ROCKLAND
William A. Farnsworth Library and Art Museum (19 Elm Street; telephone: 207-596-6497). Collection by artists who worked in Maine, including Rev Jona, the Wyeth family, Louise Nevelson, and others.

WATERVILLE
Colby College Museum of Art (Mayflower Hill; telephone: 207-872-3228). Collection of paintings by John Marin and Winslow Homer, as well as folk arts.

MARYLAND

ANNAPOLIS
(For tours and information call Historic Annapolis Foundation: 410-267-7619). Perhaps the best examples in the nation of Georgian architecture with its red brick and white trim facades can be found in the capital city of Annapolis. The well-preserved Georgian district, in addition to examples of Federal and Victorian styles, make Annapolis a must for architecture buffs. A National Historic Landmark, Annapolis also has several important museums and beautiful gardens. Don't miss the Chapel of the United States Naval Academy, a beaux-arts masterpiece designed by Ernest Flagg in 1904. Note its attractive Tiffany windows. Tours are available, as are self-guided walking tours.

COLLEGE PARK
The Art Gallery of the University of Maryland (Art and Sociology Building; telephone: 301-405-2763). WPA mural studies, African sculpture.

COLUMBIA
Maryland Museum of African Art (5430 Vantage Point Road; telephone: 410-730-7105). Large selection of African art and artifacts.

ELLICOTT CITY
National Quilting Association (8510 Highridge Road; telephone: 410-461-5733). The headquarters of the National Quilting Association are housed in this converted elementary schoolhouse, where you'll find an upbeat environment of quilters, as well as other craft artists, busy at work. Half of the school building houses the offices and gallery

spaces of the Association, and the other half is devoted to artists' studios. The Association (of which there are some six thousand American quilters, in addition to many foreign members) puts on monthly changing exhibits. The quilts you can see range from the traditional, familiar patterns, to very contemporary designs. Occasionally, antique quilts are also on exhibit.

HAGERSTOWN
Washington County Museum of Fine Arts (City Park; telephone: 301-739-5727). Collection of European, Oriental, and American art, with a focus on Maryland artists.

ROCKVILLE
Jane and Robert H. Weiner Judaic Museum (6125 Montrose Road; telephone: 301-881-0100). Judaica art and archaeology.

WOODLAWN
The Social Security Administration Building. Richard Fleischer has created a huge environmental work covering three acres on these grounds.

MASSACHUSETTS

ACTON
Discovery Museum (see page 121)

AMHERST
Mead Art Museum, Amherst College (telephone: 413-542-2335). Paintings, sculpture, graphics.
University Gallery, University of Massachusetts at Amherst (Fine Arts Center, 35D; telephone: 413-545-3670). Collection of twentieth century American photography, prints, and drawings.

ANDOVER
Addison Gallery of American Art, Phillips Academy (telephone: 508-749-4025). Excellent American art collection.

BROCKTON
Fuller Museum of Art (453 Oak Street; telephone: 617-588-6000). Nineteenth and twentieth century American art, Sandwich glass.

BROOKLINE
Frederick Law Olmsted National Historic Site (99 Warren Street; telephone: 617-566-1689). Drawings and other materials relating to the famed landscape architect.

CHESTNUT HILL
Boston College Museum of Art (Devlin Hall 140; telephone: 617-552-8587). European art, Japanese prints, and American art.

DEERFIELD
The Street (telephone: 413-774-5581). An eighteenth century village, Deerfield has been preserved as an example of colonial New England life; under stately elms and maples this entire village of architecturally interesting colonial houses and churches is open to the public (not in winter). While there, note the Charles P. Russell Gallery, Reed Art Center at Deerfield Academy (telephone: 413-772-0241).

DENNIS
Cape Museum of Fine Arts (Route 6A; telephone: 617-385-4477). Contemporary American art.

DUXBURY
Art Complex Museum (189 Alden Street; telephone: 617-934-6634). Oriental, European and American paintings, Shaker artifacts, and a Japanese Tea House.

FITCHBURG
Fitchburg Art Museum (185 Elm Street; telephone: 508-345-4207). European, American, and pre-Columbian art.

FRAMINGHAM
Danforth Museum of Art (123 Union Avenue; telephone: 617-620-0050). Paintings, sculpture, graphic arts.

GLOUCESTER
Cape Ann Historical Association (27 Pleasant Street; telephone: 508-283-0455).
North Shore Arts Association (197R E. Main Street; telephone: 508-283-1857). Art gallery in a circa 1870 barn.

HARVARD
Fruitlands Museums (102 Prospect Hill Road; telephone: 508-456-3924). Americana, including material relating to transcendentalists, a Shaker house, and American paintings.

LENOX
The Morris School (West Street, on the way toward Tanglewood). George L. K. Morris and his wife, Suzy Frelinghuysen, were leading American abstractionists in the 1930s and '40s who built the first modern house in the entire area. Their home became a meeting place for artists (both American and French). The Morris School, which adjoins the original property, is adorned with a three-paneled outdoor mosaic by Morris. You may drive into the school grounds to see it.

The Mount (at the junction of routes 7 and 7A, Plunkett Street; telephone: 413-637-1899). The Mount was Edith Wharton's Gilded Age mansion and summer "retreat." Now a certified landmark with tours, resident theater company, etc., it is quite a tourist attraction. But if you enjoy gardens and interior design, or are familiar with her influential books called *The Decoration of Houses* and *Italian Villas and Their Gardens*, it's a "must-see" spot, for she based the design of the imposing house and extensive gardens on her own design precepts.

LINCOLN
De Cordova Museum and Sculpture Park (see page 217).
Gropius House (68 Baker Bridge Road; telephone: 617-259-8843). The residence of Walter Gropius, the famous architect, where he combined Bauhaus principles with New England building materials.

LOWELL
New England Quilt Museum (Clock Tower, Boott Mills, foot of John Street; telephone: 508-452-4207). Vintage and contemporary quilts.
Whistler House and Parker Gallery (243 Worthen Street; telephone: 508-452-7641). James Abbott McNeill Whistler was born in this house, and a nice collection of the expatriate artist's etchings is on view here.

MEDFORD
Tufts University Art Gallery (Aidekman Arts Center; telephone: 617-627-3518). Nineteenth and twentieth century paintings, prints, and drawings.

MIDDLEBOROUGH
Robbins Museum, The Massachusetts Archaeological Society (17 Jackson Street; telephone: 508-947-9005). Native American art and artifacts.

NEWBURYPORT
(For information: Historical Society of Old Newburyport, Cushing House Museum, 98 High Street; telephone: 617-462-2681). The buildings lining the High Street and Market Square of Newburyport make up one of New England's most architecturally interesting districts. A colonial seaport, Newburyport went on to become a political and commercial center during the Federal period. Important statesmen, writers, and sea captains resided here, and the architecture of their homes and meeting houses reflects the town's illustrious past. (Most are closed in winter.)

NORTHAMPTON
Smith College Museum of Art (Elm Street at Bedford Terrace; telephone: 413-585-2760). Extensive collection of seventeenth to twentieth century European and American paintings, sculpture, drawings,

and prints. While in Northampton see also The Botanic Garden of Smith College (Lyman Plant House, College Lane).

PITTSFIELD
Berkshire Museum (39 South Street; telephone: 413-443-7171). Eighteen separate galleries include everything from rocks to costumes, and an especially nice collection of paintings. You will find many nineteenth century American works and contemporary art by well-known painters and sculptors with ties to the Berkshires (there are quite a few of them).
Berkshire Artisans/Pittsfield Community Arts Center (28 Renne Avenue; telephone: 413-499-9348). Craft workshops, galleries, murals, glass, sculpture, and works of many artisans.
Hancock Shaker Village (at the junction of Routes 20 and 41; telephone: 413-443-0188). Once a Shaker community (at its peak in the 1830s), this collection of simple houses and barns—including a round stone example—is an architectural pleasure. You can also watch crafts being made in traditional Shaker style.

PROVINCETOWN
Cape Cod's well-known art colony. Provincetown Art Association (see page 48)

ROCKPORT
Rockport Art Association (12 Main Street; telephone: 508-546-6604). In a 1787 building the Rockport Art Association displays works by American artists.

SALEM
(For information see Salem Historical Society, 174 Derby Street; telephone: 508-744-4323). Salem's Puritan past is reflected in its simple gabled wood houses. Architecturally among the purest examples of the New England colonial style, many of Salem's historic homes and assembly buildings are open to the public. In addition to visiting its historic district, note two major museums in Salem.
The Essex Institute (132 Essex Street; telephone: 617-744-3390). Large collection of Americana; also arranges guided tours.
Peabody Museum of Salem (E. India Square; telephone: 508-745-1876). Ethnology and archaeology of the world; arts and crafts, manuscripts.

SANDWICH
Sandwich Glass Museum (129 Main Street; telephone: 508-888-0251). Historic glass collection.

SHEFFIELD
Butler Sculpture Park (Shunpike Road; telephone: 413-229-8924). A sculptor named Robert Butler has turned his hilltop grounds with a

panoramic view of the Berkshires into an outdoor sculpture park. His works are contemporary and abstract and you can walk around and enjoy them.

SOUTH HADLEY
Mount Holyoke College Art Museum (telephone: 413-538-2245). Extensive collection of art of all periods, including ancient, medieval, Renaissance, Asian and American.

STOCKBRIDGE
Naumkeag (Prospect Hill; telephone: 413-298-3239). A lovely 1886 historic house designed by Stanford White, with charming gardens.
The Norman Rockwell Museum at Stockbridge (Route 183; telephone: 413-298-3822). The illustrator's originals and archives in a brand new setting.

TYRINGHAM
Tyringham Art Gallery (Tyringham Road; telephone: 413-243-3260). Sculpture garden and original Hansel-and-Gretel-style house designed by the sculptor Sir Henry Kitson.

WALTHAM
Rose Art Museum of Brandeis University (415 South Street; telephone: 617-736-3434). Outstanding collections of nineteenth and twentieth century European and American painting and sculpture, Oceanic art, contemporary art, and early ceramics.
Armenian Library and Museum of America (65 Main Street; telephone: 617-926-2562). Armenian folk and fine art, ceramics, religious art.

WELLESLEY
Davis Museum and Cultural Center, Wellesley College (106 Central Street; telephone: 617-283-2051). World art collection, including European and American paintings, sculpture, Asian and African works.
On the Wellesley College campus see two environmental works: Nancy Holt's *Wild Spot*, two rings of steel fencing enclosing wild flowers; and Robert Irwin's *Untitled*, a filigreed steel line.

WILLIAMSTOWN
As most art lovers know, Williamstown has become a major museum site, deserving a day's visit by itself. The two important museums in Williamstown are:
The Sterling and Francine Clark Art Institute (South Street; telephone: 413-458-9545) is a first-rate museum, whose collection includes priceless masterpieces of Western, Asian, and African art, from medieval to contemporary. Don't miss it!
The Williams College Museum of Art (telephone: 413-597-2429) is a newly renovated (and beautifully designed) museum, which houses

both a fine permanent collection and special exhibitions of unusual interest.

WORCESTER
Worcester Art Museum (55 Salisbury Street; telephone: 508-799-4406). This museum includes forty-two galleries with works from Egyptian and Classical periods to recent European and American art.
Iris and Gerald Cantor Art Gallery, College of Holy Cross (1 College Street; telephone: 508-793-3356). Large sculpture collection, including works by Rodin.
Worcester Center for Crafts (25 Sagamore Road; telephone: 508-753-8183). Ten six-week exhibitions of crafts annually.

NEW HAMPSHIRE

CANAAN
A mile-long historic district in this little village includes many examples of eighteenth and nineteenth century architecture, including two fine New England churches, a meetinghouse still in use, and an early school house—now a museum.

DURHAM
The Art Gallery, University of New Hampshire (Paul Creative Arts Center; telephone: 603-862-3712). Collection of nineteenth and twentieth century works on paper, including Japanese woodblocks.

MANCHESTER
Zimmerman House, designed by Frank Lloyd Wright (see page 96).

ORFORD
Considered the finest group of Federal-style houses in the country, this collection of spectacular homes was built between 1780 and 1820. The large, imposing houses that line the road through town are elegant examples of a particularly graceful style.

PORTSMOUTH
Strawberry Banke, Inc. (454 Court Street; telephone: 603-433-1100). A colonial seaport, Portsmouth still retains the narrow winding streets and forty-two historic houses dating from 1695. Many are open to the public (except in winter) and one, the Sheafe Warehouse, exhibits a collection of folk art and ship models.

NEW JERSEY

BEDMINSTER
Environmental sculptor Beverly Pepper created a site-specific work called *Amphisculpture* in 1974 on the grounds of the A.T. & T. building in Bedminster. This series of concentric cement terraces some

two hundred feet in diameter is punctuated with sloping walls and platforms; it resembles an ancient arena.

CAMDEN
Campbell Museum (Campbell Place; telephone: 609-342-6440). Here you'll find an extraordinary collection of dinner services and soup tureens dating from 500 B.C. to the present.

CLINTON
Hunterdon Art Center (7 Lower Center Street; telephone: 908-735-8415). Changing contemporary art exhibits.

EAST BRUNSWICK
The Quietude Garden Gallery (24 Fern Road; telephone: 201-257-4340). The Quietude Garden Gallery is a small, private sculpture garden outside of East Brunswick. One of few such gardens in our region, "Quietude" was so named by its owners and creators, Sheila and Ed Thau, to be a place of quiet reflection where art and nature could coexist in harmony.

This 4-acre oasis around their home is surrounded by a rather ordinary suburb. But the landscaped hilly woodland, meandering rustic paths, stream, and footbridges provide the naturalistic setting for a surprising amount of sculpture on display.

There are as many as 300 works—small items and maquettes of large outdoor works are shown within the owners' house—by some 30 to 40 promising artists, many from New Jersey. The art can best be described as "eclectic" in both style and substance. You might see a jagged multi-colored abstract aluminum bird and then an understated Noguchi-like stone form, almost camouflaged in its surroundings.

HAMILTON
Grounds for Sculpture (18 Fairgrounds Road; telephone: 609-586-0968) This is a new twenty-two acre sculpture park and museum located on the former site of the New Jersey State Fair. Landscaped grounds are dotted with dozens of contemporary sculptures, water features and an amphitheater. The museum houses smaller works, as well as providing a glass-walled view of the dramatic installations outdoors. Exhibits change periodically. Some one thousand trees (over one hundred varieties) form an arboretum setting for the art.

LAMBERTVILLE
Old English Pine artists' studios (202 North Union Street; telephone: 609-397-4978). Upstairs from this fine antique haven are six painters' studios open to visitors on an informal basis.

LYNDHURST
The Hackensack Meadowlands Environmental Center (2 De Korte Park Plaza; telephone: 201-460-8300)
Here you'll find an entire environmental sculpture by Bob Richardson. Made of garbage ranging from detergent bottles to bicycle wheels to a carousel horse and old appliances, it is a startling sight. In the artist's words, "My first concern was whether the garbage was to look like art, or was the garbage to look like garbage? I was told that the garbage was supposed to look like garbage—but artistically placed."

MONTCLAIR
The Montclair Art Museum (3 South Mountain Avenue; telephone: 201-746-5555). Important collection of American and Native American art.

MADISON
The Museum of Early Trades and Crafts (Main Street at Green Village Road; telephone: 201-377-2982). Towered Gothic miniatures, Tiffany medallions in leaded glass windows, changing displays of craft making and demonstrations.

MORRISTOWN
The Morris Museum (6 Normandy Heights Road; telephone: 201-538-0454). Fine arts, archaeology, decorative arts, and folk art.

NEW BRUNSWICK
The Voorhees Zimmerli Art Museum of Rutgers, The State University of New Jersey (George and Hamilton streets; telephone: 908-932-7237). Paintings, Russian and Soviet art, contemporary prints.

ROOSEVELT
This planned community built in 1936 was an experiment in cooperative living; its homes were designed by Bauhaus-trained architects Alfred Kastner and Louis Kahn. The School and Community Building still houses murals by Ben Shahn, a resident for many years.

TENAFLY
African Art Museum of the S.M.A. Fathers (25 Bliss Avenue; telephone: 201-567-0450). This surprising collection—open and free to the public—is operated by the missionaries of the S.M.A., an order of the Catholic Church whose members work primarily in West Africa. Since the order's founding in 1856 they have amassed a fine collection of art and artifacts. This is the only museum in the state devoted entirely to African art. The exhibitions are organized in a variety of imaginative ways, including by tribe, by usage, by country, and recently in a show

called "Values in African Art and Culture." Some exhibits show Christian subjects made in tribal styles.

NEW YORK

ALFRED
The Museum of Ceramic Art at Alfred University (telephone: 607-871-2421). World ceramic works from historic to contemporary.

ANNANDALE-ON-HUDSON
Edith C. Blum Art Institute, Bard College (telephone: 914-758-7437). Inventive exhibits of nationally and internationally known artists of today.

BINGHAMTON
University Art Museum at the State University of New York (telephone: 607-777-2634). Collections of Chinese art, modern graphics, and decorative arts.

BLUE MOUNTAIN LAKE
Adirondack Museum (Route 28N and Route 30; telephone: 518-352-7311). Early American art and Adirondack artifacts.

BROOKVILLE
C.W. Post Campus of Long Island University (telephone: 516-299-2464). This Long Island campus is a surprising treasure trove of contemporary outdoor sculpture set on a rolling green landscape only a few miles from New York City. (You can pick up a sculpture map of their Public Art Program at the campus gallery in Hillwood Commons at the center of the campus.) Art on the site ranges from charming turn-of-the-century landscape architecture and brick arches at the original Post House and Gardens to avant-garde steel and concrete works all across the sprawling campus.

Notable modern sculptures (some of which are permanently installed, with others on long-term loan) include: Alfred Görig's centrally placed, megalithic *Tent*; a whimsical steel and cast iron piece by Nancy Graves; *Humanity's Birches,* a setting of twenty-six vertical birch logs by Sandy Gellis; a characteristic steel George Rickey work; a contemporary figurative sculpture by Brigid Kennedy; and close to fifty major works by such artists as Vito Acconci, Seymour Lipton, Grace Knowlton, Kyong Park, Gail Rothschild, and Christy Rupp. You can also visit workshops and studios of student sculptors and welders, and see their works dotted over a hillside near the art building at the distant end of the campus.

CANAJOHARIE
Library and Art Gallery (2 Erie Boulevard; telephone: 518-673-2314). A treasure-trove of American art, including a large number of Winslow

Homer watercolors. Among the surprising collection are works by Gilbert Stuart, John Singleton Copley, some Hudson River painters, and artists of the "Ashcan school."

CLAYTON
Thousand Island Craft School Textile Museum (314 John Street; telephone: 315-686-4123). More than eight thousand examples of textiles and fabric and fiber art.

CLINTON
The Emerson Gallery, Hamilton College (198 College Hill Road; telephone: 315-859-4396). Nineteenth and twentieth century European and American paintings and prints, decorative arts, Native American collections.

COOPERSTOWN
The Fenimore House (Route 80; telephone: 607-547-2533). An extraordinary collection of American painting, including works by Thomas Cole, Asher B. Durand, and Samuel F. B. Morse, whose painting *On Apple Hill* (1828) is a view of nearby Otsego Lake. (You can admire the same view today.) An outstanding 500-piece collection of Native American art will soon be displayed in a new wing.

CORNING
Corning Glass Center, Centerway (telephone: 607-974-8276).
Corning Museum of Glass (telephone: 607-937-5371). The making of glass, including Steuben art glass, is displayed in these two museums devoted to the history of glassmaking, and in open demonstrations of today's techniques.
The Rockwell Museum (111 Cedars Street; telephone: 607-937-5386). American paintings of the Western frontier, including works by Remington, Bierstadt, and Russell.

CORTLAND
Dowd Fine Arts Gallery, State University of New York (telephone: 607-753-4216). Nineteenth and twentieth century European and American paintings, prints, drawings, and sculpture.

FONDA
The Mohawk–Caughnawaga Museum (Route 5, west of Fonda; telephone: 518-853-3646). Native American art and artifacts at the site of Caughnawaga Village.

FREDONIA
Michael C. Rockefeller Arts Center Gallery, State University College (telephone: 716-673-3538). Contemporary sculpture, prints, drawings.

GENESEO
Bertha V. B. Lederer Fine Arts Gallery, State University College (telephone: 716-245-5814). Paintings, sculpture, ceramics, graphics.

GLENS FALLS
The Hyde Collection (161 Warren Street; telephone: 518-792-1761). Superior collection of European and American arts from the fourteenth to the twentieth centuries.

HAMILTON
The Picker Art Gallery, Colgate University (telephone: 315-824-7634). Collections of pre-Columbian art, paintings, sculpture, and modern Chinese woodcuts.

HASTINGS-ON-HUDSON
The sculptor Jacques Lipchitz lived and worked in this village on the Hudson for more than twenty years. His studio is on Aqueduct Lane (off Washington Avenue) and a bronze sculpture called *Between Heaven and Earth*, which he presented to the village, can be seen in front of the Public Library.
The Jasper Cropsey House, home of the Hudson River painter (on Washington Avenue between Broadway and Warburton) is a charming yellow gabled gingerbread house containing Cropsey paintings and furnishings, open by appointment. Call Newington Cropsey Foundation (telephone: 914-478-7039).

HEMPSTEAD
Fine Arts Museum of Long Island (295 Fulton Avenue; telephone: 516-481-5700). Pre-Columbian, primitive, and contemporary art.
Hofstra Museum, Hofstra University (telephone: 516-463-5672). African, Asian, Oceanic, and contemporary art.

HUNTINGTON
Heckscher Museum (2 Prime Avenue; telephone: 516-351-3250). Excellent collection of sixteenth to twentieth century European and American painting, sculpture, and works on paper with emphasis on American artists.

ITHACA
Herbert F. Johnson Museum of Art, Cornell University (telephone: 607-255-6464). Extensive collection of Asian art, European and American painting, sculpture, drawings, and art from Africa, Oceania, and the Americas.

KATONAH
Caramoor Center for Music and the Arts (Girdle Ridge Road; telephone: 914-232-5035). This château-style mansion of fifty-five rooms houses

an eclectic and always surprising collection of art and artifacts from Europe and China. Tours through the house and Moorish courtyard are available year-round.

Katonah Museum of Art (Route 22 at Jay Street; telephone: 914-232-9555). Museum-created loan exhibits in a most attractive setting.

NEW PALTZ

College Art Gallery, The College at New Paltz (telephone: 914-257-3854). Asian and American graphic arts, pre-Columbian artifacts.

Huguenot Street (Brodhead Avenue; telephone: 914-255-1660). District of seventeenth and eighteenth century historic houses.

NIAGARA FALLS

Castellani Art Museum, Niagara University (telephone: 716-286-8200). Some four thousand works including paintings, sculpture, prints, and pre-Columbian pottery.

Native American Center for Living Arts (25 Rainbow Boulevard; telephone: 716-284-2427). Native American archaeological, ethnographic, and contemporary art from Mexico, Canada, and the United States.

NORTH SALEM

Hammond Museum (Deveau Road; telephone: 914-669-5033). Asian art, decorative arts, and a delightful strolling garden.

NYACK

Hopper House (82 North Broadway; telephone: 914-358-0774). The painter Edward Hopper was born in this modest clapboard house dating to 1858. Today it is a landmark building presenting a variety of art exhibitions. Hopper, who said he always wanted to paint "sunlight on the side of a house" did so, using Nyack's houses as subjects.

ONEONTA

The Museums at Hartwick, Hartwick College (telephone: 607-431-4480) Eclectic collection of South American, pre-Columbian, Renaissance, and Baroque art.

PEEKSKILL

Artists' studios open to the public informally or by tour. Fourteen studios and ten galleries are open in this newest of art colonies. For map and information on guided tours call 914-737-3600. Tours meet on Saturdays at 1:00 P.M. from the Chocolate Tree at 929 South Street in Peekskill. Additional studios are open by appointment.

PLATTSBURG

SUNY Platsburg Art Museum (telephone: 518-564-2813)
Asian and American art, including a large collection of paintings by Rockwell Kent.

PLEASANTVILLE
Reader's Digest Collection (Reader's Digest Headquarters, Route 117; telephone: 914-241-5125). Lila Acheson Wallace, the eminent patron of the arts, collected thousands of paintings, sculptures, and prints during her lifetime. Today, much of her impressive collection hangs in the corporate headquarters of the Reader's Digest, which she and her husband co-founded in 1922.

Approximately 6,000 works—some by great 19th and 20 century masters—adorn the walls of offices, hallways, and conference rooms. (Mrs. Wallace believed that art should be an integral part of daily life.) Visitors on guided tours can see about forty of these works, including paintings by Cezanne, Modigliani, Chagall, Monet, Manet, Matisse, Van Gogh, and American impressionists.

There are two daily tours, at 10:30 A.M. and 2 P.M., Monday-Friday. Telephone in advance for reservations.

POUGHKEEPSIE
Frances Lehman Loeb Art Center at Vassar College (telephone: 914-437-5235). Fine collection of classical sculpture, medieval to contemporary art, and paintings by Hudson River School artists.

PURCHASE
Neuberger Museum of Art, State University of New York at Purchase (telephone: 914-251-6133). Twentieth century painting, sculpture, prints, Constructivist and contemporary art.

SARATOGA SPRINGS
The Schick Art Gallery, Skidmore College (North Broadway; telephone: 518-584-5000). Paintings, graphics, ceramics, sculpture.

SCHENECTADY
Schenectady Museum (Nott Terrace Heights; telephone: 518-382-7890). Primitive and contemporary art.

SOUTHAMPTON
The Parrish Art Museum (25 Job's Lane; telephone: 516-283-2118). Works of the Italian Renaissance, nineteenth and twentieth century American paintings (including several works by William Merritt Chase), Japanese stencils, and woodblock prints.

SYRACUSE
Everson Museum of Art (401 Harrison St.; telephone: 315-474-6064). Fine collection of American, Chinese, and contemporary art.

WOODSTOCK
An artists' colony in the Catskills. (See page 66)
Quarryman's Museum. (See page 66)

YONKERS
The Hudson River Museum of Westchester (telephone: 914-963-4550). Nineteenth and twentieth century American painting, sculpture, and decorative arts.
Philipse Manor Hall (see page 153)

PENNSYLVANIA

ALLENTOWN
Allentown Art Museum (Fifth and Court Streets; telephone: 215-432-4333). European and American art.

AUDUBON
Mill Grove, The Audubon Wildlife Sanctuary (telephone: 215-666-5593). Examples of every major art work published by John James Audubon.

BETHLEHEM
Lehigh University Art Galleries (telephone: 215-758-3615). Art from antiquity to contemporary, including Etruscan bronzes, paintings from the "Ashcan school"; sculpture garden.

BOALSBURG
Columbus Chapel, Boal Mansion Museum (Business Route 322; telephone: 814-466-6210). Sixteenth century chapel interior brought from Spain, Colonial relics and decorative artifacts.

BRYN ATHYN
Glencairn Museum: Academy of the New Church (1001 Cathedral Road; telephone: 215-947-9909). Ancient Near Eastern and classical sculpture, medieval art and artifacts.

CARLISLE
The Trout Art Gallery (High Street; telephone: 717-245-1344). African and Asian artifacts; large collection of graphic arts.

CHADDS FORD
Brandywine River Museum (U.S. Route 1 at Pa. Route 100; telephone: 215-388-2700). American art and illustration, Wyeth collection.

CHESTER
Widener University Art Museum (1300 Potter Street; telephone: 215-499-1189). Asian art, and eighteenth, nineteenth, and twentieth century European and American arts, including genre painting.

COLLEGEVILLE
Philip and Muriel Berman Museum of Art at Ursinus College (Main Street; telephone: 215-489-4111). Old Masters, nineteenth and twentieth century American landscapes, contemporary Japanese graphic arts.

262

DOYLESTOWN
James A. Michener Art Museum (138 South Pine Street; telephone: 215-340-9800). American impressionists and abstract expressionist paintings.

EASTON
Lafayette College Art Gallery, Williams Center for the Arts (telephone: 215-250-5000). American and British portraits and historical art.

ELKINS PARK
Tyler School of Fine Art of Temple University. (See page 202)

EPHRATA
Ephrata Cloister (672 West Main Street; telephone: 717-733-6600). Twelve mid-eighteenth century buildings of Germanic architectural style located at original site of communal celibate religious society.

ERIE
Erie Art Museum (411 State Street; telephone: 814-459-5477). Asian porcelains and jades, American ceramics, paintings, sculpture, contemporary baskets.

FALLSINGTON
Fallsington Historic District (4 Yardley Avenue; telephone: 215-295-6567). Some twenty-five eighteenth century houses and a stagecoach inn make up the historic district in this Delaware River village where William Penn worshiped.

GLENSIDE
Beaver College. (See page 202)

KENNETT SQUARE
Longwood Gardens (Junction Routes 1 and 52; telephone: 215-388-6741). Once the country estate of industrialist Pierre S. du Pont, Longwood is famous (and well-known by tours and tourists) for its glorious formal gardens, conservatories and fountains covering 350 acres. With self-guided tour map in hand you can roam through flower gardens, an Italian water garden, a lake area, a rose arbor, a topiary garden, meadows, forests and spectacular indoor displays. You can also tour the du Pont house and expect to see period furnishings, paintings, and memorabilia.

LEWISBURG
Center Gallery of Bucknell University (Seventh Street and Moore Avenue; telephone: 717-524-3792). Renaissance art, nineteenth and twentieth century European and American paintings, Japanese art.

MILL RUN
Fallingwater (telephone: 412-329-8501). Frank Lloyd Wright house and furnishings, sculpture by Lipchitz, Arp, Picasso, Rivera and other twentieth century masters. (See page 95)

NEW BRIGHTON
The Merrick Art Gallery (Fifth Avenue and Eleventh Street; telephone: 412-846-1130). European masters including Courbet, Proudhon, American nineteenth century paintings.

PAOLI
The Wharton Esherick Museum (Horseshoe Trail; telephone: 215-644-5822). Two hundred pieces of art by Esherick, one of the fathers of the contemporary American crafts movement.

SCRANTON
Everhart Museum (telephone: 717-346-7186). Ethnographic collection, American folk art, native American art.

UNIVERSITY PARK
Palmer Museum of Art, The Pennsylvania State University (Curtin Road; telephone: 814-865-7672). World collection of art and artifacts, including Peruvian and Japanese ceramics.

RHODE ISLAND

BRISTOL
Haffenreffer Museum of Anthropology, Brown University (Mt. Hope Grant; telephone: 401-253-8388). Large ethnographical collection and primitive arts.

NEWPORT
Mansions from the gilded age (call Newport Historical Society for information and guided walking tours: 401-846-0813). (See page 000) Redwood Library and Atheneum (50 Bellevue Avenue; telephone: 401-847-0292). Collection of paintings by Gilbert Stuart and Charles Bird King.

NORTH KINGSTON
Gilbert Stuart's birthplace (see page 159).

PEACE DALE
An impressive and poignant work by Daniel Chester French can be seen on the grounds of the library here. A memorial to the Hazard family—two sons lost in the First World War and their father—it is a lovely neoclassical bronze depicting a male weaver and two graceful

Grecian women; it bears the quotation "Life spins the thread/ time weaves/ God designs the fabric of the stuff he leaves to men of noble mind."

VERMONT

BELLOWS FALLS
Native American petroglyphs. (See page 192)

BENNINGTON
The Bennington Museum (West Main Street). (See page 42)

BROOKFIELD
Museum of the Americas (Route 14; telephone: 802-276-3386). Hispanic, American and Latin American decorative and folk arts; pre-Columbian art.

BURLINGTON
Robert Hull Fleming Museum at The University of Vermont (Colchester Ave.; telephone: 802-656-0750). World arts and artifacts, including Native American and pre-Columbian arts and American and European paintings.

JOHNSON
The Vermont Studio Center (telephone: 802-635-2727). The Vermont Studio Center is a year-round community serving a number of emerging and mid-career artists from various parts of the country and around the world. Here, in the picturesque setting of this quaint Vermont village—amid barns, a converted grist mill, and a rushing waterfall—artists come to paint, draw, sculpt, or write, and to interact with other artists.

Although their studios are not officially open to the public, during the summer many artists can be seen painting or sketching out of doors in the idyllic landscape and occasionally their work is on exhibit at the art gallery near the dining hall. If you are in the vicinity, you will enjoy a walk in this charming and stimulating spot.

MIDDLEBURY
The Middlebury College Museum of Art (Fine Arts Center, Route 30; telephone: 802-388-3711). Prints, drawings, paintings, sculpture.

MONTPELIER
Wood Art Gallery (Vermont College Art Center; telephone: 802-828-8743). Nineteenth and twentieth century American art.

265

NORTHFIELD
Vermont Quilt Festival (see page 125).

NORWICH
Montshire Science Museum (see page 241).

SHELBURNE
Shelburne Museum Inc. (U.S. Route 7; telephone: 802-985-3346). Vast museum complex featuring American folk and decorative arts, and including European art, as well.

ST. JOHNSBURY
Fairbanks Museum (Main and Prospect streets; telephone: 802-748-2372). Far Eastern, African, Polynesian sculpture and other ethnological material.
St. Johnsbury Atheneum (30 Main Street; telephone: 802-748-8291). In addition to a collection of paintings by Hudson River school artists, this building—one of the oldest art galleries in the nation—houses a monumental Bierstadt painting of Yosemite scenery.

WAITSFIELD
Bundy Art Gallery (Route 100; telephone: 802-496-2389). Eighty acres of lawn and woodland sculpture park surround the Icefire Performance Theatre with its unusual collection of contemporary art. Sculpture and paintings by Central and South Americans, as well as works by artists from the United States are exhibited here.

WINDSOR
Historic town and covered bridge. (See page 191)

CHOOSING AN OUTING

CHOOSING AN OUTING

INDEX OF ARTISTS AND ARCHITECTS

INDEX OF SELECTED ART SITES*

---

*Major museums in large urban centers are not included

INDEX OF SELECTED ART SITES

INDEX OF SELECTED ART SITES

INDEX OF SELECTED ART SITES

CREDITS

John Frederick Kensett. *View from Cozzen's Hotel, West Point, NY,* 1863. Courtesy of the New-York Historical Society, New York City.

Robert Havell, Jr. *West Point.* Private Collection.

Samuel Lancaster Gerry. *West Point, Hudson River.* Private Collection.

Samuel Colman. *Storm King on the Hudson,* 1866. Courtesy National Museum of American Art, Smithsonian Institution. Gift of John Gellatly.

Georgia O'Keeffe. *From the Lake No. 1,* 1924. Purchased with funds from the Coffin Fine Arts Trust, Nathan Emory Coffin. Collection of the Des Moines Art Center, 1984.3. Photo by Ray Andrews.

David Smith, *Hudson River Landscape.* 1951. Whitney Museum of American Art.

Thomas Cole. *Falls of Kaaterskill,* 1826. The Warner Collection of Gulf States Paper Corporation, Tuscaloosa, Alabama. Photo by Helga Photo Studio.

Jasper Francis Cropsey. *Starrucca Viaduct, Pennsylvania,* 1865. The Toledo Museum of Art. Purchased with funds from the Florence Scott Libbey Bequest in Memory of her Father, Maurice A. Scott. (1947.58)

Childe Hassam. *Isle of Shoals Garden* or *The Garden in its Glory,* 1892. Courtesy National Museum of American Art, Smithsonian Institution. Gift of John Gellatly.

John Marin. *Mark and Andrews Island from Deer Isle, Maine.* 1920. Courtesy of Kennedy Galleries, Inc., New York.

Grandma Moses. *White Creek.* Copyright © 1993, Grandma Moses Properties Co., New York.

Niles Spencer. *Back of the Town (Provincetown).* 1926. Private Collection.

Morris Davidson. *Fishing Boats in Harbor.* 1948. Private Collection.

Helen Frankenthaler. *Seascape with Dunes.* 1962. Oil on canvas. 70 × 140 inches. Grey Art Gallery and Study Center, New York University Art Collection. Gift of the artist, 1963.

Edward Hopper. *Mouth of the Pamet River.* ca. 1937. Photo courtesy of Gerold Wunderlich & Co., New York.

William Sidney Mount. *Dance of the Haymakers.* 1845. Collection of The Museums at Stony Brook. Gift of Mr. and Mrs. Ward Melville, 1950.

Mystery Hill photo by Susan Stainback.

New Castle photographs by Susan Stainback.

Jackson Pollock. *Untitled (after Number 7, 1951),* 1951/1964. Courtesy Collection Pollock–Krasner House and Study Center, East Hampton, NY. Photo by Noel Rowe.

Tim Prentice. *Plasmobile* and *Giant Spider.* 1985. Courtesy Tim Prentice. Photo by Nicholas Jacobs.

John McQueen. *Untitled #189.* 1989. Permission of the artist.

Topiary bear at Green Acres.

283

CREDITS

William Chadwick. *On the Porch*, ca. 1908. Collection Florence Griswold Museum. Gift of Mrs. Elizabeth Chadwick O'Connell.

Winslow Homer, *The Lifeline*. 1884. New York Public Library Picture Collection.

Frederick E. Church. *The Catskills from Olana*. 1870-72. New York State Office of Parks, Recreation and Historic Preservation, Olana State Historic Site.

Augustus Saint-Gaudens. *The Adams (Memorial) Monument*. 1891.

J. Alden Weir, *Upland Pasture*. ca. 1905. National Museum of American Art, Smithsonian Institution. Gift of William T. Evans.

Louise Nevelson, *Atmosphere and Environment X*. 1969. Princeton University.

Jean Dubuffet. *Kiosque L'Evide*. 1985. Donald M. Kendall Sculpture Gardens, PepsiCo. Photo by James S. Harrison.

Claes Oldenburg. *The Giant Trowel II*. 1982. Donald M. Kendall Sculpture Gardens, PepsiCo. Photo by James S. Harrison.

Isamu Noguchi. *Momo Taro*, 1977. granite, 9′ × 35′2″ × 22′8″. Storm King Art Center, Mountainville, NY. Purchase 1978.4. Photo by Jerry L. Thompson.

José Clemente Orozco. *The Epic of American Civilization* 1932-34, Panel #6, *The Pre-Columbian Golden Age*. Courtesy of the Trustees of Dartmouth College, Hanover, NH.

Also by Marina Harrison and Lucy D. Rosenfeld:

ARTWALKS IN NEW YORK $14.95

A WALKER'S GUIDEBOOK
Serendipitous Outings Near New York City $13.95

To order, please send a check for the listed price to:

Michael Kesend Publishing, Ltd.
1025 Fifth Avenue
New York, NY 10028

Add $4.00 for shipping and handling plus 50¢ for each additional copy with the same order.

For quantity discounts, contact the special sales department at:

Tel: 212 249-5150
Fax: 212 249-2129